QUESTIONS & ANSWERS:
CONTRACTS

QUESTIONS & ANSWERS: CONTRACTS

Multiple Choice and Short Answer
Questions and Answers

SECOND EDITION

SCOTT J. BURNHAM
Curley Professor of Commercial Law
Gonzaga University School of Law

CAROLINA ACADEMIC PRESS
Durham, North Carolina

ISBN: 978-1-6304-3149-5
eBook ISBN: 978-0-7698-9119-4

This publication is designed to provide authoritative information in regard to the subject matter covered. It is sold with the understanding that the publisher is not engaged in rendering legal, accounting, or other professional services. If legal advice or other expert assistance is required, the services of a competent professional should be sought.

Carolina Academic Press, LLC
700 Kent Street
Durham, North Carolina 27701
Telephone (919) 489-7486
Fax (919) 493-5668
www.caplaw.com

Printed in the United States of America
2016 Printing

Dedication

To John Kidwell, *bon ami*

About the Author

Scott J. Burnham is the Curley Professor of Commercial Law at Gonzaga University School of Law in Spokane, Washington. For many years he taught at The University of Montana School of Law and has visited the law schools at Santa Clara, University of Tennessee, Western New England, UNLV, Hawaii, Memphis, The Ohio State, and Cardozo, as well as law schools in Uruguay, Lithuania, Vietnam, and China. He also teaches online at Concord Law School.

Professor Burnham is the author of numerous books, articles, and CALI lessons in the areas of Contracts, Commercial Law, and Copyright Law. He is a member of the American Law Institute.

Preface

Answering Multiple Choice Questions

Multiple Choice and short answer questions are an excellent way to review your knowledge of the concepts of Contracts by requiring you to apply that knowledge to new fact situations. Some of the questions test your ability to recall or recognize a concept or a definition. But most of them are analytical. I believe that a good multiple choice question is similar to an essay question and is best approached through the IRAC method. First, try to spot the issue raised by the facts. This is easier when the questions are organized by topic, for the topic will help you narrow the area from which the issue will be drawn. It will be harder in the Practice Final Exam, where the topics are interspersed.

Note the call of the question — exactly what is the question looking for? Take a moment to try to answer the question without looking at the options. Try to recall the relevant rule. The facts will often suggest whether a rule or an exception to a rule is being tested. For example, if the facts say "a buyer made a telephone call to a seller," ask why the author thought it was important to tell you that this transaction took place over the telephone. It was probably to indicate that the rule may involve oral contracts. If the facts say, "a merchant buyer made a telephone call to a merchant seller," ask why the author told you the parties were merchants. It was probably to invoke a rule or an exception applicable only to merchants.

Then apply the rule to the facts. As with an essay question, make sure you account for all the facts — there is a reason the author included them. And don't make up facts that aren't there. This analysis should lead you to a conclusion found in one of the options. If the question is tricky, you will probably narrow the choice down to two options that both seem correct. To distinguish between the options that seem close, you might employ some of the following techniques:

- Ask what body of law is applicable. One option might be right under the common law, and another under the UCC.

- Review the facts to determine whether you are being tested on a factual distinction. One option might be correct when the contract is *oral*, another when the contract is *written*. Or one option might be correct when the seller is a *merchant*, another when the seller is a *non-merchant*.

- Make sure you are applying the right rule. Rule A might lead you to one option, while Rule B might lead you to another.

- Check whether you are being tested on the exception to a rule. The rule might lead you to one option, while the exception might lead you to another.

- If the facts of two questions are similar, the assessor is probably trying to get you to spot a factual distinction that affects the outcome. Review the earlier question to help determine whether the different facts suggest a different outcome.

- Be skeptical of options that are stated in terms of absolutes like *always* or *never*.

The Sources of Contract Law

Traditionally, Contracts was a common law course. The law of contracts is state law, and the common law varies from state to state. However, your Contracts course likely involves the study of general principles rather than the law of a particular state. Similarly, the bar exam tests general principles rather than local rules. In theory, to know what the common law rule is, you would have to read all the cases and synthesize them. The good news is that our friends at the American Law Institute have done this for us. They have digested all the cases and stated the rules as black-letter law in the Restatement (Second) of Contracts.

This book relies heavily on the common law rules and principles as found in the Restatement (Second) of Contracts, which I will refer to as "the Restatement" — any other Restatement will be designated by name. However, every time you see a citation to the Restatement, you should imagine that there is a footnote stating:

> *WARNING! The Restatement is not the law of any particular U.S. jurisdiction. It is a handy short-cut for finding the general principles of contract law. But judges are not bound to follow it, and when you practice in a particular jurisdiction, you will have to find the case law and rules that have developed in that jurisdiction.

Statutes are an increasingly important part of the study of law. In some U.S. jurisdictions, such as Louisiana and California, the law of contracts is found in the form of a code rather than the common law, though the common law still has an important role in interpreting the statutes. All U.S. jurisdictions have enacted most of one very important statute — the Uniform Commercial Code (UCC). More specifically, all jurisdictions have enacted Article 1, which contains general principles and definitions, and all but Louisiana have enacted Article 2, which codifies the law of the sale of goods. Most basic Contracts courses introduce you to the UCC, so it is discussed in this book.

Just as the common law is different in each state, so is the UCC. While our friends at the Uniform Law Commission promulgate a uniform version of the Code, each state legislature enacting the Code is free to make changes, and often does. This book uses the Code as found in the uniform version. But just as with the common law, when you are in practice you will need to consult the law of a particular jurisdiction to see what the Code section looks like and how it has been interpreted in that jurisdiction.

There have been many attempts to revise the UCC over the years. Revised Article 1 (2001) has been enacted in most states and is the source for the bar exam, so this book uses that version of Article 1. Attempts to revise Article 2 have all failed (other than changes made to coordinate it with the adoption of Revised Article 1). Therefore, you should make sure you are using a recent version of Article 2 as promulgated by the ULC and not Revised Article 2 or Amended Article 2, both of which have been withdrawn from consideration by the states.

The United States and many of its trading partners have joined in the United Nations Convention on the International Sale of Goods (CISG), which governs international commercial contracts for the sale of goods. Because most Contracts courses regrettably do not include study of the CISG, and because it is not tested on the bar, I have not included questions about the CISG beyond a basic understanding of when it applies to a transaction.

How to Use This Book

I suggest you work with the questions in this book after you have studied each topic in order to review and reinforce your understanding of that topic. The topics are not always studied in the same order in every Contracts course, but you should be able to find the appropriate topic by its description or by using the Index. If you get a question wrong, make sure you review the reasoning to find out why you got it wrong. Then take the Practice Final Exam before you take your final. You might also want to review the questions when you study Contracts in preparation for the bar exam. The multiple choice portion of the bar exam includes Contracts and Sales questions, and there are often essay questions in those areas as well.

If you have questions or comments, feel free to contact me at sburnham@lawschool.gonzaga.edu.

Acknowledgments

I am grateful to Keith A. Rowley, William S. Boyd Professor of Law at the Boyd School of Law, University of Nevada Las Vegas, for authoring the first edition of this work. I thank the Uniform Law Commission and the American Law Institute for permission to reproduce sections of the Uniform Commercial Code, the Restatement (Second) of Contracts, and the Restatement (Third) of Restitution and Unjust Enrichment. I am grateful to Chelsea Porter, a student at Gonzaga University School of Law, for her assistance and advice. I also thank Leslie Levin and Cristina Gegenschatz at LexisNexis for their confidence in me. Most importantly, I am grateful to all my Contracts students who have allowed me to hone my skills by writing multiple choice questions in order to assess them.

Table of Contents

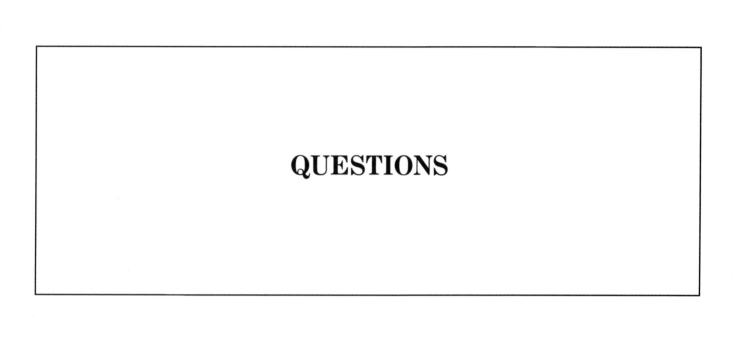

QUESTIONS

1.   What is the difference between an *agreement* and a *contract*? (Hint: *see* U.C.C. §§ 1-201(b)(3) and (12).)

ANSWER:

2.   Byron, a law student, needed a pen to write an exam. Sarah, another law student, sold him her spare pen for $1.29. During the exam, the pen stopped working. Frustrated, Byron stopped taking the exam and failed the course. His grade point average slipped below the required standard, and he flunked out of law school. Thinking that he learned something useful in law school, he sued Sarah for the $2 million difference between what he would have earned as a lawyer and what he was likely to earn without a law degree.

What body of law applies to this transaction?

(A)   The common law of contracts, because neither Byron nor Sarah is a merchant with respect to pens.

(B)   The common law of contracts, because the sale price of the pen was under $500.

(C)   U.C.C. Article 2, because a pen is a good.

(D)   U.C.C. Article 2, because pens are commonly sold in interstate transactions.

3.   A corporation in Oregon ordered 10,000 feet of lumber from a corporation in British Columbia, Canada. The lumber was supposed to be delivered to the buyer's ship in the port of Seattle, Washington. The seller never delivered the lumber and the buyer sued the seller.

What body of law should the court apply to this transaction?

(A)   Applicable British Columbia law.

(B)   The Oregon U.C.C.

(C)   The Washington U.C.C.

(D)   The United Nations Convention on the International Sale of Goods.

4.   A corporation in Oregon ordered 10,000 feet of lumber from a corporation in British Columbia, Canada. The lumber was supposed to be delivered to the buyer's ship in the port of Seattle, Washington. The contract contained a provision stating that "[t]he UCC of the State of Oregon shall govern this transaction." The seller never delivered the lumber and

the buyer sued the seller.

What body of law should the court apply to this transaction?

(A) Applicable British Columbia law.

(B) The Oregon U.C.C.

(C) The Washington U.C.C.

(D) The United Nations Convention on the International Sale of Goods.

5. U.C.C. § 2-503(1) provides in part: "Tender of delivery requires that the seller put and hold conforming goods at the buyer's disposition and give the buyer any notification reasonably necessary to enable him to take delivery."

A contract between a commercial buyer and a commercial seller contains this provision:

Tender of delivery. After seller gives the buyer notice that the goods are available, the buyer shall have until 4 p.m. of the next business day to take delivery of the goods.

Is this provision enforceable? (Hint: *see* U.C.C. § 1-302.)

ANSWER:

6. What is the Uniform Commercial Code?

(A) The principal federal statute governing interstate commerce.

(B) Legislation that has been enacted uniformly in every state, so that commercial law is the same throughout the country.

(C) A model for a statute, but it has been enacted with variations in every state.

(D) An international treaty governing commerce between countries that have signed it.

7. The answer to the previous question cited the Restatement (Second) of Contracts. What is the Restatement and where does it come from?

ANSWER:

8. A woman who resided in Montana owned a parcel of land in Idaho. In a contract signed in Idaho, she hired a contractor that was incorporated and located in the state of Washington to build a house on the property. A dispute arose between the parties about defects in construction, and the woman sued the contractor for breach of contract in Federal District Court in Washington.

What body of contract law should the court apply to the transaction?

    (A) Federal contract law.

    (B) Montana contract law.

    (C) Idaho contract law.

    (D) Washington contract law.

9. You are writing a brief on the issue of the enforceability of a "choice of forum" clause in a contract that is being litigated in your state's court of general jurisdiction. You have found cases on point that have been decided in the following courts.

Which decision has the greatest weight as authority?

    (A) The highest court in the state system in your state.

    (B) The federal district court in your state.

    (C) The federal Circuit Court of Appeals in your circuit.

    (D) The United States Supreme Court.

10. A rich uncle said to his niece, "I understand that you have been accepted by a number of law schools and can't decide which one to choose. I would like to make that decision easier for you, so I will pay your tuition wherever you go." The niece was ecstatic and said, "Thank you, uncle. I accept your offer and I will make you proud." When the niece presented the uncle with the first tuition bill, the uncle refused to pay.

Is the uncle legally obligated to pay the tuition?

(A) Yes, because he made an offer and the niece accepted it.

(B) Yes, because the niece relied on his offer.

(C) No, because he made a promise that is not legally enforceable.

(D) No, because his promise was not in writing.

11. A rich uncle said to his niece, "I understand that you have been accepted by a number of law schools and can't decide which one to choose. If you go to my alma mater, I will pay your tuition." The niece was ecstatic and said, "Thank you, uncle. I will go to your law school and I will make you proud."

Was a contract formed between the uncle and the niece?

(A) No, because the uncle did not make an offer.

(B) No, because the niece did not accept the offer because at this point she has not yet gone to the alma mater.

(C) Yes, because the niece could only accept the offer by promising to go to the uncle's alma mater, and she promised to do so.

(D) Yes, because the niece could accept the offer either by promising to go to the alma mater, or by going to the alma mater, and she promised to do so.

12. A rich uncle said to his niece, "I understand that you have been accepted by a number of law schools and can't decide which one to choose. If you promise to go to my alma mater, I will pay your tuition." The niece was ecstatic and said, "Thank you, uncle. I will go to your law school and I will make you proud."

The niece then went to another law school. Was she in breach of contract?

ANSWER:

13. A man said to his friend, "I will sell you my Ted Williams autographed baseball for $400." The friend responded, "It's a deal." When the friend later came by with the money, the man was shocked. "I was just making a joke," he said. "I would never part with that baseball."

Which of the following statements best describes the legal situation between the parties?

(A) If the man was really joking, there is no contract.

(B) If the friend really thought the man was serious, there is a contract.

(C) If a reasonable person in the shoes of the friend would have thought the man was serious, there is a contract.

(D) There is a contract even if the man was joking and the friend knew he was joking.

14. A store advertised "Brand X 48" Big Screen TVs $800." A woman drove to the store and said to a clerk, "I'd like one of those Brand X 48" Big Screen TVs, please." The clerk said, "Sorry. We all sold them out."

How would you characterize what has happened?

(A) The store made an offer. The woman accepted. A contract was formed and the store is in breach.

(B) The store made an invitation to make an offer. The woman made an offer. The store did not accept the offer. No contract was formed.

(C) The store made an offer but it was limited to a reasonable number of offerees and that number had presumably expired when the woman made her acceptance so the offer had lapsed. No contract was formed.

(D) The store made an invitation to make an offer. The woman made an offer. The store must give her a "rain check" good on their next shipment of the TVs. A contract may be formed when she presents the rain check.

15. A woman said to her friend, "I'll sell you my bicycle for $75." Two months later, the friend saw the woman and said, "I accept."

Is there a contract?

(A) Yes, because the offer was open for a reasonable period of time, and two months is probably reasonable.

(B) Yes, because the woman did not specify the time the offer was open, it is open for three months.

(C) No, because there was no offer.

(D) No, because the offer was open for a reasonable period of time, and it probably lapsed before two months were up.

16. Under the facts of the previous question, in addition to lapse of time, which of the following

events would also terminate the friend's power to accept the woman's offer?

(A) The woman dies.

(B) The friend says, "I'll give you $65 for it."

(C) The woman revokes (takes back) the offer.

(D) All of the above.

17. A woman said to her friend, "I'll sell you my bicycle for $75." The friend said, "I need some time to think it over. I'll give you a quarter if you give me two weeks to make up my mind." The woman agreed, but the friend did not give her the quarter. The next week, the woman ran into her friend and said, "I have sold the bicycle. I take back my offer." The friend then said, "I accept your offer to sell the bike for $75."

Is there a contract for the sale of the bicycle?

(A) Yes, because the offer was still open when the friend accepted.

(B) No, because the friend did not pay the quarter to keep the offer open, so the offer was revoked before acceptance.

(C) No, because the friend knew that the woman had sold the bicycle when she accepted the offer.

(D) No, because the offer was open only for only a reasonable time, so it had expired even if the woman had not revoked it.

18. The owner of a hotel on the Las Vegas strip offered $1,000 to the first person who ran to the hotel from Phoenix in three days or less. One runner decided to give it a try. He began running without notifying the owner, and as he approached the "Welcome to Las Vegas" sign on the strip, the owner jumped out from behind the sign and said, "Ha Ha. I revoke my offer!" The runner then completed his run to the hotel in less than three days.

Is the owner bound to pay the runner?

(A) Yes, because the runner accepted the offer when he began running, so the revocation came too late.

(B) Yes, because the runner prevented the owner from revoking the offer when he began running; therefore, the attempted revocation was ineffective and the runner accepted when he completed the performance.

(C) No, because an offeror may revoke at any time before acceptance, and the runner had not accepted at the time the owner revoked.

(D) No, because the runner did not notify the owner that he had begun performance.

19. A man said to a friend who paints houses, "I'm going on vacation for the month of July. I will give you $5,000 if you paint my house during that time. You can accept either by

promising to do it, or by doing it. See you in August."

When the man returned in August, he saw that the friend had slapped some paint on part of the house, but had then stopped. Is the friend in breach of contract?

ANSWER:

20. A business that regularly sells nails sent a letter on its letterhead to one of its best customers that said, "We are offering to sell you up to 10 barrels of nails at $100 per barrel. This is a firm offer and it is open for the next 10 days."

A week later, the customer walked into the business and the manager said, "If this is about that offer on the nails, I'm sorry to say we are going to have to take it back." The customer then said he wanted to buy four barrels of nails. Was a contract formed between the parties?

(A) Yes, because the offer could not be revoked during the time stated in the offer.

(B) Yes, because the customer had begun performance in reliance on the offer.

(C) No, because the offeror can revoke an offer at any time before acceptance, and in this case the offeror did so.

(D) No, because the business's letter to the customer was an invitation to make an offer and not an offer.

21. On Monday, a man mailed an offer to a woman. On Tuesday, the man thought better of it, and mailed a revocation of the offer to the woman. On Wednesday, the woman received the offer and mailed her acceptance. On Thursday, the woman received the revocation. On Friday, the man received the acceptance.

Is there a contract between the parties?

(A) No, because the man sent the revocation before the woman sent the acceptance.

(B) No, because the woman received the revocation before the man received the acceptance.

(C) Yes, because the woman accepted the offer when she mailed her acceptance, and that was before she received the revocation.

(D) Yes, because the woman reasonably relied on the offer since she did not know of the revocation.

22. In an email, a man offered to sell to a woman 10,000 widgets and told her the offer would be open for a week. The woman found retail space for a widget store and rented it for a year. She then went to the newspaper office and took out advertising that announced the opening of her widget store. She then went to the man's office and was about to tell him that she accepted the offer, but before she said anything, he said, "I revoke the offer." She then said, "I accept."

Was a contract formed between the parties?

(A) Yes, because of her performance.

(B) Yes, because of her reasonable reliance.

(C) No, because she accepted after the offer was effectively revoked.

(D) No, because the offer was by email and the acceptance was oral.

23. A contractor sent a fax to a lumberyard with which he regularly dealt, instructing the lumberyard to ship 1,000 4" x 4"s to a certain construction site by a certain day. The lumberyard had a shortage of 4" x 4"s at that time, but knew that contractors often attained the same result by putting together two 2" x 4"s. Thinking the contractor would rather have the 2" x 4"s than no wood at all, the lumberyard shipped 2,000 2" x 4"s instead of the 1,000 4" x 4"s.

The contractor claimed breach of contract. Is the lumberyard in breach?

(A) No, because the acceptance did not match the offer; therefore, there was no contract, so there could not be a breach of contract.

(B) No, because the lumberyard sent the 2" x 4"s as an accommodation, thinking the contractor could use them.

(C) Yes, because it accepted by shipping nonconforming goods.

(D) Yes, because the lumberyard's expression of acceptance operated as an acceptance even though it contained additional or different terms.

24. On April 2, Mercury, a manufacturer of indoor and outdoor thermometers, discussed with Tubular, a manufacturer of precision glass tubing, its needs for glass tubing for its thermometers. Immediately following their discussions, Tubular faxed to Mercury a Sales Order for 5,000 1-foot lengths of glass tubing, at a price of $5.00 per foot, to be delivered to Mercury's plant no later than May 1. The Sales Order contained other terms on the front and back of the form. Later that same day, Mercury faxed Tubular a written Acknowledgment, agreeing to the purchase of 5,000 1-foot lengths of glass tubing, at a price of $5.00 per foot, to be delivered to Mercury's plant no later than May 1. At the bottom of the Acknowledgment, Mercury wrote and underlined, "After accepting the delivery, we may have the glass tested for durability by a chemist of our choosing, and may reject it if it is not suitable for our purpose."

Did Mercury and Tubular form a contract by this exchange?

(A) No, because Mercury's Acknowledgment contained a term that was not included in Tubular's offer, making Mercury's Acknowledgment a counteroffer that was never accepted.

(B) No, because Mercury's acceptance was conditional on Tubular's agreement to the additional term, and Tubular did not agree to it.

(C) Yes, because Mercury responded with a definite and timely expression of acceptance that stated a term additional to those in the offer, and its acceptance was not conditional on Tubular's assent to those terms.

(D) Yes, because the additional term in Mercury's Acknowledgment did not materially alter the terms of Tubular's offer.

25. Assume the same facts as in Question 24, except that Mercury also wrote at the bottom of its Acknowledgment: "This acceptance is expressly made conditional on your assent to this additional term." Tubular nevertheless shipped the goods. When they arrived, Mercury had them inspected by a chemist and rejected them. Tubular claimed that that was a wrongful rejection because the term regarding inspection by the chemist was not part of the contract.

Is that term part of the contract?

(A) Yes, because it does not materially alter the contract.

(B) Yes, because Mercury made clear that it would not have a deal except on those terms.

(C) No, because there is no contract between the parties.

(D) No, because the contract does not include terms on which the writings of the parties do not agree.

26. Return again to the facts of Question 24. To refresh your recollection, Mercury stated in its Acknowledgment: "After accepting the delivery, we may have the glass tested for durability by a chemist of our choosing, and may reject it if it is not suitable for our purpose." It has not made its acceptance conditional on assent to that term.

Is that term part of the contract between the parties?

(A) Yes, because it does not materially alter the contract.

(B) Yes, because both parties are merchants.

(C) No, because the additional term would be "knocked out" and the default rule of the Code would be read in.

(D) No, because it materially alters the contract.

27. Return again to the facts of Question 24. This time, assume that Tubular stated conspicuously in the boilerplate of its Sales Order, "**Seller hereby disclaims all implied warranties, including but not limited to the implied warranty of merchantability.**" In its Acknowledgment, Mercury conspicuously stated, "**Seller gives buyer all applicable U.C.C. implied warranties.**" After accepting the shipment, Mercury made a claim for breach of the implied warranty of merchantability. Tubular responded, "Ha Ha! We didn't give you an implied warranty of merchantability."

How would a court determine whether the implied warranty of merchantability is part of the contract between the parties?

(A) It would find that the term of the contract is the term that is in the offeror's form.

(B) It would conduct the analysis under § 2-207(2).

(C) It would knock out both party's terms and read in the default term of the Code.

(D) All of the above, depending on the jurisdiction.

28. A rich uncle said to his niece, "I understand that you have been accepted by a number of law schools and can't decide which one to choose. If you go to my alma mater, I will pay your tuition." The niece was ecstatic and said, "Thank you, uncle. I will go to your law school and I will make you proud." The niece then enrolled in the uncle's alma mater, but when she sent him the first tuition bill he refused to pay, claiming that the contract was not enforceable.

Was there consideration for the uncle's promise to pay the tuition?

(A) Yes, the consideration was the niece's promise to go to the law school.

(B) Yes, the consideration was the niece's going to the law school.

(C) No, there is no consideration because the uncle was not benefitted by the niece's going to the law school.

(D) No, there is no consideration because the niece did not bargain for anything.

29. A manufacturer had a contract with a distributor to provide the distributor with 10 widgets a month for a year. In the middle of the third month, the distributor wrote to the manufacturer, explaining that because of a shift in the market, it wanted to terminate the contract. As it happened, the contract was not favorable to the manufacturer, so the manufacturer agreed to terminate the contract. A month later, the market shifted again, and the distributor claimed that the contract was still in effect.

Was there consideration for the agreement to terminate the agreement?

(A) Yes, because each party gave a bargained-for consideration to the other.

(B) Yes, because each party thought it would benefit from the termination.

(C) No, because neither party bargained for anything in order to terminate the agreement.

(D) No, because the agreement was for one year and could not be terminated before that time.

30. A rancher was driving by a neighbor's ranch when she saw some men loading cattle into a truck. She called the county sheriff, who arrested the men for cattle rustling. Later, when the men were convicted, a representative of the state Sheep and Cattleman's Association called both the sheriff and the rancher and told them that they were eligible for the Association's reward for actions or information leading to the arrest and conviction of cattle

rustlers. "Reward?" the rancher responded, "I didn't know there was a reward."

As a matter of contract law, is the Association obligated to pay the reward?

(A) To the sheriff only.

(B) To the rancher only.

(C) To both the sheriff and the rancher.

(D) To neither the sheriff nor the rancher.

31. A 25-year-old man became ill in a city far from his home. In the expectation of payment, an innkeeper provided him with food, lodging, and medical care that were worth $1,000, but through no fault of the innkeeper, the man died. When the man's father heard about the kindness of the innkeeper, he called him and promised to pay him $2,000. Later the father changed his mind and refused to pay the innkeeper anything.

Does the father have a contractual obligation to pay the innkeeper?

(A) Yes, he has an obligation to pay $2,000, the amount of the promise.

(B) Yes, he has an obligation to pay $1,000, the value of the benefit conferred on his son.

(C) No, because his performance was not bargained for.

(D) No, because his promise was not in writing.

32. A woman was hired as a secretary by a corporation. After she had been on the job for a week, the president sent her a letter informing her that the corporation would pay her a pension when she retired. Fifty years later, she decided to retire. When she went to the Human Resources department, she was told that she would not be receiving a pension because the new management was trying to save money.

Assuming there are no relevant statutes, is the corporation contractually obligated to pay her a pension?

ANSWER:

33. A man agreed to give his autographed baseball to a friend for either $100 or an autographed baseball cap at the friend's discretion, and the friend agreed.

Is there consideration for the exchange?

ANSWER:

34. A man orally hired a broker to perform a task for a 5% commission. After the broker successfully performed the task, the man honestly, but mistakenly, claimed that his recollection was that the broker was only entitled to a 4% commission. The broker agreed

to accept that amount and the man paid it. The broker then found and showed to the man an email in which the man acknowledged that the commission was 5%. The man nevertheless refused to pay the broker any more than the 4% he had already paid.

Is the man legally obligated to pay the broker the additional 1%?

(A) Yes, because there was no consideration when he paid only what he was obligated to pay anyway.

(B) Yes, because even though he thought he did not owe the 5%, a reasonable person would have known he owed that amount.

(C) No, because the man honestly believed he had a defense to the broker's claim for 5%.

(D) No, because the law favors the settlement of disputes.

35. In writing, a man offered an elderly woman $100,000 for her house, and the woman accepted in writing. The woman then discovered that her house was worth $250,000 and claimed that no contract was formed.

Will the woman be successful in her claim that no contract was formed because the consideration was not adequate?

ANSWER:

36. A woman who was a successful fashion designer agreed to give a man the exclusive right to the use of her name on endorsements in return for his agreement to pay her 50% of the profits he made on the endorsements. The woman then got a better offer, and looked for a way to get out of this contract. Her lawyer argued that while the man promised to pay her 50% of the profits from endorsements, he did not actually promise to seek endorsements. Therefore there was no consideration.

Will this argument be successful?

(A) Yes, because under the rule of mutuality of obligation, if he is not bound to do anything, then she is not bound to do anything either.

(B) Yes, because a promise requires a commitment, and he did not make a commitment.

(C) No, because the court will find an implied obligation on his part to make reasonable efforts to obtain endorsements.

(D) No, because the court will find an implied obligation on his part to obtain endorsements.

37. An artist induced a woman to agree to have her portrait painted for a certain price by telling her that she did not have to pay him if she was not satisfied with the painting. The artist then claimed that the contract was illusory because the woman was not obligated to do anything — she could just say she was not satisfied, and she would not have to pay.

Is the contract illusory?

(A) Yes, because the woman has a free out that will result in her not being bound.

(B) Yes, because her performance is subject to a condition.

(C) No, because the woman has to exercise her satisfaction in good faith.

(D) No, because a reasonable person can determine whether she should have been satisfied with the painting.

38. A lumberyard produced sawdust as a byproduct of its operations. It agreed with a producer of artificial logs to sell the log producer all the sawdust it produced in the next year at a certain price per pound. The lumberyard then got a better offer on the sawdust and sought to escape from the contract with the log producer on the grounds that the contract was illusory.

Is the contract illusory?

(A) Yes, because it lacks a quantity and there is no gap-filler for quantity.

(B) Yes, because the lumberyard is free to produce no sawdust, so it has not committed to do anything.

(C) No, because the quantity is whatever the log producer requires.

(D) No, because the output of the lumberyard can be determined in good faith.

39. A woman who was in the business of breeding horses sent a letter to a customer, informing him that she had a colt that was perfect for his needs. She told him the price was $2,000 and that she would hold that offer open for him for a month. He responded in a letter, "That sounds great, but I'd like to see how the colt develops. Can you keep the offer open for six months? I enclose a dollar to 'make it legal.'" The woman responded, "We have a deal."

Is the six month option contract enforceable?

(A) Yes, because there is a bargained-for consideration.

(B) Yes, because there is a firm offer that makes the option enforceable without consideration.

(C) No, because a firm offer is not enforceable beyond three months.

(D) No, because the consideration was nominal.

40. A man agreed to give his autographed baseball to a friend in return for the friend's everlasting gratitude, and the friend agreed.

Is there consideration for the exchange?

ANSWER:

41. On February 15, a professional singer and the entertainment manager of a hotel entered into a written contract whereby the singer agreed to perform at the hotel for the week of July 1–7 for a fee of $25,000. In early May, the singer had a hit song that, virtually overnight, made him a star who could command at least $75,000 for a one-week engagement. On June 1, the singer told the manager he would not perform unless he received $75,000 for his July 1–7 performances. The manager told him that "a deal is a deal," and refused to pay more than the previously-agreed upon $25,000.

Assuming the singer turned 18 on June 1, would he be entitled to refuse to perform the contract?

(A) Yes, because any contract he entered into while he was a minor was void.

(B) Yes, this contract was voidable at his option because he entered into it while he was a minor.

(C) No, because he was earning so much money that he would be considered an emancipated minor, capable of entering enforceable contracts.

(D) No, because he implicitly reaffirmed the contract when he asked the manager for more money to perform the same services.

42. Assume that, within days of his hit single's release, the singer from Question 41 signed a multi-album contract with a record company. The singer spent the whole week following his 18th birthday in the company's studios, recording and mixing songs. At the end of the week, the singer called the company's president. The singer told her that he appreciated all that the company had done for him, but he had received a better offer from another label. When the president sputtered, "But we have a contract," the singer replied, "Ha Ha! I was underage when I signed it."

Could the singer disaffirm his contract with the record company because he signed it when he was a minor?

(A) Yes, because any contract he entered into while he was a minor was void.

(B) Yes, this contract was voidable at his option because he entered into it while he was a minor.

(C) No, because he was earning so much money that he would be considered an emancipated minor, capable of entering enforceable contracts.

(D) No, because he implicitly reaffirmed the contract when he used the company's studio time and equipment following his 18th birthday.

43. A 17-year-old woman, who appeared to be older, purchased a car from a used car dealer for $1,000. Shortly after the purchase, she wrapped the car around a tree. She had the wreckage hauled to the dealer and demanded the return of her money. Is she entitled to disaffirm the contract?

(A) Yes, and the dealer must return the consideration she paid for the car.

(B) Yes, but the dealer must only return the remaining value of the car.

(C) No, because she did not appear to be a minor.

(D) No, because a minor is liable for necessaries.

44. A minor ate a meal at a local restaurant. When the bill was presented, he said, "Ha Ha! I don't have to pay because I am a minor!" Is the minor correct?

ANSWER:

45. A businessman who suffered from bipolar disorder contemplated the purchase of a small company. He could tell from the balance sheets, business plan, and other information that the business was in such distress that it was unlikely to recover. However, because he was in the manic phase of his illness and thought he had extraordinary business powers, he purchased the company in spite of his awareness of the problems. When he and his family realized that his mental illness had caused him to make the decision, he sought to avoid the contract. Will he be able to avoid the purchase?

(A) Yes, because he lacked the capacity to understand the nature and consequences of the transaction.

(B) Yes, because even though he had the capacity to understand the nature and consequences of the transaction, he was unable to act in accordance with that understanding.

(C) No, because he understood the nature and consequences of the transaction, and the other party did not know he was suffering from a mental illness.

(D) It depends on the jurisdiction.

46. A woman had a retirement fund contract under which she would be paid a fixed amount for her lifetime with the remainder paid to her heirs on her death. Because of her clinical depression, the woman's family had her declared incompetent and a guardian appointed. The woman then made a study of her retirement plan and came to the conclusion that it would be preferable to change the plan to one that paid her a higher amount for her lifetime with no remainder paid to her heirs on her death. This would be a rational choice if she lived longer than average life. She made this change to her contract with the retirement fund, but shortly after that she died, making the choice unwise in retrospect.

Will her heirs be able to avoid the new contract she made?

(A) Yes, because the contract is void.

(B) Yes, because the contract is voidable since she did not understand the nature and consequences of the transaction.

(C) No, because even though she understood the nature and consequences of the transaction and was unable to act in accordance with that understanding, the other party was not aware of her mental illness.

(D) No, because the change was a rational choice when she made it.

47. Assume that under the facts of Question 41, when the singer said he would not perform unless the manager agreed to pay him more money, the manager relented. After a lengthy face-to-face discussion the morning of June 8, the manager prepared a new contract with the same language as the first contract except that the singer's compensation changed from $25,000 to $50,000. After they tore up the old contract, the parties signed the new one. Thereafter, the singer kept the engagement, but the manager refused to pay more than the $25,000 he had originally promised. The singer sued.

What is the manager's best argument that he should not be held to the June 8 (second) contract?

(A) He signed it under duress.

(B) He signed it under undue influence.

(C) The contract is unconscionable.

(D) None of the above.

48. Assume under the facts of Question 41 that when the singer met with the manager on June 8, the singer was accompanied by a couple of older men, whom he introduced to the manager as his "advisors." When the manager rejected the singer's initial demand for more money, the elder of the two men motioned for the manager to come closer. When he did, the younger of the two men casually opened his suit jacket to reveal a pistol. Threatened by the gesture, the manager's negotiating strategy changed, and he and the singer soon came to an accommodation and signed the new contract.

Under these facts, would the manager have grounds to refuse to pay the singer more than the original $25,000?

(A) The manager should not be bound by the June 8 contract because he signed it under duress.

(B) The manager should not be bound by the June 8 contract because he signed it under undue influence.

(C) The manager should not be bound by the June 8 contract because to do so would be unconscionable.

(D) None of the above.

49. Returning to the facts of Question 47, assume that the manager drank heavily the day he
     and the singer negotiated and signed the agreement increasing the singer's compensation
     to $50,000.

     Can the manager defend the singer's suit by arguing that he was too intoxicated to form
     the requisite intent to be bound by the new contract?

     (A) No, because the manager voluntarily became intoxicated, and should not now be able
          to argue that he was not responsible for his actions while intoxicated.

     (B) No, because the manager's actions indicate that he was not sufficiently intoxicated so
          as to relieve him of his contractual obligations.

     (C) No, because the manager reaffirmed the June 8 contract by letting the singer
          perform at his hotel the week of July 1–7.

     (D) Yes, because the manager was so intoxicated that he could not form the requisite
          intent to contract, and the singer knew or should have known that the manager was
          intoxicated.

50. Having completed a very successful summer tour, in August the singer began hunting for
     housing befitting a rising music star. After some searching, he found a co-op apartment in
     New York City. Having agreed with the seller, Sam Sharman, on a price of $2.5 million, the
     singer paid $250,000 cash and signed a five-year installment purchase contract for the
     balance. Upon full satisfaction, Sharman would deliver title to the apartment, free of any
     liens or encumbrances (other than those in favor of the apartment building owner or
     cooperative).

     After moving into the apartment, the singer was visited by an attorney, who introduced
     himself as a representative of Otis Owen, the actual owner of the apartment that the singer
     was presently occupying. Owen was preparing to return to the city and had sent the
     attorney to notify Sharman, who was subletting from Owen, that he had 14 days to vacate
     the premises. When the singer told the attorney he must be mistaken because the singer
     had purchased the apartment from Sharman, the attorney responded, "I'm sorry, sir, but
     you're the one who is mistaken. Mr. Sharman has never owned this apartment, and had no
     right to sell it to you. You have fourteen days to vacate."

     When the singer received a payment due notice from Sharman a day or two later, he
     returned it unpaid with a note stating that he would not pay Sharman one cent more and
     that he would see Sharman in court. Sharman sued the singer for breach of the installment
     purchase contract. The singer countersued, seeking judicial rescission of the installment
     purchase contract and the return of his $250,000 down payment.

     Was the singer obligated to pay Sharman the remainder of the installments as promised,
     despite the fact that Sharman did not have the right to sell the singer the apartment?

     (A) No, because the singer lacked the requisite capacity to form a binding contract.

(B)   No, because the singer was mistaken in his belief that Sharman had the right to sell the apartment.

(C)   No, because Sharman misrepresented that he had title, or could give title, to the apartment to the singer.

(D)   Yes, because the singer did not ask Sharman whether he had title to the apartment before agreeing to purchase it from him.

51.   Assume, instead, that Sharman did have good title or the right to convey good title on Owen's behalf, and that the singer has been comfortably ensconced in the apartment since he moved in several months ago. Assume also that the contract included a provision for interest on the unpaid balance at 18% per year, and that the maximum interest rate permitted by applicable New York law is 16% per year.

Would the singer have grounds to avoid the contract with Sharman under these circumstances?

(A)   Yes, because the contract rate of interest is usurious, and therefore illegal.

(B)   Yes, because the contract rate of interest is usurious, and therefore unconscionable.

(C)   Yes, because Sharman breached the duty of good faith and fair dealing he owed the singer when he gave the singer a contract to sign that contained a usurious interest rate.

(D)   Yes, because Sharman actually or impliedly misrepresented that the interest rate included in the contract was not usurious.

52.   While he was strolling down the street one afternoon, a young woman approached the singer, handed him a piece of paper, and asked for his autograph. The singer obliged. A few days later, the singer received a phone call from an attorney at his record company, who explained that a young woman had delivered what appeared to be an agreement, signed by the singer, assigning her one-half of his royalties for the next five years in exchange for her domestic services. The singer denied signing any such agreement, and asked the attorney to describe the young woman. When the attorney did so, the singer realized it must have been the young woman who had asked for his autograph a few days earlier. The next morning, the same young woman appeared at the singer's door and asked, "Where shall I begin?" The singer responded, "What do you mean?" She replied, "We have an agreement. I clean your apartment once a week, and you pay me one-half of your royalties. You signed it, remember?"

Has the singer entered into an enforceable contract?

ANSWER:

53.   One night when he was looking for some excitement, the singer decided to read his contract with the recording company for the first time. He was horrified to discover that he was

bound for a 10-year term and that when that term expired, the company could renew it for another 10 years. If he had been aware of those terms, he never would have bound himself for such an extended period.

What is the singer's best argument that the contract, or at least that portion of it, is not binding on him?

(A) Because the company had a duty to disclose the term of the contract to him, their failure to disclose was the equivalent of fraud.

(B) The term is unconscionable.

(C) The term is illegal.

(D) Since he had a duty to read the contract before signing it, none of the above claims will be helpful to him.

54. Which of the following contracts, if oral, would likely *not* be within a state's statute of frauds?

   (A) A creditor and a friend of the debtor agree that the friend will guaranty the debt in exchange for the creditor's binding extension of time for payment of the debt.

   (B) A landlord and a tenant agree for the lease of land for two years.

   (C) A school board and a teacher enter into an agreement on January 10 for nine months of service to begin on September 1.

   (D) A retailer agrees to sell a television set to a consumer buyer for $399.

55. On January 10, the dean of a law school called a professor who taught in a distant state and asked her if she was interested in teaching at the law school for a year. The professor said she was, and they agreed that the professor would be employed at the law school from August 15 until May 30. They also agreed that the law school would pay a salary of $100,000 but would not pay any moving expenses.

   In August, the professor moved her family at considerable expense to the new law school, rented a house for 10 months, and commenced working. At the end of the first semester, the dean told the professor that the law school was terminating her employment effective immediately. When the professor protested that she had been hired until the end of May, the dean said, "I don't see any writing to that effect."

   Is the contract between the professor and the law school within the statute of frauds?

   (A) Yes, because it could not be performed within a year from the making.

   (B) Yes, because it was for more than $500.

   (C) No, because the professor detrimentally relied on the contract.

   (D) No, because it could have been performed within a year if the professor had quit, been fired, or died before January 10 of the following year.

56. Assume the facts of the previous question. Shortly after the conversation with the professor, the dean sent an email to the faculty that said, "I am pleased to announce that Professor Smith from Summit Law School will be joining us as a visitor during the next academic year. Please welcome her to our school." A month later, the dean sent a message typed on stationery that at the top said "From the desk of the Dean" to the payroll department. The message said, "Professor Smith's salary will be $100,000. Please make the

necessary arrangements."

Under these facts, can Professor Smith enforce the contract against the law school?

(A) No, because there was no written contract signed by both parties.

(B) No, because there was no writing signed by the professor evidencing the contract.

(C) Yes, because either one of the documents signed by the dean satisfied the writing requirement.

(D) Yes, because the documents together satisfied the writing requirement.

57. A woman said to her niece, "If you take care of me until I die, I will leave my estate to you." The niece took care of the woman for 51 years until she died. When the woman's will was read, the niece discovered that the woman had left her estate to charity.

If the niece claims the estate, is a court likely to award it to her?

ANSWER:

58. A grain buyer passed through North Dakota, stopping at various farms and making oral agreements to buy grain. When he returned to his office, he sent a signed confirmation to one farmer that stated, "This is to confirm that you agreed to sell us 100,000 bushels of winter wheat at $3 per bushel." When it came time to harvest the wheat, the market price was $3.50 per bushel, and the farmer refused to sell his wheat to the grain buyer.

If the buyer was to seek to enforce the contract, what would be the farmer's best defense?

(A) There is no writing signed by the farmer that evidences the contract.

(B) The farmer is not a merchant.

(C) The terms of the confirmation are too indefinite.

(D) The buyer sent the confirmation to the correct address, but it never got there.

59. A buyer and a seller orally agreed on the sale of a machine for $10,000. When the buyer refused to accept delivery of the machine, the seller sued for breach of contract. The attorney for the seller prepared a summons and complaint, which alleged the facts surrounding the formation of the contract and the buyer's breach, and asked for damages. The buyer responded in an answer which admitted the facts surrounding the formation and breach, but which pleaded the affirmative defense of the statute of frauds.

Will the defense of the statute of frauds be successful?

ANSWER:

60. The owner of a vacant lot of land orally agreed to sell the lot to a buyer for $50,000. The

buyer gave the seller a cash down payment of $5,000. With the owner's consent, the buyer took possession of the land and began to build a house on it. The seller then repudiated the agreement, claiming it was not enforceable because of the statute of frauds.

What is the likely result?

(A) The contract will be enforced because performance of it had begun.

(B) The contract will not be enforced, but the buyer will recover in restitution for the value of the benefit she conferred on the seller.

(C) The contract will not be enforced, but because of the buyer's reasonable reliance, the buyer will recover the out of pocket expenses she incurred.

(D) Because of her reasonable reliance, the contract will be enforced by specific performance.

61. The owner of a house located at 500 Eddy Avenue was trying to sell it for $300,000. After looking at the house, a buyer said, "I'll give you $300,000 for it, with closing in 90 days if the title is satisfactory." The seller said, "It's a deal if you give me a down payment of $30,000 toward the price, with the balance to be paid at closing." The buyer said, "I agree to that," and they shook hands. The buyer then wrote the seller a check for $30,000. On the memo line of the check, he wrote "DP on 500 Eddy $300,000." After the seller indorsed and deposited the check, he received an offer on the house for $325,000. He tendered a check for $35,000 to the buyer, saying, "I'm sorry I'm going to have to call off our deal. Here is your money back along with a little something for your trouble." The buyer refused to take the check and sued the seller for enforcement of the contract. The seller raised the defense of the statute of frauds.

Is the contract enforceable?

(A) Yes, because it is not within the statute.

(B) Yes, because it is evidenced by a writing sufficient to satisfy the statute.

(C) No, because the transaction is too indefinite.

(D) No, because the performance exception is not applicable under these facts.

62. A student applied to a bank for a student loan. The bank told the student that she did not have enough assets to secure the loan and asked if she could have someone guaranty payment of the loan. The student returned to the bank with her father, who orally promised to pay the loan if the student did not. In reliance on that promise, the bank loaned the student $10,000 in a signed writing. When the student defaulted on the loan, the bank sought payment from the father. The father told the bank that he had promised to pay the loan, but he nevertheless claimed it was not enforceable because it was not in writing.

Is the agreement enforceable against the father?

(A) No, because the transaction is within the statute of frauds.

(B) No, because the father received no consideration for his promise.

(C) Yes, because he admitted that he made the promise.

(D) Yes, because the bank relied on his promise.

63.   A rich uncle said to his niece, "I hear that you are planning to attend the law school that I went to. I promise to give you $500 to make things a little easier for you." The niece was ecstatic and said, "Thank you, uncle. I will make you proud." During her first semester at the law school, the niece spent $400 purchasing study aids, including, of course, *Q&A: Contracts*, that she would not have bought without knowing her uncle would be helping her out. When the niece politely asked him to send the money, however, the uncle refused to pay.

Is the uncle's promise to pay the $500 enforceable?

(A)   Yes, the consideration was the niece's promise to go to the law school.

(B)   Yes, the promise to pay $500 is enforceable because of the niece's reasonable reliance on it.

(C)   No, but the promise is enforceable to the extent of $400 because of the niece's reasonable reliance on it.

(D)   No, there is no consideration because the niece did not bargain for anything.

64.   An art museum announced a $10 million fundraising campaign to build a new wing. Seeing an opportunity to immortalize the family name, Alpha contacted the museum president and told her that he would donate $5 million toward the cost of the new wing if the museum would name the wing after his family. The museum agreed. The museum then publicly announced Alpha's pledge in order to encourage others to help it reach the goal, but did not take any other action. A few weeks later, Alpha informed the museum that his finances had collapsed and he would be unable to honor his pledge.

Does the museum have a claim against Alpha?

(A)   Yes, because there is a bargained-for contract between them.

(B)   Yes, because the promise is enforceable on a theory of reliance.

(C)   No, because a charitable pledge is not a promise on which a charity can foreseeably rely to its detriment.

(D)   No, because the facts do not suggest that the museum relied to its detriment on the pledge.

65.   An art museum announced a $10 million fundraising campaign to build a new wing. Alpha contacted the museum and pledged $5 million toward the cost of the new wing. After the

museum publicly announced Alpha's pledge, other donations poured in and the museum quickly reached its goal. The museum then announced that the campaign was officially concluded, and an architect and a contractor were hired. Shortly after ground was broken on the construction site, Alpha informed the museum that his finances had collapsed and he would be unable to honor his pledge.

Does the museum have a claim against Alpha?

(A) Yes, because there is a bargained-for contract between them.

(B) Yes, because the promise is enforceable on a theory of reliance.

(C) No, because a charitable pledge is not a promise on which a charity can foreseeably rely to its detriment.

(D) No, because the facts do not suggest that the museum relied to its detriment on the pledge.

66. An art museum announced a $10 million fundraising campaign to build a new wing. Alpha contacted the museum and pledged $5 million toward the cost of the new wing. After the museum publicly announced Alpha's pledge, other donations poured in and the museum quickly exceeded its goal, receiving over $5 million in pledges. Then, before the museum took any action, Alpha informed the museum that his finances had collapsed and he would be unable to honor his pledge.

Does the museum have a claim against Alpha?

(A) Yes, because there is a bargained-for contract between them.

(B) Yes, because the promise is enforceable on a theory of reliance.

(C) No, because a charitable pledge is not a promise on which a charity can foreseeably rely to its detriment.

(D) No, because the facts do not suggest that the museum relied to its detriment on the pledge.

67. A woman was hired as a secretary by a corporation. After she had been on the job for a week, the president sent her a letter informing her that the corporation would pay her a pension when she retired. Forty years later, suffering from an illness, she decided to retire. For a few months, the corporation paid the pension. Then, new management took over and looked for ways to save money.

Disregarding any relevant statutes, can the corporation stop paying the pension to the former secretary?

(A) No, because it is contractually bound to pay her.

(B) No, because she reasonably relied on the promise.

(C) Yes, because the promise was a gift promise.

(D) Yes, but the payment will be limited to the extent to which she relied on the promise.

68. In a telephone call, a school board offered a school teacher in a distant city a two-year teaching job for a salary of $40,000 per year. The teacher accepted the offer, and spent $5,000 relocating to the new city. Shortly after she got settled there, the school board told her that it did not have a position for her, and raised the statute of frauds as a defense to her claim for breach of contract.

What is the teacher's most likely recovery?

(A) Expectation damages of $80,000 for breach of contract.

(B) Reliance damages of $80,000.

(C) Reliance damages of $5,000.

(D) No recovery.

69. A 25-year-old man became ill in a city far from his home. In the expectation of payment, an innkeeper provided him with food, lodging, and medical care worth $1,000, but through no fault of the innkeeper, the man died. When the man's father heard about the kindness of the innkeeper, he wrote to the innkeeper and promised to pay him $2,000. Later the father changed his mind and refused to pay the innkeeper anything.

What is the innkeeper's best claim for recovery?

(A) Against the father for $2,000, the amount of the promise.

(B) Against the father for $1,000, the value of the benefit conferred on his son.

(C) Against the son's estate for $1,000, the extent of his reliance.

(D) Against the son's estate for $1,000, the value of the benefit conferred.

70. An elderly widower had two children, a son and a daughter. When the father became unable to care for himself, his daughter gave up her employment and moved in with him to take care of him full-time. During the time she cared for him, her father often said things to her such as, "You have been good to me. I will be sure to take care of you in my will." After a year, the father died and in his will he left his entire estate to the son. The daughter asked the estate to pay her $20,000, representing the reasonable value of the care she had provided. The son, as executor of the estate, refused to pay her anything.

What is the daughter's likely recovery?

(A) $20,000, as expectancy damages for breach of contract.

(B) $20,000, as the reasonable value of the benefit conferred on the father.

(C) The amount she forewent when she gave up her job in order to take care of her father.

(D) Nothing, because it is presumed that she conferred the benefit as a gift.

71. Glenn and Nick own adjoining lots along the Willamette River in Oregon. One day, while sitting on his boat dock, Glenn noticed that one of Nick's boats had broken loose from its moorings and was floating away down the river toward a set of rapids that would probably destroy it. Glenn grabbed some rope and a gaffing hook, hopped into his canoe, and managed to retrieve the stray boat. An hour later, Nick returned just as Glenn was re-securing Nick's boat. Glenn explained what had happened and Nick thanked him profusely for rescuing his boat.

Does Glenn have a viable claim against Nick?

(A) Yes, because Glenn conferred a benefit on Nick that was not a gift and was not officious.

(B) Yes, because a reasonable person in Nick's shoes would reward Glenn for his actions.

(C) No, because Glenn did not act with the intent of being rewarded for his actions.

(D) No, because Glenn's actions did not cost him anything.

72. Assume the facts of the previous question, but Nick's child was in the boat when it drifted away, and in the process of successfully rescuing the child, Glenn broke his arm and incurred medical expenses. Do these facts change the answer to the question?

ANSWER:

73. Assume that Nick was present when the boat floated away from the dock, but was unable to do anything about it because he had recently had knee surgery and was on crutches. Seeing his cherished boat begin to float away, he called out to Glenn, who was nearby: "If you will fetch my boat and bring it back to me, I'll pay you $100." Glenn, seeing an opportunity to make a few extra bucks, set out to retrieve the boat and return it to Nick. When he returned with the boat, Nick thanked him, handed him $10, and said, "Sorry, that's all I have on me."

Does Glenn have a viable claim against Nick for the balance of the money promised?

(A) Yes, based on reliance.

(B) Yes, based on restitution.

(C) Yes, based on contract.

(D) No, because rescuers are presumed to act as volunteers.

74. Assume that under the same facts as Question 72, after Glenn explained to Nick that he had injured himself while rescuing Nick's child, Nick promised to pay him $1,000. If Nick later refused to pay, what is the best theory for a claim by Glenn against Nick?

(A) There is a bargained-for contract.

(B) There is reliance.

(C) There is unjust enrichment.

(D) There is some combination of promise and restitution that makes the promise enforceable.

75. A buyer made an offer to enter into a contract with a seller. The seller wrote to the buyer, "I refuse to deal with you because about five years ago I sold you some goods and you did not pay the $1,200 contract price. My lawyer tells me it is too late for me to make a legal claim against you because of something called the statute of limitations, but I still don't like it." The buyer responded in writing, "I understand your situation. I didn't pay for the goods because I thought they were defective. I thought we would negotiate a settlement, but we never did. I am now willing to pay you $1,000 for them." Nevertheless, the buyer failed to pay the seller anything.

Does the buyer have an obligation to pay the seller?

(A) No, because the parties can't contract around the statute of limitations.

(B) No, because there is no consideration for the buyer's promise of $1,000.

(C) Yes, the buyer has an obligation to pay $1,000.

(D) Yes, the buyer has an obligation to pay $1,200.

76. Two parties negotiated the terms of an agreement, and then reduced the agreement to a writing that they both signed. Which of following statements most accurately describes where the terms of their agreement may be found?

    (A) The terms of the agreement are found exclusively in the writing.

    (B) The terms of the agreement may be found in both the writing and in oral understandings.

    (C) Whether the terms of the agreement are found exclusively in the writing or may be supplemented by oral understandings depends on the intention of the parties.

    (D) The terms of the agreement may be found in their negotiations as well as in their writing and their oral understandings.

77. Which of the following agreements is most likely partially integrated?

    (A) Two friends discussed the terms under which one would sell his car to the other. They then wrote on a piece of paper, "Sam agrees to sell his car to Becky for $5,000," and they signed the paper.

    (B) Two friends discussed the terms under which one would sell his car to the other. They then found a form for the transaction online, filled in the blanks, and signed it.

    (C) Two commercial parties negotiated an agreement for the rental of a fleet of cars, and signed a writing incorporating their understanding. One provision of the agreement stated, "This writing represents the complete and final understanding of the parties. There are no other understandings, oral or written."

    (D) Two commercial parties negotiated a 27-page agreement for the rental of a fleet of cars, and signed the document. The written agreement did not state that it represented the complete and final understanding of the parties.

78. When demonstrating a copy machine to a potential buyer for a business, the salesperson told the buyer that it made 30 copies per minute and could collate 20 copies at once. The buyer then purchased the copier. The written agreement prepared by the seller and signed by both parties contained terms that stated:

    Performance standards. This copier makes 20 copies per minute and collates 10 copies at once.

Entire agreement. This writing is intended by the parties as a final expression of their agreement and is intended also as a complete and exclusive statement of the terms of their agreement.

After using the copier, the buyer discovered that it made only 20 copies per minute and could collate only 10 copies at once. Is the buyer likely to succeed in a claim against the seller for breach of warranty?

(A) Yes, because the statements by the salesperson constituted express warranties.

(B) Yes, because the seller fraudulently misrepresented the copier.

(C) No, because the statements by the salesperson do not supplement the agreement because the agreement is found entirely in the writing.

(D) No, because the oral statements by the salesperson are not part of the agreement because they contradict the writing.

79. When demonstrating a copier to a potential buyer, the salesperson told the buyer that it made 30 copies per minute and could collate 20 copies at once. The buyer then purchased the copier. The written agreement prepared by the seller contained terms that stated:

Entire agreement. This writing is intended by the parties as a final expression of their agreement and is intended also as a complete and exclusive statement of the terms of their agreement.

After using the copier, the buyer discovered that it made only 20 copies per minute and could collate only 10 copies at once. Is the buyer likely to succeed in a claim against the seller for breach of warranty?

(A) Yes, because the statements by the salesperson constituted express warranties.

(B) Yes, because the seller fraudulently misrepresented the copier.

(C) No, because the statements by the salesperson do not supplement the agreement because the agreement is found entirely in the writing.

(D) No, because the oral statements by the salesperson are not part of the agreement because they contradict the writing.

80. A man sold his house for a fair price. The written agreement was very detailed and contained a clause that stated:

Merger. This writing contains the entire agreement of the parties. There are no other understandings, oral or written.

After the closing, the man sought to avoid the contract, claiming that the seller held a gun to his head and made him sign the contract.

Will this evidence be admissible?

(A) No, because the writing is a complete integration.

(B) No, because even if the writing is not a complete integration, this evidence contradicts it.

(C) Yes, because the evidence is offered to prove a defense to contract formation.

(D) Yes, because the writing is only a partial integration.

81. A man sold his house for a fair price. The written agreement was very detailed and contained clauses that stated:

> **Personal Property**: The following personal property is included in this sale: <u>none</u>.

> **Merger**. This writing contains the entire agreement of the parties. There are no other understandings, oral or written.

After the closing, the buyer noticed that there was no refrigerator in the kitchen. The seller pointed out that no personal property was included in the sale. The buyer pointed out that while they were negotiating the terms of the deal, the buyer asked the seller if he would sell the refrigerator for $300 and the seller had said yes.

Will this evidence be admissible?

ANSWER:

82. When demonstrating a copy machine to a potential buyer for a business, the salesperson told the buyer that it made 30 copies per minute and could collate 20 copies at once. The buyer then purchased the copier. The written agreement prepared by the seller contained a term that stated:

> **Entire agreement**. This writing is intended by the parties as a final expression of their agreement and is intended also as a complete and exclusive statement of the terms of their agreement. In particular, no representations about the specifications of the copier have been made.

After using the copier, the buyer discovered that it made only 20 copies per minute and could collate only 10 copies at once.

Is the buyer likely to succeed in a claim against the seller for *fraud*?

ANSWER:

83. A manufacturer of salad dressing ordered 1,000 dozen eggs from a supplier with a delivery date of June 1. The written agreement stated that it was the final and complete agreement of the parties. Just before they signed the writing, the manufacturer explained that it was having a new storage unit built and that it could accept delivery only if construction was finished. The supplier said that would not be a problem. When the eggs were tendered on June 1, the manufacturer claimed that it was not obligated to accept them because the storage unit had not been finished. The supplier said, "I don't see that in the contract."

Will evidence of that understanding be admissible in court?

(A) No, because the writing is a final and complete agreement between commercial parties.

(B) No, because the oral understanding contradicts the writing.

(C) Yes, because the oral understanding is offered to prove a formation defense.

(D) Yes, because the oral understanding is offered to prove a condition to performance of the contract.

84. A seller agreed to sell a buyer a certain quantity of a fertilizer compound for $100,000. The written agreement stated that it was the final and complete agreement of the parties. The seller delivered the fertilizer and submitted a bill for $103,000 to the buyer. The buyer called the seller and claimed there must have been a mistake, but the seller said that the bill was correct because in the chemical fertilizer business, with which they were both familiar, there is a trade usage that says that a stated price is only an estimate, and if the price of a raw material goes up, a seller may pass along that increase to the buyer. That, says the seller, is what happened.

Is the buyer liable for the price of $103,000?

(A) No, because the writing is a final and complete agreement between commercial parties.

(B) No, because even if the trade usage were admitted, it would contradict the express terms of the contract.

(C) Yes, because trade usage governs over the express terms of a contract.

(D) Yes, because trade usage is admissible to supplement even a final and complete agreement.

85. A seller sold a buyer a machine. The contract provided that the seller would service it "regularly." The seller serviced it every week. The seller then sold the buyer another similar machine with the same contract terms, and later sold a third machine. Immediately after the sale of the third machine, the seller discovered that in the trade, these machines are serviced only monthly. The seller told the buyer that because of that practice, it would be servicing the third machine monthly rather than weekly.

How often does the seller have to service the third machine?

(A) Regularly, as that term is defined by the court.

(B) Every week, because that is the course of dealing.

(C) Every week, because that is the course of performance.

(D) Monthly, because that is the trade practice.

86. An auto insurance policy stated that the insurance company would pay "all sums which the insured shall become legally obligated to pay as damages because of bodily injury" if he

was involved in an accident. The driver was involved in an accident and required by a court to pay $10,000 in damages for bodily injury and $50,000 in punitive damages. The insurance company refused to pay the punitive damages.

Which of the following rules of interpretation would best assist the driver in his claim that the insurance company was required to pay the punitive damages?

(A) *Expressio unius est exclusio alterius* ("the expression of one is to the exclusion of another").

(B) *Ejusdem generis* ("of the same kind").

(C) *Noscitur a sociis* ("known by the company it keeps").

(D) *Contra proferentem* ("construed against the drafter").

87. A party claims that the language of a contract is ambiguous, but the ambiguity is not clear from the face of the writing. Will the court allow the party to introduce evidence to prove that the language is susceptible to more than one meaning?

(A) It will not allow any evidence, because the "four corners" of the contract do not indicate that there is an ambiguity.

(B) It will admit all relevant evidence, because whether the meaning is clear and unambiguous can never be determined from the face of the writing alone.

(C) Whether the meaning is clear and unambiguous can never be determined from the face of the writing alone, but the court should admit only objective evidence supplied by disinterested third parties.

(D) It depends on the jurisdiction.

88. A contract contains a patent ambiguity (*i.e.*, it is clear from looking at the language that it could be interpreted in more than one way). To resolve this ambiguity, which evidence is a court *least* likely to admit?

(A) Prior drafts of the document.

(B) The conduct of the parties subsequent to execution of the agreement.

(C) Testimony by a person in the same trade or business who is not a party.

(D) Testimony by the lawyer who drafted the contract as to what she intended.

89. A material term of a contract is written in language that is ambiguous. Each party attributes a different meaning to the language and is not aware of the meaning attributed by the other party. Moreover, the evidence admitted indicates that each party's meaning was reasonable.

What should the court do?

(A) Interpret the language against the party that drafted it.

(B) Interpret the language against the plaintiff, who was unable to carry the burden of proving that its meaning should prevail.

(C) Conclude that the contract is voidable because of mutual mistake.

(D) Conclude that no contract was formed because the parties did not manifest mutual assent to the exchange.

90. The buyer for a software company shopped for a surge protector. She went to an electronics shop and saw a model that would serve the company's purposes. She asked the seller how much it cost, and the seller said, "Thirty-two-fifty." The buyer, having purchased surge protectors before, knew that this model should be worth around $3,000, and agreed to buy it. The seller sent the buyer an invoice for $3,250, while at the same time, the buyer sent the seller a purchase order for $32.50.

Is there a contract, and if so, for how much?

(A) There is a contract for $32.50, because the language should be construed against the seller, who created the ambiguity.

(B) There is a contract for $3,250, because the buyer knew the meaning attached to the language by the seller.

(C) There is a contract, but since no price was agreed upon, the price is a reasonable price.

(D) There is no contract because there is a misunderstanding about the price.

91. The owner of a home contracted with a real estate broker to assist with the sale of the home. The contract stated that the broker was to be the owner's exclusive broker and that the owner would pay the broker a fee of 6% of the sale price when the broker found a buyer ready, willing, and able to purchase the house.

     Several weeks later, the owner noticed that, other than putting a "For Sale" sign in front of the house, the broker had made no efforts to find a buyer. When confronted by the owner, the broker said, "Look at your contract. You promised to pay me *if* I found a buyer. I didn't promise to find a buyer."

     How would a court likely characterize the obligation of the broker?

     (A) To find a buyer.

     (B) To show the home to the average number of potential buyers that the average broker in the community would show it to.

     (C) To make reasonable efforts to find a buyer.

     (D) The broker had no obligation.

92. A student took a standardized exam administered by a national testing organization. Six months later, the student took the exam a second time and scored so much higher that the organization flagged the score for further examination. Pursuant to a provision in the contract for handling such a matter, the organization conducted an internal investigation and concluded that because of a handwriting disparity, the score was invalid. The organization informed the student of this conclusion, and informed him that he could supply additional information. In response, the student supplied the following:

     Verification that he was suffering from mononucleosis during the first examination; diagnostic test results from a preparatory course he took prior to the second examination (he had taken no similar course prior to the first examination) that were consistent with his performance on that test; a statement from a proctor who remembered his presence during the second examination; and statements from two students — one previously unacquainted with him — that he had been in the classroom during that test. He further provided a report from a document examiner obtained by his family who concluded that he was the author of both sets of answer sheets.

     The organization nevertheless concluded that on the basis of the handwriting, his score was invalid.

     What is the student's best cause of action if he sues the organization?

(A) Breach of the duty of good faith and fair dealing.

(B) Failure of the organization to follow its own rules and regulations.

(C) Breach of the duty to use reasonable efforts to make a determination.

(D) The relevant contract provision is voidable because it is unconscionable.

93. A plaintiff buyer of goods claims that the defendant seller breached the obligation of good faith.

What does the plaintiff have to prove?

(A) That the defendant was not honest in fact.

(B) That the defendant did not observe reasonable commercial standards of fair dealing.

(C) Either (A) or (B).

(D) It depends whether the seller is a merchant or not.

94. How does proving that the defendant breached the covenant of good faith and fair dealing enhance the remedies available against the defendant?

ANSWER:

95. Which of the following warranties is not found in contracts governed by U.C.C. Article 2?

(A) The warranty of fitness for a particular purpose.

(B) The warranty of good title.

(C) The warranty of habitability.

(D) The warranty of merchantability.

96. A manufacturer hired a painting contractor to supply paint matching its specifications for the job and to apply the paint to its buildings "in a manner satisfactory to the manufacturer."

If a dispute subsequently arose about the painter's performance, what standard should a court use to decide whether the painter performed satisfactorily?

(A) Whether the manufacturer was honestly dissatisfied with the painter's performance.

(B) Whether a reasonable person in the manufacturer's position would have been dissatisfied with the painter's performance.

(C) Whether the painter's performance met industry standards.

(D) Whether the painter performed in good faith.

97. Assume that under the facts of the previous question, the manufacturer was justifiably dissatisfied with the painter's performance. Investigation proved that the problem was with the quality of the paint used. The painter made a claim against the paint store that sold him the paint.

    If the paint store had supplied poor quality paint, would the painter have a claim against it for violating any U.C.C. Article 2 implied warranty?

    (A) Yes, the seller would have violated the implied warranty of merchantability.

    (B) Yes, the seller would have violated the implied warranty of fitness for a particular purpose.

    (C) No, because the seller was an innocent party since it merely resold paint that it received from the maker of the paint, who was ultimately responsible for the quality.

    (D) No, the seller would not have violated any implied warranty.

98. An interior design business that was expanding into graphic design and advertising ordered software from a company that produced software. The business informed the software company what its needs were, and the software company chose the software that would perform those tasks. The software came with the following statement:

    Warranty: This software will operate free of any errors for a period of one year from the date of purchase. During this time, the company will repair or replace the software. Other than the foregoing, **there are no warranties, express or implied, including but not limited to the implied warranty of merchantability.**

    Is this transaction governed by U.C.C. Article 2?

ANSWER:

99. Considering the same facts as the previous question, assume that a few weeks after the purchase, the business began to notice a recurrent glitch when it ran the software that made their work unusable. Assuming that U.C.C. Article 2 governs the dispute, does the business have a viable claim against the software company for breach of an express warranty or for breach of the implied warranty of merchantability?

    (A) Yes, for breaching both the express warranty and the implied warranty of merchantability.

    (B) Yes, for breaching the express warranty, but not the implied warranty of merchantability.

    (C) Yes, for breaching the implied warranty of merchantability, but not the express warranty.

    (D) No, neither the express warranty nor the implied warranty of merchantability was breached.

100. Assuming that U.C.C. Article 2 governs the dispute in the previous question, does the business have a viable claim against the software company for breach of the implied warranty of fitness for a particular purpose?

   (A) Yes, because the software company is a merchant dealing in goods of the kind.

   (B) Yes, because the software company knew the purpose for which the business wanted the software and selected the software for that purpose.

   (C) No, because the implied warranty of fitness for a particular purpose was effectively disclaimed.

   (D) No, because the facts did not give rise to the implied warranty of fitness for a particular purpose.

101. In a small town in Montana, there are only a few housepainters, and Betty has a reputation for doing the best job. Because of the short painting season, Betty only takes the number of jobs that she feels she can complete. Well in advance of the painting season, Sam hired Betty to paint his house for $6,000 in a written contract. Betty then discovered that because of a high demand for her services that season, she could charge more for each contract. She went back to Sam and told him, "I'm sorry, but I can't paint your house unless you agree to pay me $6,600." Sam agreed to pay her the additional money.

After she completed performance, Betty sent Sam a bill for $6,600. Sam paid her $6,000, claiming that that amount discharged his obligation to her.

Is Sam liable for the additional $600?

(A) No, because under the pre-existing duty rule, there is no consideration for Sam's promise to pay Betty $600 more.

(B) No, because Betty used economic duress to obtain Sam's consent.

(C) No, because the modification was not in writing.

(D) Yes, because the modification was fair and equitable in light of circumstances not anticipated by the parties when the contract was made.

102. Assume that under the facts of Question 101, Sam and Betty agreed to tear up their old contract and entered into a new written contract in which Betty agreed to paint Sam's house for $6,600. Does this make the agreement to pay $6,600 enforceable?

ANSWER:

103. Assume that under the facts of Question 101, after Betty began work, she discovered a number of spots where water had damaged the clapboards on Sam's house, requiring that they be replaced before she painted them. The painter is responsible for this work, but the number of problems is unusual. Betty requested that Sam pay $6,600 for the work instead of $6,000 and Sam agreed.

Is Sam liable for the additional $600?

(A) No, because under the pre-existing duty rule, there is no consideration for Sam's promise to pay Betty $600 more.

(B) No, because Betty used economic duress to obtain Sam's consent.

(C) Yes, because there is consideration for the modification.

(D) Yes, because the modification was fair and equitable in light of circumstances not anticipated by the parties when the contract was made.

104. A metal fabricator agreed to make a machine to the specifications of the buyer for a price of $6,000. During construction, the fabricator found that the work was more difficult than it had believed when it bid on the contract. The fabricator sent an email to the buyer explaining this situation, and asked if the buyer would pay an additional $600. The buyer responded in an email that it would. When it was completed, the fabricator sent the machine to the buyer with a bill for $6,600. The buyer refused to pay more than the original contract price of $6,000.

Is the buyer liable for the additional $600?

(A) No, because under the pre-existing duty rule, there is no consideration for the buyer's promise to pay the fabricator $600 more.

(B) No, because the fabricator used economic duress to obtain the buyer's consent.

(C) Yes, because consideration is not needed for the modification.

(D) Yes, because the modification was fair and equitable in light of circumstances not anticipated by the parties when the contract was made.

105. Assume that under the facts of Question 104, the buyer had agreed to pay the additional $600 because the fabricator, knowing that the buyer needed the machine for its assembly line, had threatened to delay its production unless the buyer paid the additional sum.

Would the modification still be enforceable?

ANSWER:

106. A buyer and a seller entered into a written contract that required the seller to deliver produce on November 1. The contract has a provision that states:

> **No oral modification.** No modification of this agreement is enforceable unless found in a writing signed by both parties.

On October 30, the seller telephoned the buyer and told him that he was having some problems with deliveries. The seller asked if it would be okay if he delivered first thing on November 2 instead of on November 1 and the buyer agreed. After the seller delivered on November 2, the buyer claimed that the seller was in breach of contract.

Is the seller in breach?

(A) Yes, because there is no consideration for the modification.

(B) Yes, because the modification is not enforceable under the "no oral modification" clause of the contract.

(C) No, because the buyer waived its right to claim breach when it agreed to the oral modification.

(D) No, because the modification is enforceable even though there is no consideration for it.

107. A man contracted with a contractor to make improvements to his house. Pretty soon, the man got carried away and made more improvements than he could pay for. The contractor threatened suit for nonpayment. The man told his parents about the situation, and the parents made an agreement with the contractor under which they agreed to be liable for the son's obligation and the contractor agreed that the son would not be liable.

Which of the following terms best describes the parents' agreement with the contractor?

(A) Suretyship.

(B) Modification.

(C) Novation.

(D) Substituted agreement.

108. If under the facts of Question 107, the parents did not pay the contractor, could the contractor enforce its agreement with the son instead?

ANSWER:

109. Sam, a homeowner, agreed with Betty that Betty would paint his house for $6,000. When Betty completed the job, she said, "Whew. That was a lot harder than I thought it would be. A reasonable painter would have charged you $7,200. But I'm going to bill you for only $6,600."

Does Sam have to pay the $6,600 bill?

ANSWER:

110. Assume that under the facts of Question 109, Betty completed performance and sent Sam a bill for the contract price of $6,000. Sam sent Betty a check for $5,400 along with a note saying that if she accepted this amount, then she had no further claim against him.

If Betty cashes the check, can she recover the additional $600 from Sam?

(A) No, because the parties made an enforceable accord and satisfaction.

(B) No, because the parties made an enforceable modification.

(C) Yes, because Sam used coercion to get Betty to agree to accept less.

(D) Yes, because there is no consideration for the accord.

111. Assume that under the facts of Question 110, Betty completed performance and sent Sam
      a bill for the contract price of $6,000. Sam called Betty and told her that he did not believe
      he owed her that much because she had not replaced all the rotten wood where she had
      painted. He told her he thought $5,400 was fair, and offered to pay her that much if she
      agreed that his payment of that amount would discharge the debt. She reluctantly agreed.
      Sam sent the check for $5,400 and Betty cashed it.

      Can Betty now claim the additional $600?

      (A) No, because the parties made an enforceable accord and satisfaction.

      (B) No, because the parties made a substituted contract.

      (C) Yes, because the accord was not in writing.

      (D) Yes, because there is no consideration for the accord.

112. A wallboard supplier promised a housing contractor 100,000 wallboard sheets by Novem-
      ber 1. After the supplier placed its order with its usual source, a wallboard manufacturer
      in China, the U.S. government, due to concern about the presence of toxic ingredients,
      unexpectedly placed an embargo on the importation of wallboard from China.

      When the supplier was unable to deliver wallboard to the contractor on November 1, was
      the supplier in breach?

      (A) Yes, because a party's contractual obligation is presumed to be unconditional unless
           the contract says otherwise.

      (B) Yes, because this event was reasonably foreseeable.

      (C) No, because performance has been made impracticable by the occurrence of a
           contingency the non-occurrence of which was a basic assumption on which the
           contract was made.

      (D) It depends on whether the contract provided that the supplier's exclusive source of
           supply was the wallboard manufacturer in China.

113. Assume that under the facts of Question 112, by the time the supplier obtained the sheets
      for delivery to the contractor, the cost of the sheets had gone up 10%, wiping out his profit
      and causing him a slight loss on the deal.

      Is the supplier excused because of impracticability?

ANSWER:

114. A wallboard supplier promised a housing contractor 100,000 wallboard sheets by Novem-
      ber 1. Prior to the delivery date, the housing market collapsed because of the subprime
      mortgage crisis and construction of all new homes came to a halt.

      On which of the following grounds is the housing contractor likely to be excused from the
      contract?

(A) Failure of a condition precedent.

(B) Frustration of purpose.

(C) Impracticability.

(D) None of the above.

115. In March, a woman made a number of bets on the Red Sox to win the World Series in October (this must have occurred in Nevada, the only state in which sports betting is legal). Enthusiastic about her chances, she showed a contractor friend the plans she had drawn up by an architect for her dream house. She said to the contractor, "If the Red Sox win the World Series, I'd like to go forward with the building of this house. How much would you charge to build it?" The contractor emailed her, "I will build the house to those specifications for $500,000." The woman emailed back, "It's a deal."

Are there any express conditions in this contract?

ANSWER:

116. Assume now the Red Sox win the World Series (we would say the condition has been *satisfied*). Who has to perform first: the woman by paying or the contractor by building the house?

   (A) The woman has to pay first and then the contractor has to build the house.

   (B) The contractor has to build first and then the woman has to pay for it.

   (C) The building and the paying are simultaneous.

   (D) The woman has to make "progress payments" as the building proceeds.

117. The situation described in the previous question is bad news for the contractor, who has to perform and then take a chance that he might not get paid. Is there anything the contractor can do about it when he negotiates the contract?

ANSWER:

118. A man agreed in writing to sell his car to a woman for $10,000. On the agreed date for performance, the man tendered the car but the woman did not tender the $10,000, telling the man she would pay him later. Is the man justified in not giving her the car?

   (A) No, because he had promised to tender the car on that date.

   (B) No, because there is no express condition making his performance a condition of her performance.

(C) Yes, because performance by each party is an implied condition of performance by the other party.

(D) Yes, because her material breach discharges the man's duty.

119. A man agreed in writing to sell his car to a woman for $10,000. They agreed that he would give her the car immediately, and she would have 30 days to pay the money. Thirty days after he gave her the car, she did not pay him. What is the man's remedy?

(A) Repossess the car.

(B) Rescind the contract.

(C) Sue her for $10,000.

(D) All of the above.

120. Let's go back to the contract for the construction of a house to certain specifications for $500,000 in Questions 115–17. Assume that the contractor did not contract around the default rule, and the $500,000 was payable on completion of his performance. After he told her the house had been completed, the woman inspected it. She told the contractor, "You did not satisfy the condition of building the house to specifications. There is no molding around the bedroom ceilings and the lawn was not sodded. Therefore, I don't have to pay you."

Is the woman correct?

(A) Yes, because an express condition was not satisfied.

(B) Yes, because the contractor has not brought about the event that had to occur before her performance became due.

(C) No, because the contractor substantially performed.

(D) No, because the contractor did not breach since his failure to perform according to the specifications was immaterial.

121. An insurance company has a policy with a homeowner that covers theft. The policy conspicuously states:

> **If the homeowner does not report a loss within 30 days of the loss, the insurer is not responsible for it.**

A homeowner suffers a loss from theft and reports it to the insurance company 32 days later. What is the homeowner's best argument that the insurance company is responsible for the loss?

(A) The homeowner substantially performed.

(B) Although the condition was not satisfied, the condition should be excused.

(C) The provision is contrary to public policy.

(D) The homeowner's breach was immaterial.

122. A lawyer, who was currently leasing space in a building owned by Alpha, wanted to lease space for her growing law practice in a building owned by Beta. However, the lawyer could not afford to pay rent on two places. On July 1, she signed a contract agreeing to lease space in Beta's building commencing September 1, subject to her being released by Alpha from her current lease, and commencing January 1 if Alpha did not release her.

By September 1, the lawyer had been unsuccessful in getting Alpha to release her from her current lease. Can Beta begin charging the lawyer rent as of September 1?

(A) Yes, because she promised to pay rent to Beta starting September 1.

(B) Yes, because she promised to induce Alpha to release her from her present lease and she failed to do so.

(C) Yes, because otherwise Beta, who could not arrange to lease the space to someone else if the lawyer was unable to move in by or shortly after September 1, would suffer a forfeiture if the space went unleased.

(D) No, because the lawyer's obligation to move in was conditioned on Alpha releasing her from her current lease.

123. Assume that the specifications for the woman's home in Question 115 stated that the contractor was to use exclusively "Acme No. 63" bricks in constructing the circular fireplace, hearth, and chimney. When the contractor ordered the bricks, his supplier told him he did not have a sufficient inventory of Acme No. 63 bricks to fill the order, and would not have them for another three weeks, which would set the construction schedule back considerably. The contractor found another style of brick, Brown No. F-17, which appeared to be identical in every respect to Acme No. 63 bricks, except that they had "Brown," rather than "Acme," molded into the face of each brick. Because the contractor intended to install the bricks so that the "logoed" side of the bricks was not showing anyway, he ordered a sufficient supply of Brown No. F-17 bricks to timely complete the job.

Did the contractor materially breach its contract by using Brown bricks instead of Acme bricks?

(A) Yes, because the contractor's use of Brown bricks, rather than Acme bricks, substantially deprived the woman of the benefit of her bargain.

(B) Yes, because the contractor cannot adequately compensate the woman for any diminution in the value of the house to the woman as a result of the contractor's use of Brown bricks rather than Acme bricks.

(C) Yes, because the contractor's substitution of Brown bricks for Acme bricks was inconsistent with the contractor's duty of good faith and fair dealing.

(D) No, because the contractor's use of Brown bricks when Acme bricks proved to be unavailable in adequate quantities did not substantially deprive the woman of the benefit of her bargain, was consistent with the contractor's duty of good faith and fair dealing, and the contractor can adequately compensate the woman for any diminution in the value of the house as a result of the contractor's use of Brown bricks rather than Acme bricks.

124.   Suppose that the specifications stated that the "Acme" label was to face out on every third brick because the woman planned to have *Architectural Monthly* shoot a photo spread of the new house and she knew that Acme would be very generous to a homeowner who featured its product so favorably. Unfortunately, the contractor was unable to timely acquire a sufficient supply of Acme bricks to satisfy that specification.

If the contractor laid all of the hearth, fireplace, and chimney bricks "face in" — so that the appearance of the brick would be uniform, rather than having bricks stamped "Acme" and bricks stamped "Brown" showing, which of the following would be true?

(A)   The contractor materially breached its contract with the woman.

(B)   The woman's duty to pay the contractor upon completion of the house would be suspended until the contractor cured the nonconformity by dismantling and relaying the brick hearth, fireplace, and chimncy.

(C)   The woman's duty to pay the contractor upon completion of the house would be discharged because of the contractor's uncured, material breach.

(D)   The contractor's sole liability to the woman would be for any diminution in the value of the house to the woman as a result of the contractor's use of Brown bricks rather than Acme bricks when the supply of Acme No. 63 bricks ran out.

125.   Assume a contractor did such a poor job constructing a building that a court found that the contractor did not substantially perform. Is the contractor barred from any recovery?

ANSWER:

126. On May 1, a buyer agreed in writing to purchase a house from the seller for $250,000, with payment to be made on closing on July 1.

    Which of the following statements by the buyer on June 1 would constitute an anticipatory repudiation of the contract?

    (A) The buyer told the seller, "I recently lost my job and I am not sure I'll be able to pay you the entire $250,000 on July 1."

    (B) The buyer told his friend, "I know the seller is planning to blow the money I promised to pay him for the house on a trip to Vegas. That just seems such a waste that I'm not going to pay him anything. I'm not crazy about the house anyway."

    (C) The buyer told the seller, "I have thought this over, and I am not going to pay you the money I promised you."

    (D) The buyer told the seller, "The more I think about it, the more I am convinced that you are asking too much for the house. Would you agree to sell it to me for $225,000, instead of $250,000?"

127. Assume the facts are the same as in Question 126, except that the seller said nothing and on June 1 the buyer saw in the newspaper that the house had been sold. Has the seller repudiated?

ANSWER:

128. Assume the facts are the same as in Question 126, except that on June 1 the buyer told the seller, "I absolutely, unequivocally am not going to close on the house and pay you the $250,000 until July 2." Has the buyer repudiated?

ANSWER:

129. Assuming that the buyer's statement in Question 126 constituted an anticipatory repudiation, which of the following would the seller be entitled to do in response to the buyer's repudiation?

    (A) Do nothing, hoping that the buyer would, in fact, perform as promised.

    (B) Cancel the contract and retain the house.

(C) Sell the house to another buyer for $245,000 and sue the buyer for the $5,000 difference between the contract price and the resale price, plus whatever other damages the seller incurred.

(D) All of the above.

130. Under the facts of Question 126, assume that after the buyer's repudiation, the seller chose to do nothing, hoping the buyer would, in fact, perform as promised. In fact, the buyer called the seller the next day and said, "I don't feel comfortable being a dirty contract breaker. I fully intend to keep my promise and pay you $250,000 for the house and close on July 1."

Would the seller still be entitled to cancel the contract, sell the house to another buyer, or sue the buyer for damages?

(A) Yes, because the seller did not seek the buyer's retraction.

(B) Yes, because the buyer's repudiation preceded the seller's sale of the house to another buyer.

(C) No, because the buyer retracted his repudiation before July 1.

(D) No, because the buyer retracted his repudiation before the seller acted in reliance on the buyer's repudiation or indicated that he considered the repudiation to be final.

131. In Question 126, assume that in order to sell the house to the buyer "free and clear" of any liens or other impediments of title, the seller had to pay the last $5,000 he owed the sellers from whom he had bought the house 18 months earlier, and had to obtain and record a release of that lien.

If the buyer repudiated, did the seller have to pay off the loan prior to July 1 if the remaining $5,000 was not otherwise due until December 31?

ANSWER:

132. On May 1, a contractor agreed to buy 100 barrels of nails from a supplier, with payment and delivery on June 1. On May 10, the supplier called the contractor and said, "The price of nails is going up. I just don't know if we are going to be able to make that June 1 delivery to you." Which of the following statements best characterizes the legal situation of the parties?

(A) The supplier has breached by anticipatory repudiation, entitling the contractor to choose a remedy.

(B) The contractor is required to demand adequate assurance of due performance from the supplier and must make his demand in writing.

(C) The contractor is entitled to demand adequate assurance of due performance from the supplier and may make his demand by any reasonable means.

(D) The contractor is entitled to demand adequate assurance of due performance from the supplier and must make his demand in writing.

133. Returning to the facts of Question 126, assume that on June 1 the buyer said to the seller, "I recently lost my job and I am not sure I'll be able to close on July 1." The seller responded, "You are making me nervous about this whole deal. If you don't pay me the $250,000 by June 15, I am going to cancel the deal."

How should the attorney for the buyer analyze this exchange?

(A) The buyer committed a breach by anticipatory repudiation, so the seller was not required to demand reasonable assurances.

(B) The seller had reasonable grounds to believe that the buyer might breach, but the seller did not demand reasonable assurances.

(C) The seller had reasonable grounds to believe that the buyer might breach, and the seller demanded reasonable assurances.

(D) The seller did not have reasonable grounds to believe that the buyer might breach, so the seller was not entitled to demand reasonable assurances.

134. Under the facts of the previous question, assume that the seller had simply demanded assurance by June 10. Which of the following statements or acts by the buyer would have best satisfied the seller's demand?

(A) The buyer told the seller on June 3, "I'll do everything I can to make sure that I have the money by July 1."

(B) On June 10, the seller received a letter from the buyer's bank informing the seller that the buyer had been having cash flow problems, but would have sufficient cash on hand on July 1 to purchase the house.

(C) On June 14, the buyer called the seller and told him, "I just got off the phone with my financial adviser, who was on vacation all of last week, and I told her to sell some of the stocks I bought with the money I inherited from my rich uncle. She said it would take a couple of days to get me a check, but I will have the $250,000 before July 1."

(D) On June 30, the buyer showed up at the seller's house with a certified check for $250,000 in cash to purchase the house.

135. Assuming that the buyer adequately assured the seller that he would perform as and when promised, would the seller nevertheless be entitled to sell the house to a third party or otherwise dispose of it prior to July 1 because of the buyer's behavior?

ANSWER:

136. If the buyer failed to timely satisfy the seller's reasonable request for adequate assurances of performance, which of the following would the seller have been entitled to do?

(A) Urge the buyer to reconsider and perform as and when promised.

(B) Cancel the contract and retain the house.

(C) Sell the house on June 24 to a new buyer for $245,000 and sue the original buyer for $5,000, plus any incidental and consequential damages the buyer's repudiation caused the seller.

(D) All of the above.

137. In a jurisdiction that has enacted the U.C.C. but has not had a case involving a demand for assurances, a supplier of electricity demanded assurances from the buyer, but the buyer claimed that it was not required to respond to a demand for assurances under the law of the state.

Which of the following would constitute an appropriate way for the court to reach the conclusion that the buyer was required to respond to a demand for assurances?

(A) Because electricity is a good, the U.C.C. applies to the transaction and it contains a provision for demand for assurances.

(B) Electricity is not a good, but it is like a good, so by analogy to the U.C.C. the law recognizes a demand for assurances.

(C) Electricity is not a good and is not analogous to a good, but a demand for assurances is recognized as a part of the common law.

(D) All of the above.

138. A contractor agreed in writing to build a building on an owner's land for $100,000. The contractor's expected cost to complete the project was $90,000. The owner repudiated the contract after the contractor spent $60,000. The owner did not pay the contractor anything, and the contractor cannot salvage any value from the money spent. The value to the owner of the partially completed building was $40,000.

What amount can the contractor claim (1) under expectancy damages, (2) under reliance, and (3) under restitution?

ANSWER:

139. The owner of a plot of land entered into a contract with a builder to build a house to certain specifications on the land for $200,000, to be paid on completion. The builder expected to spend $180,000 on labor and materials, and make a profit of $20,000. When the builder had completed 75% of the construction, the builder repudiated the contract without cause. The owner had another builder complete the house for the reasonable cost of $75,000. How much should the owner pay the builder?

(A) Nothing, because the builder materially breached.

(B) $125,000, because that amount will compensate the builder for the benefit conferred.

(C) $135,000, because that is the amount the builder is out of pocket for labor and materials.

(D) $150,000, because the builder completed 75% of a $200,000 contract.

140. Assume under the facts of the previous question that after the breach the owner was able to find another builder who completed the house for $40,000. What is the most the owner should pay the builder?

ANSWER:

Questions 141–45 are based on the following fact pattern: A restaurant contracted with a seller to buy a certain pizza oven for $10,000 and gave the seller an $800 down payment. The seller knew that if the oven was not delivered on time, the restaurant would be unable to sell pizzas. Prior to delivery, the restaurant hired a contractor to construct a base on which the oven would stand for $500. The seller then breached the contract and did not deliver the oven. The restaurant then reasonably spent $100 hiring a restaurant supply broker to find a comparable oven. The comparable oven cost $11,000 but did not fit on the base, so the restaurant had to spend an additional $500 to build a new base. Because the restaurant did not have the oven, it was unable to sell pizzas for 30 days and lost $6,000 in profit.

How would you characterize the following claims by the restaurant?

141. The $800 down payment.

ANSWER:

142. The $500 cost of the base.

ANSWER:

143. The $100 spent finding another oven.

ANSWER:

144. The $1,000 additional cost of the new oven.

ANSWER:

145. The $6,000 lost profit.

ANSWER:

146. A student bought a new computer from a computer store for $2,000. The specifications stated that the computer had a terabyte of memory. After he used it for a while, the student discovered that it had only one-half of a terabyte of memory. The store sells the same model of computer with one-half of terabyte of memory for $1,800. A computer repair shop will install another one-half of a terabyte of memory for $240.

    What is the Code remedy for the breach of warranty?

    (A) The seller must repair or replace the computer so that it conforms to what was promised.

    (B) The seller must pay the student $200.

    (C) The seller must pay the student $240.

    (D) The seller must pay the student the difference in value between the goods as promised and the goods as delivered, which could be either $240 or $200 depending on the measure used.

147. A manufacturer of high-end computers desperate to attract customers promised that a new model, costing only $5,000, had specified features that are normally found only in computers costing $12,000. A purchaser of the computer discovered that in fact the computer did not have all of the promised features, and only had the features of a computer costing $6,000.

In a claim for breach of warranty, how much is the purchaser entitled to?

ANSWER:

148. A buyer contracted to purchase a home for $300,000, with a closing date two months later. Before the closing date, the city announced that it would build a park next to the home, and its value increased to $400,000. On the closing date, the seller refused to sell the home. What is the buyer's remedy?

(A) $100,000, the difference between the purchase price and the value of the home.

(B) Specific performance requiring the seller to convey the home.

(C) Either A or B.

(D) The buyer is not entitled to a remedy because the unanticipated event excuses the seller's nonperformance.

149. A professional football player signed a contract to play with an NFL club. His standard player's contract states:

The Player hereby represents that he has special, exceptional and unique knowledge, skill and ability as a football player, the loss of which cannot be fairly or adequately compensated by damages and therefore agrees that the Club shall have the right . . . to enjoin him by appropriate injunction proceedings against playing football . . . for any person, firm, corporation or institution.

The player's club had a number of other players in his position, and he did not get much game time. When the player was offered an opportunity to play football in Europe for more playing time and more money, he breached his contract and signed with a European team. What is his club's likely remedy?

(A) It will hire another player to fill his position and recover the difference between what it had to pay the replacement and the contract price of the player.

(B) It can get an order of specific performance ordering the player to play for the club.

(C) Because the player agreed to injunctive relief in the contract, the court will enjoin the player from playing for another team.

(D) The court is not bound by the contract, but is nevertheless likely to enjoin the player from playing for another team.

150. A party willfully and intentionally breached a contract. In addition to the standard contract

remedies, which of the following can the non-breaching party recover?

(A) Attorney's fees.

(B) Punitive damages.

(C) Both attorney's fees and punitive damages.

(D) Neither attorney's fees nor punitive damages.

151. On March 14, Mercury, a thermometer manufacturer, entered into a contract with Tubular, a manufacturer of precision glass tubing, to purchase 5,000 1-foot lengths of glass tubing, at a price of $5.00 per foot, to be delivered to Mercury's plant no later than May 1.

On April 15, Mercury agreed to purchase the tubing from another seller at a price of $4.50 per foot, and refused to accept the shipment from Tubular when it arrived on May 1.

What remedies does Article 2 afford Tubular against Mercury?

ANSWER:

For Questions 152–55, use the facts from the previous question and also assume that:

1. Tubular has the manufacturing capacity to produce orders on demand.
2. On May 15, Tubular entered into a contract to sell 4,000 feet of the glass tubing originally destined for Mercury to a new buyer for $6.00 per foot, and the new buyer agreed to transport the glass at its own expense from Tubular's plant to its factory no sooner than June 1.
3. Tubular did not notify Mercury of its sale to the new buyer.
4. The market price of the glass tubing on April 15 was $5.00 per foot.
5. The market price of the glass tubing on May 1 was $5.50 per foot.
6. The market price of the glass tubing on May 15 was $6.00 per foot.
7. The transportation cost between any two locations involved in these Questions is $100 per 1,000 feet of glass tubing.
8. The cost of storing glass tubing is $0.05 per foot per month.
9. Tubular's cost of manufacturing the tubing ordered by Mercury was $4.50 per foot.

152. What resale damages could Tubular recover under U.C.C. § 2-706 as of June 1, taking into account Tubular's contract with the new buyer?

(A) $0.

(B) $1,500.

(C) $1,750.

(D) $2,150.

153. Assuming that Tubular is entitled to recover contract-market differential damages under

U.C.C. § 2-708(1), what is the measure of those damages?

(A) $0.

(B) $500.

(C) $750.

(D) $3,250.

154. What lost profit damages under U.C.C. § 2-708(2) is Tubular eligible to recover, if any?

(A) $0.

(B) $1,250.

(C) $2,500.

(D) $3,250.

155. Is Tubular eligible to sue for the contract price under U.C.C. § 2-709, and if so, what is the measure of those damages?

ANSWER:

156. On July 14, Monica, a fruit merchant, mailed Chandler, a fruit stand operator, a written offer to sell up to 500 crates of mangoes for $6.00 per crate. By the terms of Monica's offer, Chandler had the exclusive right to accept or decline the offer until July 25 at 5:00 p.m. Chandler received Monica's offer at 2:00 p.m. on July 16.

On July 17, Monica wrote to Chandler revoking the offer. Later that same day, Monica sold all 500 crates of mangoes to a new buyer for $6.50 per crate.

On July 19, Chandler wrote to Monica stating that he would purchase 100 crates of mangoes from Monica for $6.00 per crate, provided that Monica deliver the mangoes no later than September 1.

Monica received Chandler's letter on July 21. Monica immediately sent a fax to Chandler informing him that she had revoked her offer and sold the mangoes to a new buyer. Chandler received Monica's July 17 letter a few hours after receiving Monica's fax.

Do Monica and Chandler have a contract?

(A) No, because Chandler's response to Monica's offer contained an additional term, making it a counteroffer rather than an acceptance.

(B) No, because Monica revoked the offer on July 17 before Chandler accepted the offer on July 19.

(C) Yes, because a contract was formed on July 19 when Chandler dispatched his acceptance.

(D) Yes, because a contract was formed on July 21 when Monica received Chandler's acceptance.

157. Assume the facts of the previous question and also assume that:

1. Monica could acquire another 100 crates of mangoes in time to deliver them to Chandler by September 8.

2. Chandler could purchase replacement mangoes for delivery on or before September 1 from another seller for $7.00 per crate (including delivery).

3. The market price of mangoes on July 21 was $6.50 per crate.

4. The market price of mangoes on September 1 was $7.00 per crate.

5. There are 30 mangoes in a crate and Chandler sells 50 crates of mangoes per week to his customers at a price of three mangoes for $1.

If Chandler sued Monica, which U.C.C. Article 2 remedy would afford Chandler the most complete recovery against Monica?

(A) Cover damages under U.C.C. § 2-712.

(B) Contract-market differential damages under U.C.C. § 2-713.

(C) Damages for nonconformity under U.C.C. § 2-714.

(D) Specific performance under U.C.C. § 2-716.

158. A small interior design business wanting to expand into graphic design contracted with a computer software company to design customized graphics software for it. The design business told the software company that it needed the software to produce a product for an advertising company it planned to contract with. The computer company promptly designed and delivered software at a cost of $3,000 and promised that the software would perform the required functions. The contract conspicuously stated: **"There are no warranties, express or implied, including but not limited to the implied warranty of merchantability."**

Less than two weeks after taking delivery of the software, the design business noticed a recurrent glitch that prevented the software from performing one of the promised functions. It complained to the software company, but the software company was unable to solve the problem. While the software company was trying to fix the problem, the design company lost the advertising contract on which it would have made a profit of $1,000. Worse, the advertising company threatened to sue for breach of contract. The design company had to pay a lawyer $500 and the lawyer negotiated a settlement in which the design company agreed to pay the advertising company damages of $600. Finally fed up with it all, and wanting to prevent any further loss of business, the design company purchased software that would perform all of the required functions for $4,000.

In a suit against the software company, how much is the design company likely to recover?

(A) $1,000.

(B) $2,000.

(C) $2,600.

(D) $3,100.

159. A man purchased a life insurance policy from an insurance company. The insurance company promised that in the event of his death, the company would pay $100,000 to the person he named as beneficiary of the policy on the appropriate form. On that form, the man wrote: "My wife Magdalena." When the man died with the policy in force, the company refused to pay the benefit to Magdalena. She tried to get the executor of his estate to make a claim, but the executor begged off, claiming it was not his responsibility since the insurance money did not pass through the estate.

Can Magdalena sue the insurance company herself?

(A) Yes, because she is a third-party beneficiary of the contract.

(B) Yes, because the man effectively assigned his rights to the money to her.

(C) No, because she is not in privity of contract with the insurance company.

(D) No, because she is not the executor of the estate.

160. A woman needed money to purchase a house. She was able to borrow the money from a friend, who required that she pay back the loan with interest in monthly payments over 20 years. A few years later, the woman sold the house. Because the loan had a favorable rate of interest, the woman and the buyer entered into a contract in which they agreed that the buyer would pay the remaining balance on the loan to the friend. After a few years, the buyer stopped making payments to the friend.

Can the friend sue the buyer for repayment of the loan?

(A) Yes, because the friend is a third-party beneficiary of the contract.

(B) Yes, because the parties entered into a novation in which the buyer became obligated on the loan instead of the woman.

(C) No, because the friend is not in privity of contract with the buyer.

(D) No, because the friend is only an incidental beneficiary of the buyer's promise.

161. A man did not take very good care of his house, to the annoyance of his neighbor, who repeatedly complained to the man that the poor appearance of his house was causing the value of neighboring properties to decline. One day, the man said to his neighbor, "I have good news for you. I have retained Peter's Painting to fix up and paint my house." The neighbor was pleased, but when nothing happened for a few months, the neighbor asked what was going on. The man said, "Yeah, those dirty contract breakers told me they were

not going to do the job. I am really annoyed, but I don't have the time to do anything about it and I'm afraid I'm not in any hurry to get someone else to do the job."

The neighbor wants to know if he can bring a claim against Peter's Painting for breach of contract.

ANSWER:

162. A cereal company regularly purchased its supply of corn from FirstCo because it found FirstCo to be a very reliable supplier. On June 1, it agreed to buy 100,000 bushels of U.S. No. 2 yellow corn at a price that included delivery to the company. On June 3, the company received notice from FirstCo that the contract would be performed by SecondCo and that payment should be made to SecondCo.

What rights and remedies does the company have?

(A) It does not have to accept performance by SecondCo because it had a substantial interest in having FirstCo perform, but it has to pay SecondCo.

(B) It does not have to accept performance by SecondCo because it had a substantial interest in having FirstCo perform, and it does not have to pay SecondCo.

(C) It has to accept performance by SecondCo and pay SecondCo, but it can hold either FirstCo or SecondCo liable for breach.

(D) It has to accept performance by SecondCo and pay SecondCo, and it can hold only SecondCo liable for breach.

163. Assume in Question 162 that the company had chosen FirstCo because it had problems in the past with SecondCo delivering late and delivering goods that did not conform to the contract. Would these facts change your answer to Question 162?

ANSWER:

164. The President of the United States contracted with Murphy, a famous artist, to paint her portrait. The President then informed Murphy that because she needed the time that she had planned to sit for the portrait for other business, she has asked the Vice-President to sit for the portrait instead. Murphy then informed the Vice-President that she has asked Roseman, another famous artist, to paint the portrait of the Vice-President.

What is the best legal analysis of the situation?

(A) Neither the President nor Murphy can delegate their duties.

(B) The President cannot assign her right and Murphy cannot delegate her duty.

(C) Neither the President nor Murphy can assign their rights.

(D) The President cannot assign her right but Murphy can delegate her duty.

165. Returning to the facts of Question 162, the cereal company learned from its experience. The next time it contracted with FirstCo, the company negotiated for a provision that stated: "Duties under this contract may not be delegated and rights may not be assigned." FirstCo then delegated its duties and assigned its rights under the contract to SecondCo. Is the restriction on assignment and delegation effective?

    (A) Yes, because parties have the freedom of contract in this situation to bar assignment and delegation.

    (B) Yes, but only if the provision is conspicuous.

    (C) No, because under Article 9, a provision restricting assignment is ineffective.

    (D) No, because the provision will be interpreted as barring the delegation of duties, but not the assignment of rights.

166. Assume again that the agreement between FirstCo and the company contained a provision that stated: "Duties under this contract may not be delegated and rights may not be assigned." Assume also that FirstCo had a security agreement with a lender in which it had put up its accounts (the money it was owed by its account debtors, like the cereal company) as collateral for the loan. FirstCo defaulted on the loan, and the lender, pursuant to its security agreement with FirstCo, claimed that it had an assignment of the account and demanded payment from the company. The company refused to pay, claiming that the lender had no right to the account since the contract provided that rights may not be assigned. Will the company prevail?

ANSWER:

167. Assume the same facts as Question 166, but the drafter for the company wrote the provision as follows: "This contract may not be assigned." Is this an effective restriction on assignment and delegation?

    (A) Yes, because parties have the freedom of contract in this situation to bar assignment and delegation.

    (B) No, because the provision will be interpreted to bar the assignment of rights, but not the delegation of duties.

    (C) No, because under Article 9, a provision restricting assignment is ineffective.

    (D) No, because the provision will be interpreted to bar the delegation of duties, but not the assignment of rights.

168. A homeowner wants to have a swimming pool installed in the back yard. The homeowner asks around and finds that ABC Construction has the best reputation in the community for being a reliable contractor. She hires ABC Construction, but she knows that contractors often delegate their duties under their contracts, a practice known as "subcontracting."

Being pretty sophisticated in matters of contract law, she doesn't want that to happen, so she gets ABC to agree to a provision that states: "Duties under this contract may not be delegated."

The homeowner is shocked when she sees an XYZ Construction truck roll into the yard. When she confronts the workers, they tell her that the work was subcontracted to them by ABC Construction. Because of the provision she negotiated in the contract, she believes that the delegation is ineffective and she does not have to let XYZ proceed with the work. Is she correct?

(A) Yes, because parties have freedom of contract to restrict assignment and delegation of contracts.

(B) Yes, because it is a material breach by ABC, canceling the contract between herself and ABC.

(C) No, because even though ABC has breached the contract, that only entitles her to damages and does not make the delegation ineffective.

(D) No, because free delegation is so important in construction contracts that as a matter of policy the prohibition will not be enforced.

PRACTICE FINAL EXAM:
QUESTIONS

169. A contractor sought the submission of bids from subcontractors to do a portion of the work on a parking lot. The contractor received 10 bids. The bid from one subcontractor was for $112,000, which was $45,000 less than the next lowest bid. The discrepancy was due to the omission of a $46,000 item on the part of the subcontractor's staff. The contractor accepted the bid. When the subcontractor explained what had happened, the contractor demanded either performance or damages from the subcontractor. Which of the following best describes the subcontractor's legal situation?

   (A) It is bound by the acceptance at a price of $112,000.

   (B) It is not bound by the acceptance only if the contractor actually knew a mistake had been made at the time it accepted the bid.

   (C) It is not bound by the acceptance if the contractor should have known a mistake had been made at the time it accepted the bid.

   (D) It is not bound by the bid submitted because there was no meeting of the minds.

170. On January 1, a buyer and a seller entered into a written agreement that provided that the buyer would buy a widget from the seller on the first of every month for a year for $100 per month. The agreement had a No Oral Modification (NOM) clause stating that it could be modified only by a signed writing. In June, the buyer called the seller, told him that he had been offered a better price for widgets, and asked if the seller would drop the price to $95 for the rest of the year. The seller agreed, so the buyer turned down the better deal. On July 1, the buyer tendered the seller $95 for the widget. The seller said, "Ha Ha! The price is $100. That modification doesn't count."

   Is the modification enforceable?

   (A) No, because there is no consideration for the modification.

   (B) No, because the contract had an NOM clause and the modification was oral.

   (C) Yes, because NOM clauses are not enforceable.

   (D) Yes, because the NOM clause is subject to waiver.

171. A contract between an employer and an employee stated that the employee promised not to say any bad things about the employer during employment and for six months following the termination of employment. The contract also stated that this provision is enforceable against the employee irrespective of any breach by the employer. The employer wrongfully discharged the employee, and the employee said bad things about the employer. Does the employer have a claim against the employee?

(A) No, because it is not a material breach by the employee.

(B) No, because the employer's breach relieved the employee of his obligations to the employer.

(C) Yes, because the employee's promise was not conditional on the employer's actions.

(D) Yes, because an employee owes an employer an implied duty of loyalty.

172. At a ski resort, a snowboarder went over a jump and hit a skier in the head; the skier was rendered unconscious by the blow. Shortly thereafter, a local radiologist skied by. One of the Ski Patrol members on the scene knew the doctor and asked her if she would examine the skier before the Ski Patrol loaded him on the rescue sled to transport him to the main lodge in the valley.

The doctor determined that the skier was suffering from extreme shock, that a vertebra in his neck was fractured and that the sled trip to the lodge could irreparably damage his vertebra and spinal cord. Based upon the doctor's advice, the Ski Patrol called for a helicopter. Two hours later, it arrived and transported the skier and the doctor to the local hospital. The doctor stayed with the skier and was unable to return to the ski area that day. Later, the doctor sent a bill to the skier for $3,000, representing six hours of her professional medical service at her standard billing rate of $500 per hour.

What is the skier's best defense against having to pay the doctor's claim for fees?

(A) There was no contract because neither the skier nor anyone else on his behalf had consented to the medical assistance.

(B) A rescuer cannot recover in restitution unless there is a subsequent promise by the rescued person.

(C) The doctor did not have a reasonable expectation of being compensated for her medical advice.

(D) The skier had not requested the medical assistance.

173. In a written contract, a hot dog distributor granted a woman the "non-exclusive" right to sell hot dogs on a college campus. The woman sued the distributor when she found another vendor selling the distributor's hot dogs on the campus. The distributor pointed out that the contract states that her right is non-exclusive, and therefore they can use other hot dog sellers. The agreement also contains a merger clause stating that it is complete and final. The woman wants to offer testimony that before they entered the contract, the distributor told her that she would have exclusive rights but they didn't want to put that in writing because they were concerned the term might violate the college's rules.

Is a court likely to admit evidence offering to prove that there is such a term in the agreement?

ANSWER:

174. Under the facts of the previous question, assume instead that the woman claims that the agreement is ambiguous and she wants to offer evidence that the parties agreed that "non-exclusive" means "exclusive."

Is a court likely to admit the evidence?

ANSWER:

175. Mary borrowed $1,000 from John. After she made a number of payments, she told him that she thought the debt was fully paid. John said that according to his records, he believed she still owed him $100. Mary admitted that her records weren't very good either, and she was not absolutely sure how much she had paid him. Mary offered to give him $50 to settle the matter for good. John agreed and she paid him the $50. Mary later went through her accounts and found that she had in fact paid him $50 too much. John agreed with her calculations, but refused to give the money back. Does Mary have a good claim to get it back?

(A) Yes, because there was no consideration for her promise to pay the $50 since she didn't really owe it.

(B) Yes, because John was unjustly enriched by the payment that she made.

(C) No, because they entered into a substituted contract.

(D) No, because John honestly believed he had a claim against Mary.

176. Able owed Baker $100. Able sold a widget to Charlie for $100 and directed Charlie to pay the $100 to Baker in satisfaction of Able's debt to Baker. Charlie agreed to do so.

How would you characterize this transaction?

(A) Able has delegated to Charlie his (Able's) duty to pay Baker.

(B) Baker is an incidental beneficiary of Charlie's promise to Able.

(C) There is a novation, with Charlie being substituted for Able as the obligor.

(D) Baker is a third party beneficiary of Charlie's promise to Able.

177. A first year law student was studying in the law library and decided to take a short refreshment break. When she returned to her study desk 10 minutes later, her copy of *Q&A: Contracts* was gone. She ran into the student lounge and announced, "I will pay $20 to anyone who identifies the dirty bird who took my *Q&A: Contracts* book."

What is the legal effect of her statement?

(A) It is an offer to be accepted by performance.

(B) It is an offer to be accepted by a promise.

(C) It has no legal effect because a reasonable person would think that she was not making a serious offer but was just expressing anger that her book was missing.

(D) It is an invitation to make an offer.

178. Assume the facts of the previous question, except the student said, "I will pay $50 to anyone who returns my book." Although he hadn't taken the book, another law student was quick on the uptake because he knew that the amount offered for the book exceeded its cost. "Here it is," he said, handing her *his* copy of the book. Is the student who tendered the book entitled to claim the reward?

ANSWER:

179. Which of the following contracts is most likely governed by U.C.C. Article 2?

(A) An attorney's advice on an estate plan.

(B) The sale of crops and timber growing on a property.

(C) The purchase of a commercial building.

(D) The sale of a patent.

180. In order for an offer to be irrevocable under U.C.C. Article 2, which of the following must be true?

(A) It must be made by a merchant to a merchant.

(B) It must be in a signed writing which by its terms gives assurance that it will be held open.

(C) It must state the period of time for which it is irrevocable.

(D) It must be made by a seller.

181. An electric company entered into an agreement to buy "all the copper wiring it needs" for six months from a wire company for a fixed price per unit. Which of the following best describes the agreement between the two companies?

(A) It is unenforceable because it is too indefinite as to quantity.

(B) It is unenforceable because it lacks mutuality of obligation.

(C) It is unenforceable because of lack of consideration since the electric company might not require copper wiring during that time.

(D) It is valid and enforceable.

182. A woman owned two sailboats, a 32-foot boat and a 37-foot boat. The 32-foot boat is worth

$12–$15,000, while the 37-foot boat is worth $15–$18,000. Her friend had frequently sailed with her on both boats. In writing, the woman offered to sell "my sailboat" to the friend for $15,000 cash. The friend accepted in writing and agreed to buy "the sailboat" for $15,000 cash, which he paid.

The next day, the woman delivered the 32-foot boat to the friend, who rejected it because he thought he was buying the 37-foot boat. The woman refused to return the friend's $15,000 payment and insisted that the friend take the 32-foot boat because it was the sailboat she thought he was buying.

What is the likely result of this dispute?

(A) There is no contract because each party knew that the language could have different meanings.

(B) There is a contract for the 37-foot boat because the woman knew what the friend meant but the friend did not know what the woman meant.

(C) There is no contract because there was a mutual mistake.

(D) There is a contract for the 32-foot boat because the woman had the option of providing either boat under the contract.

183. A young woman whose parents lived in Spokane, Washington moved to New York City immediately after graduating from a local college. Her parents kept hoping she would return to Spokane, where all the family lived. To facilitate such a decision by their daughter, the parents sent an email to her stating, "We hope you will return to Spokane. If you do, we plan to give you that condo we own in town." After getting the email, the daughter made plans to return to Spokane and forfeited a deposit she had made to rent an apartment in New York. When their daughter showed up in Spokane with her boyfriend, the parents changed their minds about giving the condo to her because they did not approve of the boyfriend.

If the daughter brings suit against her parents seeking specific performance of their promise of the condo, is she likely to recover?

(A) Yes, because making the move from New York City to Spokane was consideration for her parents' promise to give the condo to her.

(B) Yes, because even if the move was not consideration, she reasonably relied upon the promise.

(C) No, because the promise of the condo was more likely a promise to make a gift on a condition rather than an offer to be accepted by performance.

(D) No, because the parents revoked the offer prior to acceptance.

184. Assume in the previous question the court finds that there is no bargained-for contract. Should the daughter be able to recover in reliance?

(A) No, because a reasonable person would not have relied on the promise.

(B)   Yes, and the reliance makes the promise of the condo enforceable.

(C)   Yes, and she can recover only the cost of moving back to Spokane because moving was the only thing the parents requested.

(D)   Yes, and she can recover both the cost of moving back to Spokane and the lost apartment deposit because both were reasonable expenses incurred in reliance.

185.   A California lawyer falsely represented to a woman living in Kansas that he was admitted to practice law in Kansas. A Kansas statute regulating attorneys requires all attorneys practicing in the state to be admitted in the state and properly licensed. The woman signed a contract agreeing to pay the attorney a fee for handling a personal injury matter in Kansas. The attorney competently represented her and secured a large settlement, but when she learned that he was not admitted to the Kansas bar, the woman refused to pay the attorney the agreed-upon fee. If the attorney sued the woman for nonpayment of the fee, what would the likely result be?

(A)   The woman is not liable on the contract, but is liable to the attorney in restitution for the reasonable value of services rendered.

(B)   The woman is liable to the attorney for the full fee under the contract.

(C)   The woman is not liable to the attorney because the contract is illegal and a court will never allow a party who enters into an illegal contract to recover under it.

(D)   The woman is not liable to the attorney because the contract is illegal and there is no public policy favoring an exception.

186.   A Washington buyer agreed to buy a home in Montana from an owner in Idaho. The contract was signed by the owner in Idaho and then by the buyer in Washington. The contract provides that Idaho law applies to the transaction. If a dispute arising from the contract is heard in Federal District Court in Idaho, which state's contract law should the court apply?

(A)   Washington, because that was the place where the last act occurred that resulted in there being a contract.

(B)   Montana, because it has the most significant contact with the transaction since the house is located there.

(C)   Idaho, because the court hearing the case is located in Idaho.

(D)   Idaho, because the contract provides that Idaho law applies.

187.   A patient went to a private hospital for treatment. The hospital required her to sign a contract containing a clause in which she relinquished the right to sue the hospital for injuries caused by its negligence (an exculpatory clause). The hospital treated her negligently, causing her death. Her personal representative sued the hospital and the hospital defended on the basis of the exculpatory clause. What is the likely result?

(A) The court will strike out the exculpatory clause because all exculpatory clauses are not enforceable.

(B) The court will strike out the exculpatory clause because the transaction involved an area of public interest in which the patient had little choice but to agree to the clause in order to get the needed services.

(C) The court will enforce the exculpatory clause because the transaction involved an area of private interest in which exculpatory clauses are permitted.

(D) The court will enforce the exculpatory clause because the patient did not have to sign it and could have shopped around to obtain the service from a different hospital.

188. A teenager who was almost 18 contracted with her 18-year-old friend to purchase the friend's used computer for $400 for her personal use. The agreement provided that the teenager would pay $200 down on delivery and $200 30 days later. The teenager took delivery and paid the $200 down payment. Twenty days later, the computer was seriously damaged as a result of the teenager's own negligence. Four days later, the teenager turned 18, and the day after that, she tendered the damaged computer to her friend and asked for her money back. Will the teenager be able to disaffirm the contract?

(A) Yes, even though she was not a minor at the time of disaffirmance.

(B) Yes, but only if she does so in writing.

(C) No, because she had failed to pay the balance of the purchase price.

(D) No, because the computer was damaged as a result of her negligence.

189. On March 1, a manufacturing company orally engaged a woman to be a district sales manager for an 18-month period commencing April 1. The manager commenced work on that date and performed her duties in a highly competent manner for several months. On October 1, the company gave the manager notice of termination as of November 1, citing a downturn in the market for its products. The manager is thinking of suing the company.

If the contract was otherwise enforceable, is the company justified in terminating her because of the downturn in the market for its products?

ANSWER:

190. Under the facts of the previous question, would the company likely prevail if it raised the statute of frauds as a defense?

(A) No, because there is an exception to the statute of frauds when a contract has been partially performed.

(B) Yes, because there was no contract signed by both the company and the manager.

(C) Yes, because there must be a writing signed by the company to make the contract enforceable.

(D) No, because the statute of frauds does not apply to contracts such as this.

191. One party to a negotiated commercial contract attempted to introduce evidence in court. The other party's lawyer objected on grounds of the parol evidence rule. Which of the following evidence is a court most likely *not* to admit?

   (A) Evidence of an oral modification that was made several days after the written contract had been executed.

   (B) Evidence of a term the subject of which is covered in detail in the contract and the contract indicates that the writing was intended as the "entire contract" between the parties.

   (C) Evidence of a mutual mistake of fact by the parties regarding the subject matter of the contract.

   (D) Evidence that language in the contract is patently ambiguous.

192. A producer of cherries offered his crop to a fruit wholesaler. The producer showed the wholesaler sample cherries from his crop and the wholesaler agreed to buy the entire cherry crop for a certain price. When the cherries arrived, most of them were less plump and ripe than the ones the producer had shown to the wholesaler. Does the wholesaler have a claim for breach of warranty?

   (A) Yes, because the producer told the wholesaler the cherries would be plump and ripe.

   (B) Yes, because the sample created an express warranty that the goods would conform to that sample.

   (C) No, because no description of the cherries was part of the contract.

   (D) No, because a reasonable buyer would not expect the goods to conform to the sample.

193. A car dealer sold a used car with 80,000 miles on it to a buyer. Shortly thereafter, the transmission failed. Assuming no other facts, did the seller breach the implied warranty of merchantability?

   (A) No, because used car dealers don't give a warranty of merchantability.

   (B) No, because the implied warranty of merchantability is not given in the sale of used goods.

   (C) Yes, because the seller impliedly promised that the car would function for a reasonable period of time.

   (D) It depends on the facts and circumstances.

194. An organic food store ordered from a wholesaler a certain type of oranges that it had ordered many times before. Unknown to the store, the producer of the oranges had started applying a spray to the oranges that some parties believed made them non-organic. The wholesaler knew about the change but honestly believed the oranges were still organic and shipped them to the store. Every other supplier, however, stopped supplying the oranges to organic food stores. When some customers of the store complained and returned the oranges, the store claimed that the wholesaler had not acted in good faith.

Did the wholesaler act in good faith?

(A) No, because it had a duty to disclose what it knew to its buyer.

(B) No, because it did not observe reasonable commercial standards of fair dealing.

(C) Yes, because it honestly believed the oranges were suitable for the store.

(D) Yes, because it supplied the goods the buyer had ordered.

195. A contractor agreed to do some construction work for an owner. After completion, the owner claimed the work was shoddy and offered to pay the contractor $8,000. The contractor did not agree that the work was shoddy, and thought it was worth more than $8,000, but was desperate for cash in order to buy materials for another job, so the contractor accepted the $8,000 offer and the money was paid. The contractor then sued the owner to recover the amount he claimed was due.

Which additional fact would be most helpful to support the contractor's recovery of additional money?

(A) The contract price was not liquidated.

(B) The owner knew the contractor was desperate for cash in order to buy materials for another job.

(C) The owner made up the claim that the work was shoddy.

(D) The agreement to settle the debt for $8,000 was oral.

196. The buyer of a house agreed with the seller that the closing would be in 60 days and the contract provided that the buyer's performance would be excused if he could not obtain mortgage financing by the time of the closing.

How would you characterize the promise by the buyer?

(A) It is an immediately performable promise.

(B) It is illusory because he might not have to perform.

(C) It is not enforceable because there is no consideration given for it.

(D) It is enforceable, but its performance is subject to a condition.

197. Assume that under the facts of the previous question, the buyer did not apply for a

mortgage. At the time scheduled for closing, he refused to participate, saying that his performance was excused because the condition had not been satisfied.

Is the buyer correct?

ANSWER:

198. On January 2, a retail corporation ordered 30 cash registers of a radically new design to be delivered by December 31 of that year. At a meeting with the cash register manufacturer on September 1, it became clear to the retailer that the manufacturer was struggling to build a prototype machine. The executive in charge for the retailer concluded the meeting by saying, "We demand to see progress within a month or we may have to consider this contract canceled." On October 1, the parties met again. The prototype was still not ready, and while the manufacturer did not say that it could not complete the prototype and build the machines by December 31, the retailer reasonably concluded that the manufacturer had breached by anticipatory repudiation and canceled the contract.

When the manufacturer sued the retailer, the retailer claimed that it was justified in canceling the contract because it had complied with U.C.C. § 2-609. What is the manufacturer's best argument that the retailer had not satisfied all of the elements of § 2-609?

(A) The retailer did not have reasonable grounds for insecurity.

(B) The retailer did not demand adequate assurance.

(C) The retailer had not made the demand for adequate assurance in writing.

(D) The manufacturer had timely responded with adequate assurances.

199. In the lumber industry, a seller is considered to be in breach if it supplies more than 7% warped boards. A buyer ordered 5,000 boards from a lumber seller, to be delivered in five monthly shipments of 1,000 each. The written contract stated, "This writing is the final and complete agreement of the parties." The first three shipments had 10% warped boards, but the buyer did not object. When the fourth shipment arrived with 10% warped boards, the buyer claimed breach of contract.

Does the buyer have a claim against the seller for breach with respect to the fourth shipment?

(A) Yes, because according to trade usage, more than 7% warped boards is breached.

(B) No, because the agreement was fully integrated, so evidence of the trade usage is not admissible.

(C) No, because course of performance trumps trade usage.

(D) No, because course of dealing trumps trade usage.

200. A homeowner decided to purchase an underground watering system for his lawn and

garden. In December he signed a $5,000 contract with a contractor, which included installing the underground watering system and all labor and materials. The contractor expected to realize a profit of $1,000 on the job. The project was to begin on March 1, and the contractor scheduled her workers to begin the project on that date. On February 1, the homeowner decided to do the work himself and called the contractor telling her that the contract was off. The contractor told the homeowner that she intended to hold him to the agreement. She then began to buy the materials necessary to complete the job at a cost of $1,500. On March 1, the contractor showed up at the homeowner's house to begin the work, but the homeowner refused to allow her access to the property. If the contractor brings suit against the homeowner for breach of contract, how much will she likely recover?

(A) $5,000, the agreed-upon price of the contract that the homeowner intentionally breached.

(B) $1,500, the cost of purchasing the materials.

(C) $1,000, her lost profit on the job.

(D) $2,500, consisting of her $1,000 lost profit plus the $1,500 cost of the materials.

201. A furniture company sells fine custom furniture. It has been encountering difficulties lately with some customers who have breached their contracts either after the furniture they have selected has been customized to their order, the fabric they have selected has been cut, or the selected fabric has actually been installed on the piece of furniture purchased. The company therefore wishes to include a liquidated damages clause in its sales contract to encourage performance or to provide an acceptable amount of damages. Regarding the company's contemplated resort to a liquidated damages clause, which of the following is correct?

(A) The company may not use a liquidated damages clause because it is a merchant and is the preparer of the contract.

(B) The company need not include a liquidated damages clause because it can simply take a very large deposit, which will be forfeited if a customer cancels the contract.

(C) The amount of the liquidated damages stipulated in the contract must be reasonable in light of the anticipated or actual harm caused by the breach.

(D) Even if the company uses a liquidated damages clause in its sales contract, it will nevertheless have to establish that the liquidated damages claimed do not exceed actual damages by more than 10%.

202. A poultry producer offered to sell a wholesaler 20,000 pounds of a specified kind of chicken at 40 cents per pound under specified delivery terms. The wholesaler sent the following response and the producer did not object to it:

> We accept your offer for 20,000 pounds of the specified kind of chicken at 40 cents per pound, the weight to be evidenced by a city scale weight certificate.

Which of the following is correct?

(A) A contract was formed on the producer's terms.

(B) The wholesaler's reply is not binding on the producer unless the producer affirmatively accepts it.

(C) The wholesaler's reply constitutes a counteroffer and no contract was formed.

(D) A contract was formed on the wholesaler's terms.

203. A woman sold some lawn furniture to her neighbor for $2,000, which he was to pay in one month. Prior to receiving payment from the neighbor, the woman became short on cash and approached a finance company. The finance company agreed to pay the woman $1,900 in return for an assignment to the company of her right to payment from the neighbor.

   The neighbor then claimed that because the furniture was not as promised, he should have to pay only $1,900 instead of $2,000 for it. Can the neighbor include an explanation with his payment and deduct $100 from the amount he pays the finance company?

   (A) No, because an assignee takes free of all claims against the assignor.

   (B) No, because a buyer cannot exercise self-help by deducting damages from a payment.

   (C) Yes, because an assignee stands in the shoes of the assignor and is subject to all claims and defenses the buyer had against the seller.

   (D) No, because the warranties were breached by the woman, not by the finance company.

204. In which of the following situations does the common law give a delegator (the one delegating the duty) the right to delegate a duty to a delegatee (the one to whom the duty is delegable)?

   (A) The contract provides that the duty is nondelegable.

   (B) The duty delegated is the payment of money and the delegatee is less creditworthy than the delegator.

   (C) The delegation will result in a material variance in performance by the delegatee.

   (D) The duty to be performed involves the personal skill of the delegator.

205. A seller and a buyer entered into a written agreement for the sale of real property. After they had signed the agreement, but before closing, they got into an argument. The seller decided the price was too low, the buyer decided the price was too high, and they both agreed in an email exchange to terminate the contract. Later the buyer changed his mind and decided he would pay what the seller wanted for the property. He contacted the seller, who refused to sell to him at any price even though the property was unchanged since they made the original agreement. If the buyer brings suit against the seller for specific performance, which party is likely to prevail?

   (A) The seller, because there was no consideration for the original agreement.

(B) The buyer, because he changed his mind before there was any change of position by the seller.

(C) The buyer, because there was no consideration for the agreement to rescind the contract.

(D) The seller, because the contract had been effectively rescinded.

206. During a telephone conversation, a man sold his Ted Williams autographed baseball to his friend Chelsea Porter for $800. The man then sent an email to his brother that stated, "I just sold my Ted Williams autographed baseball to my friend Chelsea Porter for $800." His brother then replied that he should have gotten a lot more for the ball. The man then told Chelsea, "Sorry, but the deal is off. You should have gotten it in writing."

Is the contract enforceable?

(A) Yes, because this transaction is not within the statute of frauds, it doesn't have to be evidenced by a writing to be enforceable.

(B) Yes, because it is evidenced by a sufficient writing.

(C) No, because there is no writing signed by the parties.

(D) No, because an email does not constitute a writing for purposes of the statute of frauds.

207. On May 1, a company ordered machine parts from a seller to be delivered by July 1. On June 1, the seller notified the company, "We are experiencing production problems and we do not expect to be able to deliver the parts on time." If the company asks its lawyer for advice, what advice should the company give them?

ANSWER:

208. Tempus Fugit ("Tempus") manufactures wall clocks in its factory in Tempe, Arizona. Frank's Cranks ("FC") manufactures precision gear works in its factory in Nuevo Laredo, Mexico. Gearz, FC's authorized dealer for Arizona and New Mexico, has its place of business in Albuquerque, New Mexico. On March 1, 2003, Tempus's purchasing manager telephoned Gearz and, after discussing Tempus's particular needs, faxed a purchase order for 1,000 sets of precision gear works, at a price of $50.00 per set, to be delivered to Tempus no later than April 15. Later that same day, FC faxed Tempus an acknowledgment from Nuevo Laredo, agreeing to the terms.

If a dispute arises between Tempus and FC, what body of law primarily governs?

(A) Arizona common law.

(B) The Arizona Uniform Commercial Code (U.C.C.).

(C) The U.N. Convention on Contracts for the International Sale of Goods (C.I.S.G.).

(D) The New Mexico U.C.C.

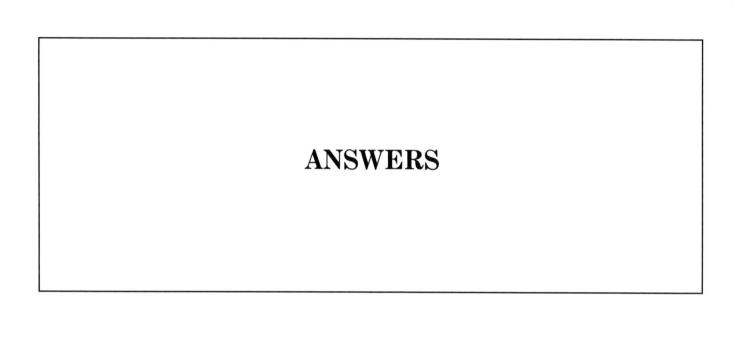

ANSWERS

1. Most of the time, this distinction is not important, and we frequently use the terms interchangeably. According to the Uniform Commercial Code ("U.C.C." or "Code"), an *agreement* is what the parties in fact agree to (together with terms supplied by any applicable course of performance, course of dealing, and usage of trade), while a *contract* is an agreement that is legally enforceable. *See also* RESTATEMENT §§ 1 and 3. So if Walter calls Tuco and agrees to sell him 100 pounds of methamphetamine and Tuco agrees to pay Walter $100,000, they have made an agreement. They might not have made a contract, however, for a number of reasons. The agreement may not be enforceable because it is oral, and it is likely not enforceable because it is illegal.

    So while *agreement* is broader than *contract*, most of the time this distinction is not important, and we often use the two terms interchangeably. An example of this can be seen in the case of *Buckeye Check Cashing, Inc. v. Cardegna*, 546 U.S. 440 (2006). There, the Supreme Court was faced with the issue of whether, in a contract with an arbitration clause in it, a court or an arbitrator should resolve a claim that the contract is illegal and void. The respondent noted that the relevant statute, § 2 of the Federal Arbitration Act (F.A.A.), applies to "a written provision in . . . a contract . . . to settle by arbitration a controversy thereafter arising out of such contract." She argued that if the agreement was void, then there was no contract, so the F.A.A. would not apply.

    The Court resolved the problem by determining that Congress was a bit careless in its choice of words, and by *contract* it meant *agreement*. The Court noted that another section of the U.S. Code, the Sherman Anti-Trust Act states that "every contract . . . in restraint of trade . . . is hereby declared to be illegal." If this language was taken literally, a defendant accused of violating the Act could argue that the agreement he made in restraint of trade was illegal; therefore, it was not a contract; therefore, he did not enter a contract in restraint of trade; therefore, he is not guilty of violating the Act. So if I get careless in my use of these terms in this book, I am in good company — or at least in the company of the U.S. Congress.

2. **Answer (C) is the best answer.** Section 2-102 of the Code states that "this Article [U.C.C. Article 2] applies to transactions in goods." Section 2-105 defines *goods*, stating that " 'Goods' means all things (including specially manufactured goods) which are movable at the time of identification to the contract for sale." A pen is movable at the time of the sale. Therefore it is a good and U.C.C. Article 2 applies to the transaction.

    Answer (D) is incorrect because while this fact may be true, it is irrelevant. Interstate commerce may be the basis for many statutes passed by Congress. The U.C.C., however, is state law enacted by each state. Moreover, when using a statute, the definitions used in that statute should be consulted to determine the meaning of words used in the statute.

    Answers (A) and (B) are incorrect because as stated in § 2-102, Article 2 applies to transactions in goods *period*. For purposes of determining the applicable law, it doesn't matter whether the parties are merchants or not and it doesn't matter what the sale price of the goods is. As we will see, there are some particular provisions of Article 2 where it does matter whether the parties are merchants. We will also see that it matters for purposes of the Statute of Frauds whether the price was under $500. But for purposes of determining whether Article 2 applies to the transaction, those things don't matter.

Byron's lawsuit might raise some issues that are not addressed in the Code, such as the principles of causation, certainty, and mitigation. The Code tells us in § 1-103(b) that "[u]nless displaced by the particular provisions of [the Uniform Commercial Code], the principles of law and equity . . . supplement its provisions." Therefore, if we have a Code transaction, we might end up looking to the common law if the Code does not have an applicable rule, but that does not mean that it is not a Code transaction.

3.   **Answer (D) is the best answer**. If you have never heard of the United Nations Convention on the International Sale of Goods (U.N.C.I.S.G. or C.I.S.G.), you are probably in the company of most lawyers. The facts of this case are based on *GPL Treatment Ltd. v. Louisiana-Pacific Corp.*, 894 P.2d 470 (Or. Ct. App. 1995). The case had been tried and was on appeal when one of the judges woke up and said, "Wait a minute. Why are we applying the U.C.C. here? The C.I.S.G. is the governing law." He was right.

The C.I.S.G. is an international treaty. According to C.I.S.G. Article 1, "This Convention applies to contracts of sale of goods between parties whose places of business are in different States [meaning nation-states or countries] . . . when the States are Contracting States [meaning they have signed the convention]." Because the U.S. and Canada have both signed it, the CISG applies to this transaction. Because the C.I.S.G. applies, **Answers (A), (B), and (C) are incorrect**.

You will probably find a copy of the C.I.S.G. in the statutory supplement to your Contracts course. Many of the provisions are similar to the U.C.C. provisions, so it is not hard to master and unlike most lawyers, you should not be afraid of it. You can also learn a lot at the web site maintained by Pace Law School at http://www.cisg.law.pace.edu/.

4.   **Answer (B) is the best answer**. U.S. lawyers who are familiar with the C.I.S.G. probably know one thing about it — that they have freedom of contract to contract around it. Parties are generally free to put a "choice of law" clause in their contract. According to U.C.C. § 1-301, they may do so in a Code transaction as long as the transaction bears a "reasonable relation" to the chosen jurisdiction. In this case, the parties could have chosen British Columbia, Oregon, or Washington law, because each one bears a reasonable relation to the transaction — one party is located in British Columbia, the other is located in Oregon, and the goods are to be delivered to Washington. Because the Oregon U.C.C. applies, **Answers (A), (C), and (D) are incorrect**.

Note that a "choice of law" clause merely determines what law the forum jurisdiction will apply to the transaction. It has nothing to do with where the case is heard — that is determined by the rules of civil procedure, though the parties also have freedom of contract to insert a "choice of forum" clause that specifies where the plaintiff may sue the defendant. But in the absence of a choice of forum clause, wherever the plaintiff gets jurisdiction over the defendant, that court will apply the chosen law of Oregon.

By the way, there is a decision that held that when the parties to an international transaction specified that "The law of California applies to this transaction," the C.I.S.G. applied. Do you see why? The court took the words literally, and reasoned that the law of

California includes applicable federal law, including treaties the U.S. has entered into. Therefore, the C.I.S.G. is the law of California. While that was obviously not the intent of the parties, the careful drafter will state, as our drafter did here, that "the U.C.C. of Oregon" shall apply. Or she could have stated, "The law of Oregon applies to this transaction. The parties specifically exclude application of the C.I.S.G."

As we will see, many of the rules of contract law are "default" rules, meaning that they apply in the absence of the parties' agreement otherwise, but the parties are free to change them. However, if the rule is a "regulatory" or "mandatory" rule, then the parties are not free to change it. One of the things that makes the study of contract law difficult is trying to figure out whether a particular rule is a default rule or a regulatory rule.

5. Yes. Section 2-503 requires that the seller give the buyer reasonable notice. A good place to start our analysis is to ask whether this is a default rule or a regulatory rule. If it is the former, we are free to change it, but if it is the latter, we are not. Some Code provisions are prefaced by the language "unless otherwise agreed," which indicates that they are default rules that the parties are free to contract around. This one does not have that language, but § 1-302(c) informs us that the fact that some provisions contain this language does not mean that other provisions may not be varied by agreement.

Section 1-302(a) states the general rule that except as otherwise provided, the provisions of the Code "may be varied by agreement" that is, they are default rules. Some exceptions are found in § 1-302(b), which tells us that "the obligations of good faith, diligence, reasonableness, and care prescribed by [the Uniform Commercial Code] may not be disclaimed by agreement." So, for example, the parties cannot agree that "seller does not have to act reasonably under this agreement."

However, subsection (b) goes on to say:

> The parties, by agreement, may determine the standards by which the performance of those obligations is to be measured if those standards are not manifestly unreasonable. Whenever [the Uniform Commercial Code] requires an action to be taken within a reasonable time, a time that is not manifestly unreasonable may be fixed by agreement.

According to this rule, while the parties can't disclaim these obligations, they can define the standards for measuring them. In our example, the parties have determined that the standard for "notification reasonably necessary to enable him to take delivery" is notification that they may be picked up by 4 p.m. the next business day. Therefore the issue becomes whether this agreement is reasonable. According to the Code provision, this is permissible as long as the standard is not "manifestly unreasonable." So while it is fair to say that the answer is "it depends," this standard is probably not manifestly unreasonable.

What would be a manifestly unreasonable expression? A provision negating the obligation, such as this:

> **Tender of delivery**. Seller has no obligation to give the buyer notification to enable him to take delivery.

6. **Answer C is the best answer.** The Uniform Commercial Code is a project of the Uniform Law Commission (U.L.C., formerly known as the National Conference of Commissioners on Uniform State Laws) with the assistance of the American Law Institute (A.L.I.), the group

that promulgates the Restatements of Law. The U.L.C. is a nonprofit group with representatives from every state that is devoted to the improvement of law. See its website at http://www.uniformlaws.org/.

To facilitate commerce within the U.S., it would be helpful if the laws were uniform. One way to make them uniform would be for Congress to use its power to regulate interstate commerce and enact national legislation. While Congress has done this in limited areas of contract law, it has left most areas of contract law to the states. So **Answer (A) is incorrect**.

The U.L.C. stepped into this void by drafting a Uniform Commercial Code that contains various Articles that address many different areas of commercial law. The Articles we will be primarily concerned with in this book are Article 1, which contains general principles and definitions that apply throughout the Code, and Article 2, which governs the sale of goods.

Once the U.L.C. finished its drafting, however, the job had barely begun. A Uniform Law is just a proposal until it has been enacted by a state legislature, and to be truly uniform, it must be enacted in the same form by each state legislature. The U.L.C. has had pretty good success on both counts with the U.C.C. Beginning in the 1960s, it began to be adopted by the states and today Article 1 has been adopted by every state and Article 2 by every state except Louisiana. However, each state has enacted its own version, so the law is not truly uniform. That is why **Answer (B) is incorrect**.

To make matters more complicated, the U.L.C. proposes revisions to the Articles of the U.C.C. from time to time. Attempts to revise Article 2 have not been successful, but a Revised Article 1 has been enacted by most of the states. So when this book refers to the Uniform Commercial Code, the U.C.C., the Code, Article 1, or Article 2, it is referring to the most recent uniform version as promulgated by the U.L.C. When you are in practice, you will have to deal with the Code as enacted in a particular jurisdiction.

There is an international treaty governing commerce between countries that have signed it, but it is called the United Nations Convention on the International Sale of Goods (C.I.S.G.). So **Answer (D) is incorrect**.

7.   Contract law is largely common law, which is to say law made by judges. Therefore, if you want to know what the rule of contract law is on a particular topic, you would have to read all the court opinions and synthesize the analysis in order to determine the rule. Fortunately, someone has already done that work for us. The Restatements of the Law are produced by the American Law Institute, which is a nonprofit group of lawyers, judges, and scholars devoted to the improvement of the law. See its website at http://www.ali.org/.

The first Restatement of Contracts came out in 1932 under the direction of Samuel Williston, who also wrote a great multi-volume treatise on contract law. The second Restatement came out in 1981 under the direction of the late E. Allan Farnsworth, who also wrote a very readable single volume treatise on contract law. There are, of course, Restatements in other areas of law. Unless otherwise indicated, when I refer to the "Restatement" in this book, I am talking about the Restatement (Second) of Contracts.

As you can tell from this description, the Restatement is not the law of the United States. It has not been enacted by any legislature and is only occasionally cited by courts. It is a just a handy shortcut to stating the general principles and rules of contract law. Like any shortcut, it has its disadvantages. For one thing, there are often "majority" and "minority" (and even "subminority") rules, but only one rule is found in the black-letter sections of the

Restatement. That section usually states the majority rule (after all, a *restatement* by definition should be merely descriptive), but occasionally the drafters couldn't help themselves and acted prescriptively, adopting a minority rule that they thought was the better rule. Another disadvantage of the black-letter provisions of the Restatement is that rules of contract law are more meaningful when seen in their application to particular facts. If you consult the entire text of the Restatement, and not just the shortened version that you get in many student supplements, you will find helpful Comments that discuss the provisions and Illustrations that demonstrate the application of the provision to a particular fact situation.

When I use the Restatement as a shortcut method of stating the legal rule, you would be wise to remember these limitations. You can cite the Restatement as persuasive authority, but that is all it is. When you are in practice, the judge is less interested in what the Restatement says on the subject than in what precedent in that particular jurisdiction has to say. So in spite of the availability of the Restatement and other sources of "black-letter law," don't neglect to work on the skill of reading and synthesizing the case law.

8. **Answer (C) is the best answer.** But let's start our analysis with the worst answer, which is Answer (A). First off, since contract law is largely state law, when a contracts case shows up in federal court, we have to ask how it got there. Most of the time, the answer is because of federal "diversity" jurisdiction, which gives federal courts the right to hear cases between residents of different states if the dollar amount in controversy is over a certain threshold (now $75,000). So if the federal court has jurisdiction over the parties, the next question is what body of law the federal court will apply.

    In Civil Procedure, you will study a case called *Erie Railroad Co. v. Tompkins*, 304 U.S. 64 (1938), which held that there is no federal common law and federal courts must apply state substantive law. Therefore, **Answer (A) is incorrect**. Since the law of contracts is a matter of state substantive law, the question now becomes which state's contract law will apply.

    This is a question answered by another body of law called Conflict of Laws, which you might study as an elective. Unfortunately, the answer to the question of which state's contract law applies varies with the jurisdiction, with some applying the "old" rule and some applying the "new" rule. When a case is in federal court, we would look at the forum state — the place where the federal court is located — and determine whether that state applies the old rule or the new rule. So in our case, that would be the law of Washington — but only to determine which Conflicts law to apply, not which contract law to apply.

    The old rule is that we use the substantive law of the jurisdiction where the last act occurred that resulted in the formation of the contract. In our case, that would be Idaho, where the contract was signed. The new rule is that we use the substantive law of the jurisdiction that has the most contacts with the transaction. Here there are contacts with Montana, where the plaintiff resides, Washington, where the contractor is incorporated and located, and Idaho, where the land is found. Since the dispute centers on a house being built on that land, that is probably the most significant contact. So the author cleverly constructed this question so that Answer (C) would be the correct answer whether Washington applies the new or the old conflict of laws rule, and **Answers (B) and (D) are incorrect answers.**

9. **Answer (A) is the best answer.** As discussed in the previous question, matters of substantive contract law, like the enforceability of a clause in a contract, are matters of state law. A decision of the highest court in the state system is mandatory authority for a lower

court in the system.

The federal court decisions will have less weight and will be merely persuasive. As we discussed in the previous question, the federal courts generally get contracts questions because of their diversity jurisdiction, and in resolving them, they apply state substantive law. The state substantive law might not even be the law of your state. And if it is, the federal district court puts itself in the position of the highest state court and tries to decide the matter the way that court would decide it. But that decision is not binding on your state court, which is free to disregard it. Therefore, **Answer (B) is incorrect**.

As with the federal district court, when you see that a federal court of appeals has heard a contracts case, you again have to ask which state's substantive law was applied. Chances are it is not your state, but even if it is, that decision is not binding on your state court, as discussed above. Therefore, **Answer (C) is incorrect**.

The U.S. Supreme Court will not take jurisdiction over a question of state substantive law since there is no federal question involved. But didn't the facts say that there was a Supreme Court case on point? In fact, there is such a case, *Carnival Cruise Lines v. Shute*, 499 U.S. 585 (1991), in which the Supreme Court decided the issue of the enforceability of a choice of forum clause. We have to ask why the Supreme Court took jurisdiction over this case. The answer is because the transaction involved a ship on the high seas, and the Court does have jurisdiction in matters of admiralty law. While you are free to cite that case in your brief, it is mandatory authority only in matters of admiralty law, so in your case it is merely persuasive. Therefore, **Answer (D) is incorrect**.

TOPIC 2:	ANSWERS
OFFER AND ACCEPTANCE	

---

10. **Answer (C) is the best answer**. We saw in Topic 1, Overview, that Restatement § 1 defines a *contract* as "a promise or set of promises" the law will enforce. Section 2 defines a *promise* as "a manifestation of intention to act or refrain from acting in a specified way, so made as to justify a promisee in understanding that a commitment has been made." Clearly, the uncle made a promise to the niece. But is it the kind of promise the law will enforce?

Societies differ in their willingness to enforce promises. Our society has elected not to enforce all promises. As a general rule, it will enforce only those promises that are "bargained-for," that is, the ones where the promisor has sought something in return from the promisee. (Remember that the *promisor* is the one making the promise, and the *promisee* is the one to whom it is made.) *See* RESTATEMENT §§ 17 and 71.

To enter into a bargain, therefore, a party must not only make a promise, but must seek something in return for that promise. We call a promise that seeks something in return an *offer*. Here, the uncle did not seek anything in return for his promise, so he did not make an offer. Therefore, **Answer (A) is incorrect**.

We call a promise that does not seek anything in return a "gift promise." Although gift promises are generally unenforceable, note that the Restatement leaves open the possibility that the law might enforce "a promise" as opposed to "a set of promises." Thus, some promises made by a promisor who does not bargain for anything in return may be enforceable. In the old days, a promise under seal might be enforceable even if the promisor sought nothing in return. Today, such promises are rare, and putting the promise in writing is not enough. In other words, even if the uncle had put his promise in writing and had the writing notarized, it would still not make the promise enforceable. Therefore, **Answer (D) is incorrect**.

We will see in Topic 6, Obligations Enforceable Without Consideration, that reliance on a promise may sometimes make the promise enforceable. But there are no facts in this question that indicate reliance by the niece. Because she was already committed to paying law school tuition, the uncle's promise did not induce her to do anything. Therefore, **Answer (B) is incorrect**. When you answer multiple-choice questions, you don't want to make up facts.

In sum, to find a bargained-for contract, look for an offer — a promise by the offeror to do something conditional on getting something in return from the offeree. Then look for acceptance — the giving by the offeree of what was requested in return for the promise. If you have offer and acceptance, then you have a contract (as long as you also have consideration, which we will examine in Topic 3, Consideration).

11. **Answer (B) is the best answer.** An offer is a promise to do something conditional on getting something in return. Here, the uncle promised to pay the tuition if the niece went to a

particular law school. This promise is an offer. Therefore, **Answer (A) is incorrect**.

But what did the uncle bargain for in return for his promise? The manner of acceptance of an offer can take three forms:

a promise,

a performance, or

a promise or a performance.

Restatement § 30(2) states:

Unless otherwise indicated by the language or the circumstances, an offer invites acceptance in any manner and by any medium reasonable in the circumstances.

Here, the uncle said he would pay the tuition "if you go to my alma mater." It seems to me that this language indicates he wanted acceptance by performance — the niece *going* to the law school — rather than by promise — the niece *promising* to go. Furthermore, under the circumstances, her promise (sometimes called a "promissory acceptance" as opposed to an "acceptance by performance") would be of little value to him. He might well say to her, "I don't care if you promise to do it. You either do it or you don't." If the offer could be accepted only by performance, then **Answers (C) and (D) are incorrect**.

12.   Yes. In this case, the uncle bargained for her to *promise* to go to the alma mater, and she gave a promissory acceptance. Note that people don't generally go around saying "I promise" to do this and that. It is enough if they express a commitment, so the niece's saying "I will go to your law school" would be considered to be a promise to go there. Therefore, a contract was formed at the moment of acceptance, and the niece breached when she did not perform as she had promised. Don't confuse formation of the contract with breach. Once there is offer, acceptance, and consideration, a contract is formed. If a party then fails to perform, it doesn't mean a contract wasn't formed — it means a contract was breached.

13.   **Answer (C) is the best answer**. Contracting is serious business. We enforce contracts because they are the expressions of autonomous parties exercising an important freedom. We should not enforce contracts that are the product of a joke. That is all well and good, but how are we going to determine whether a party is joking? We could look at it subjectively, and determine whether in their minds they are joking. The only problem with that approach is that it is nearly impossible to measure what is in someone's mind. So we have largely rejected what has been called the *subjective* view of assent. Therefore, **Answer (A) is incorrect**.

Instead, we look for *objective* manifestations of assent — not whether the person was joking in his mind but whether the surrounding facts and circumstances would lead a person to conclude that he was joking. The language is one manifestation. If you look just at the language the parties used, you would probably conclude that a contract was formed, even if they were both joking. This limited objective view would not make sense, so we look beyond the language to all the facts and circumstances. Therefore, **Answer (D) is incorrect**. But it is not the actual perceptions of the other person we are concerned with. When looking at all the facts and circumstances, we look beyond how the offeree perceived the offer. It is the perceptions of a *reasonable person* in the shoes of that person that matter. Therefore,

Answer (B) is incorrect.

People who ought to know better, including many judges, will sometimes say that formation of a contract requires a "meeting of the minds." This is sheer nonsense — since we can't even tell what is in one mind, imagine how hard it is to determine whether two of them have met. Therefore, it is better to say that a contract requires an *objective manifestation of assent*. That expression might not roll as trippingly from the tongue, but it is a far more accurate way of describing the process of determining whether there has been assent to contract and you would do well to remember it.

14. **Answer (B) is the best answer.** It is dangerous for an offeror to make an offer to a number of offerees if the offeror cannot make good on every acceptance. The law has historically protected offerors from the problem of multiple acceptances by coming up with the rule that advertisements, circulars, catalogues, and the like are not offers. Instead, they are invitations to make an offer. It may seem odd to think of the woman as going to the store and saying in effect, "I hereby offer you $800 for one of those Brand X TVs," but that is exactly what she is doing. Therefore, **Answers (A) and (C) are incorrect.**

A store may try to make disappointed customers happy by giving them a "rain check" to purchase the goods later, but that is a business decision and not a rule of contract law. Therefore, **Answer (D) is incorrect.** Notice that the store could take advantage of this rule by attracting customers in this manner, not having the goods, and then steering them to other goods — a tactic known as a "bait and switch." Contract law has no solution for that problem, but in most jurisdictions Consumer Protection Acts supplement contract law by enumerating "unfair or deceptive acts or practices," including bait and switch. A store concerned that it might be accused of a bait and switch will often protect itself by putting language in its advertisements that advise consumers that only limited quantities are available; *e.g.*, "limited to stock on hand" or "only 5 available at this price."

15. **Answer (D) is the best answer.** One test for whether a statement is an offer or merely a "preliminary negotiation" is whether a contract would be concluded by the other person responding, "I accept" without any other discussion. *See* RESTATEMENT § 26. For example, suppose the woman had said, "I'm thinking of selling my bicycle. Would you give me $75 for it?" That language seems to indicate a preliminary negotiation rather than an offer. She is testing the water, finding out how much her bike might be worth. If the other party had said, "I accept," that response doesn't really answer her question. But under the given facts, the test seems to be satisfied. The woman did not hedge and left nothing to be negotiated. Therefore, **Answer (C) is incorrect.**

So the issue becomes, once an offer is made, how long is it open before it lapses? The answer won't surprise you — it is open for a reasonable period of time. **Answer (B) is incorrect** because the three month rule only applies in the special case of the merchant's firm offer, which does not apply here.

What is reasonable depends on the facts and circumstances. An offer made on the floor of the New York Stock Exchange, for example, may be open for only a few seconds. It would not be fair to the offeror to allow the offeree to hold open the time of acceptance in such a rapidly changing market. The market for the woman's bicycle is not so volatile, however. On the other hand, she should be able to sell it to someone else without worrying about the open offer being accepted later. For this reason, some say that an offer made in a face-to-face meeting lapses when the meeting ends. In any event, I can't say exactly when it lapsed, but

I am quite sure it was not open two months later. Therefore, **Answer (A) is incorrect**.

16.   **Answer (D) is the best answer.** *See* RESTATEMENT § 36. The offer dies with either the offeror or the offeree. Therefore, **Answer (A) is correct, but (D) is a better answer**. Notice this is not true of a *contract*. If the offeree had accepted the offer, and then one of the parties had died, that party's personal representative would have the right to enforce the contract.

If the offeree responds by suggesting a deal under different terms, this is called a rejection and counteroffer, which terminates the original offer. Therefore, **Answer (B) is correct, but (D) is a better answer**. The common law rule is that the acceptance must be the "mirror image" of the offer. *See* RESTATEMENT § 58. This makes sense, for it wouldn't do for the offeree to respond to the offeror's $75 offer by saying, "I accept for $65." So when the offeree says, "I'll give you $65 for it," the offeree has now become the offeror. By making a counteroffer, the offeree risks losing out on the deal. Assume that the original offeror rejects the counteroffer, and the original offeree says, "Okay, then I'll give you $75 for it." The original offeror is free to say, "Ha Ha. My original offer is gone and I reject your $75 offer." The original offeree can avoid this problem by making an inquiry rather than rejecting the offer. She might say something to the effect of, "While holding open your offer of $75, would you be willing to consider taking $65 for the bicycle?" If the offeror says no, presumably the original offer is still open.

The implied promise to keep the offer open for a reasonable time is just that — a promise — and as we know, promises by themselves are not enforceable. So if the woman said, "I'll sell you my bicycle for $75," and before the friend could respond, the woman said, "I take it back," then the offer was effectively revoked. Therefore, **Answer (C) is correct, but (D) is a better answer**. Note that this result would be the same if the woman had said, "I'll sell you my bicycle for $75. This offer is open for a week" and two days later, before the friend had accepted, the woman said, "I take it back." The woman's revocation would be effective because her promise to keep the offer open for a week was just a gift promise.

17.   **Answer (A) is the best answer.** There are two contracts here. The first was made when the friend offered a quarter in return for the woman keeping the offer open for two weeks, and she accepted. At that moment, a bargained-for contract was formed. It should not trouble you that the quarter was not paid. The bargain was the promise of a quarter in return for the promise of keeping the offer open for two weeks. As discussed in Question 12, if the quarter was not paid, that was breach of the contract, but it did not prevent a valid contract from being formed. Therefore, **Answer (B) is incorrect**. You may be troubled by the fact that the promise to keep the offer open for two weeks was given in exchange for a mere quarter. As you will learn in Topic 3, Consideration, the respective values of the exchange are generally irrelevant.

Unlike in the gift promise situation, the offeree here promised to pay for the right to have the offer kept open for a specified period of time, a contract that is called an "option contract." *See* RESTATEMENT § 25. The option period then replaces the "reasonable time" that the offer would otherwise have been open, so **Answer (D) is incorrect**. The friend then accepted the offer during the option period, which formed the second contract. Again, the fact that the woman had already sold the bicycle does not mean that a contract was not formed. It just means she is in breach of contract. Therefore, **Answer (C) is incorrect**.

18.   **Answer (B) is the best answer.** This is a difficult problem to resolve, and the best way to

resolve it is to first identify the manner of acceptance. In this case, the manner of acceptance is clearly performance only. The offeror does not care whether someone promises to do it. A promissory acceptance is more meaningful when the offeror needs the commitment that something is going to get done, as is the case with most commercial contracts. But with a prize or contest, a commitment is not meaningful. In fact, if a person starts to perform and then quits, there should be no consequence to either party. For that reason, notice is not important. In a commercial case, for example, where a seller might accept by shipping goods, it might be important for the buyer to know that the goods are on their way. But the operator of the contest does not need to know that a person has entered. You may recall that this is the rule of the notorious case of *Carlill v. Carbolic Smoke Ball Co.*, 1 Q.B. 256 (C.A. 1892). Therefore, **Answer (D) is incorrect**. *See* RESTATEMENT § 54.

When a promissory acceptance is expected, the rule that the offeror may revoke at any time before acceptance makes sense, for the offeree, knowing that there is no contract until acceptance, would be foolish to rely on the offer. Therefore, an offeree should not be out anything if the offeror revokes. But with an acceptance by performance, no contract is formed until the requested performance is given. Therefore, **Answer (A) is incorrect**, since the contract is formed not when the runner begins running, but when he or she gives the offeror the requested performance — here, running to the hotel in three days or less.

But when acceptance is by performance rather than by promise, the offeree must begin performance while the offer is still open. This necessary reliance on the part of the offeree is enough to act like an option contract, keeping the offer open while the offeree decides whether to accept by completing performance. Therefore, **Answer (C) is incorrect**, since under these facts we need an exception to the rule that the offeror can revoke at any time before acceptance. The beginning of performance does not create a contract, for that would bind the offeree to complete and there is no reason to bind them when they have made no commitment to the offeror. But it does keep the offeror from revoking, and the offeree is free to accept by completing the requested performance or to not accept by quitting performance. *See* RESTATEMENT § 45.

19.   Yes. Start by asking: What was the manner of acceptance? Here, the man said that the offeree could accept by either promising to do it or by giving the requested performance. So this offer could be accepted by promise or by performance. In this situation, as distinguished from the situation where acceptance is by performance only, the beginning of performance has the same effect as promising to perform. At the moment the friend started performance, he was in effect saying, "I promise to do it." Since a contract was formed at that point, he is in breach if he then ceases his performance before completion. *See* RESTATEMENT § 62.

20.   **Answer (A) is the best answer.** As we have seen, the general rule is that the offeror can revoke the offer any time before acceptance. The exception applicable here was created by statute and applies only in a narrow set of circumstances. It is found at U.C.C. § 2-205:

§ 2-205. Firm Offers.

An offer by a merchant to buy or sell goods in a signed writing which by its terms gives assurance that it will be held open is not revocable, for lack of consideration, during the time stated or if no time is stated for a reasonable time, but in no event may such period of irrevocability exceed three months; but any such term of assurance on a form supplied by the offeree must be separately signed by the offeror.

Let's break down the language of this statute. It starts by requiring that there be an offer. Under our facts, was the letter an offer or an advertisement? The U.C.C. does not answer this question, so § 1-103(b) directs us to the common law. Because it was addressed to a limited number of offerees (in this case, one) and could be accepted by the offeree without any further negotiation, this was probably an offer. Distinguish this situation from an advertisement in which the business states that it has nails for sale at $100 per barrel. Therefore, **Answer (D) is incorrect**.

This rule applies only to offers by merchants to buy or sell goods. In general, Article 2 applies to all transactions involving the sale of goods, but there are a few rules (13 to be exact) that apply only to merchants. For purposes of those rules, it is important to determine whether a party is a merchant: Section 2-104(1) provides:

> (1) "Merchant" means a person who deals in goods of the kind or otherwise by his occupation holds himself out as having knowledge or skill peculiar to the practices or goods involved in the transaction or to whom such knowledge or skill may be attributed by his employment of an agent or broker or other intermediary who by his occupation holds himself out as having such knowledge or skill.

So a person can be a merchant either because they are familiar with the goods or the practices involved, or they have an agent who has this familiarity. Since this business regularly sells nails, it is a merchant, and nails are goods. Additionally, the statute only applies to an offer by the merchant that is found in a signed writing. The letter is undoubtedly a writing, but is it signed? The definition of "signed" in U.C.C. § 1-201(b)(37) provides:

> "Signed" includes using any symbol executed or adopted with present intention to adopt or accept a writing.

The Official Comment states that "[t]he symbol may be printed, stamped, or written; it may be by initials or by thumbprint. It may be on any part of the document and in appropriate cases may be found in a billhead or letterhead." If the intention of the signature is to indicate that the writing was adopted by that party as coming from them, then the letterhead would probably be adequate to conclude that the writing was signed by the business.

The statute goes on to require that the offer "by its terms gives assurance that it will be held open." This offer stated, "This is a firm offer and it is open for the next 10 days," which would probably suffice. If it satisfies those requirements, then the offer "is not revocable, for lack of consideration, during the time stated." Recall the "option contract" discussed in Question 17. This statute says that the firm offer gives the offeree an option contract, even without consideration; that is, without the offeree having to give anything in return to the offeror. During that option period, the offeror cannot revoke the offer. Therefore, **Answer (C) is incorrect**.

This offer satisfies the requirements of a merchant's firm offer and since it was not revocable, the offeror's statement to the customer attempting to revoke the offer was of no effect, and a contract was formed when the customer said he was accepting the offer. Reliance by the offeree is irrelevant, so **Answer (B) is incorrect**.

21.   **Answer (C) is the best answer.** This question invokes the notorious "mailbox rule." Simply

put, the rule is: "Acceptance is effective on dispatch, not receipt." We still apply the rule that an offer can be revoked before acceptance, but this rule tells us when acceptance occurs. Under the facts, it occurred when the woman mailed her acceptance. A revocation is not effective until the offeree receives it. *See* RESTATEMENT § 42. Therefore, **Answer (A) is incorrect**. Since the woman mailed her acceptance before she received the revocation, her acceptance was effective, and it doesn't matter when the acceptance was received, so **Answer (B) is incorrect**. In fact, according to Restatement § 63, her acceptance would be effective even if the offeror never received it. Reliance on the offer is not relevant. The offeree accepts an offer by manifesting acceptance, not by reliance, so **Answer (D) is incorrect**.

22. **Answer (C) is the best answer**. The general rule is that an offer can be revoked any time before acceptance, and these facts fit the general rule.

    The offer was to be accepted by promise, not performance, so **Answer (A) is incorrect**. The rule on the medium of acceptance is that an offer can be accepted by the same or a better medium. Here, an offer made by email could be accepted orally, so the medium is not a problem and **Answer (D) is incorrect**. *See* RESTATEMENT § 65.

    There is no doubt that the woman relied on the offer. But was that reliance reasonable? No. She knew that acceptance was to be by promise and that the offeror could revoke at any time. Before she relied, she should have accepted. If she wanted a commitment that the offer would remain open while she made a decision, she should have purchased an option. Because her reliance was not reasonable, **Answer (B) is incorrect**. You may be aware of cases — or more likely just one case — *Drennan v. Star Paving*, 333 P.2d 757 (Cal. 1958), where the offeror was prevented from revoking the offer because of the offeree's reliance. That case arose in a subcontracting situation where the offeror knew that the offeree could not accept before he relied on the offer. The rule in that case should be limited to its facts and should not be expanded to a general rule that an offeree may keep an offer open by relying on it.

23. **Answer (C) is the best answer**. This question shows how some of the U.C.C. rules differ from the common law rule. We have already seen an example of this in Question 20, where the common law rule on option contracts was changed by U.C.C. § 2-205. The "mirror image rule," discussed in Question 16, was changed by U.C.C. § 2-206, which provides in part:

    ### § 2-206. Offer and Acceptance in Formation of Contract.

    (1) Unless otherwise unambiguously indicated by the language or circumstances . . . .

    > (b) an order or other offer to buy goods for prompt or current shipment shall be construed as inviting acceptance either by a prompt promise to ship or by the prompt or current shipment of conforming or non-conforming goods, but such a shipment of non-conforming goods does not constitute an acceptance if the seller seasonably notifies the buyer that the shipment is offered only as an accommodation to the buyer.

    The common law mirror image rule states that the acceptance has to match the terms of the offer. *See* RESTATEMENT § 58. At common law, if the offeror requested 4" x 4"s and the offeree shipped 2" x 4"s, the offeree could claim that its shipment was not an acceptance since it varied the terms of the offer; if there was not an acceptance, there could not be a contract; and if there was not a contract, there could not be a breach of contract. However, § 2-206 provides that "an order or other offer to buy goods for prompt or current shipment shall be construed as inviting acceptance either by a prompt promise to ship or by the prompt or current shipment of conforming or non-conforming goods." Under this rule, acceptance occurs when the offeree ships non-conforming goods, that is, goods that don't conform to the terms of the offer. If there is an acceptance, then a contract is formed. But it is a contract on the terms of the offer; so when the offeror requested 4" x 4"s, the offeree breached by shipping 2" x 4"s. While Answer (A) might be correct at common law, this is a contract for goods, and is governed by the U.C.C. Therefore, **Answer (A) is incorrect**.

There is some relief for the seller. The subsection goes on to say: "but such a shipment of non-conforming goods does not constitute an acceptance if the seller seasonably notifies the buyer that the shipment is offered only as an accommodation to the buyer." So if the seller notifies the buyer that it is shipping the nonconforming goods as an accommodation, then the shipment is not an acceptance but a counteroffer. Here, however, the seller gave no notice to the buyer that it was shipping the nonconforming goods as an accommodation. Therefore, **Answer (B) is incorrect**.

In this instance, the seller accepted by shipping the goods, as requested by the offeror. There was no "expression of acceptance," such as a form document, sent by the seller. Therefore, **Answer (D) is incorrect**. Make sure you distinguish between those different situations. The questions that follow involve an expression of acceptance that contains additional or different terms, which is another area where the U.C.C. has changed the common law.

24.   **Answer (C) is the best answer.** As previously discussed, the common law "mirror image rule" requires that to constitute an acceptance, the response to the offer must contain precisely the same terms as the offer — no more, no less. *See* RESTATEMENT § 58. The common law considers a purported acceptance not satisfying the "mirror image rule" to be a counteroffer. *See* RESTATEMENT § 59. This contract, however, is for the sale of goods. Therefore, it is governed by U.C.C. Article 2, which rejects the common law "mirror image rule." U.C.C. § 2-207 provides:

§ 2-207. Additional Terms in Acceptance or Confirmation.

(1) A definite and seasonable expression of acceptance or a written confirmation which is sent within a reasonable time operates as an acceptance even though it states terms additional to or different from those offered or agreed upon, unless acceptance is expressly made conditional on assent to the additional or different terms.

(2) The additional terms are to be construed as proposals for addition to the contract. Between merchants such terms become part of the contract unless:

  (a) the offer expressly limits acceptance to the terms of the offer;

  (b) they materially alter it; or

  (c) notification of objection to them has already been given or is given within a reasonable time after notice of them is received.

(3) Conduct by both parties which recognizes the existence of a contract is sufficient to establish a contract for sale although the writings of the parties do not otherwise establish a contract. In such case the terms of the particular contract consist of those terms on which the writings of the parties agree, together with any supplementary

terms incorporated under any other provisions of this Act.

This provision governs "The Battle of the Forms." To solve a § 2-207 problem (and they are not easily solved!) it is necessary to carefully parse the language of the statute. The Code does not change the common law definitions of offer and acceptance, so we have to carefully analyze the facts to determine which party is the offeror and which is the offeree. Here, it seems that Tubular made the offer with its Sales Order, and is thus the offeror. Therefore, Mercury's Acknowledgment was the "expression of acceptance" referred to in § 2-207(1). To be an acceptance, it has to be "definite and seasonable." *Seasonable* means timely, and timeliness was satisfied here. There is a lot of debate about what "definite" means. I think the best view is that the forms must agree on the essential or "dickered" terms for an expression of acceptance to constitute an acceptance. Here, there was agreement on the description of the goods, the price, quantity, and delivery terms, so this was a definite acceptance. The next step is where the Code diverges from the common law. The common law requires the acceptance to be the mirror image of the offer, but the Code says that the expression is an acceptance even if it "states terms additional to or different from those offered." Here, Mercury wrote in a term that was additional to the terms in the Sales Order. Nevertheless, this does not prevent the expression of acceptance from being an acceptance. Therefore, **Answer (A) is incorrect**.

There is, however, one thing that can prevent the expression of acceptance from being an acceptance, and that arises when "acceptance is expressly made conditional on assent to the additional or different terms." Again, there is a lot of debate about what language is strong enough to satisfy this requirement. I think the best view is that the language must amount to the party saying, "We don't have a deal unless you agree to my terms." One way to do that is to track the language of the statute. Clearly, Mercury did not go that far, so **Answer (B) is incorrect**.

Notice where we are in our analysis of the statute. We have an offer and an expression of acceptance. Our analysis leads us to the conclusion that the expression of acceptance operates as an acceptance. If we have offer and acceptance (and consideration since each party has bargained for something), then we have a contract. The call of the question was whether the parties have a contract, and since we have determined that they do, **Answer (D) is incorrect**. As we will see, we may have to analyze whether the proposed term materially alters the terms of the contract when we get to the issue of whether the proposed term is part of the contract or not. But we don't have to go that far to determine that there is a contract.

25.   **Answer (D) is the best answer.** See § 2-207(3), which we will work our way up to.

Our analysis begins the same as the analysis of Question 24, but now we see that Mercury has included in its Acknowledgment language sufficient to satisfy the requirement of § 2-207(1) after the comma: "unless acceptance is expressly made conditional on assent to the additional or different terms." Since the expression of acceptance is not an acceptance, there is no contract at that point. Had the parties gone their separate ways, there would have been no harm and no foul.

But instead of going their separate ways, Tubular shipped the goods and Mercury accepted them. We are now thrown into § 2-207(3), for the parties have recognized the existence of a contract through their *conduct* even though their writings did not establish a contract.

Therefore, since there is a contract, **Answer (C) is incorrect**.

What are the terms of that contract? Subsection 3 goes on to tell us that "[i]n such case the terms of the particular contract consist of those terms on which the writings of the parties agree, together with any supplementary terms incorporated under any other provisions of this Act." In other words, we "knock out" all the terms that are not the same, and read in the default rules of the Code. Here, we would read in the Code rule on delivery and inspection of the goods rather than Mercury's term. Notice that by insisting on its terms, Mercury did not get its terms. Therefore, **Answer (B) is incorrect**.

If you chose Answer A, you were distracted by language about a material alteration. But that language is found in subsection 2 of § 2-207, and we never got to that subsection in our analysis. Therefore, **Answer (A) is incorrect**. In Question 24, we solved the problem without getting past subsection 1, and here we solved the problem by skipping over subsection 2 and going to subsection 3.

26.   **Answer (A) is the best answer.** We established in Question 24 that there is a contract between the parties. The question now is to find the terms of that contract — specifically, does it include the additional term found in the acceptance?

To analyze that question, we go to § 2-207(2). There we are told that "[t]he additional terms are to be construed as proposals to the contract." Think of Mercury as saying to Tubular, "We propose this term for inclusion in our contract." We are then told that "[b]etween merchants such terms become part of the contract." We have to analyze whether both Mercury and Tubular are merchants according to the definition in § 2-104(1). I don't think there is much doubt, for they are both experienced not only with this kind of good, but with general business practices. Therefore, we tentatively conclude that Tubular has accepted the proposal, and it is part of the contract.

By the way, you may wonder what we would do if both parties were *not* merchants. Unfortunately, § 2-207 does not tell us, and a court would have to fill in this gap in the statute. I think the sensible and logical answer is that if *between* merchants such terms *become* part of the contract, then *not between* merchants such terms do *not become* part of the contract. That is, they are not automatically included, but would be included only if the party to whom they were proposed affirmatively agreed to accept them.

The fact that both parties are merchants, however, does not mean that the proposed term is part of the contract, so **Answer (B) is incorrect**. Subsection 2 goes on to say that even between merchants, the terms are only presumptively part of the contract, and the party to whom they are proposed has three opportunities to reject them. The first would apply if the other party drafted its offer to provide that "the offer expressly limits acceptance to the terms of the offer." We don't have any facts indicating that Tubular did that here. The second is that the party to whom they are proposed objects to them after they are proposed. That rarely happens because it would require parties to read the form documents they receive, and they generally don't. We don't have any facts indicating that that happened here. The Code nicely assumes the reality that parties by and large don't read beyond the dickered terms of their contracts, so it adds a third way in which the proposal can be rejected — if the proposed additional term materially alters the terms of the contract. Note that in subsection 2, the Code does not say anything about a "knockout rule," so **Answer (C) is incorrect**.

It can be hard to determine whether a term materially alters the contract, but the Official Comments give us some guidance, Comment 4 giving examples that *do* materially alter and

Comment 5 giving examples that *do not*. The distinction seems to be whether they result in "surprise or hardship." Here, we would have to ask if it would cause surprise or hardship for Tubular if Mercury had the glass examined by a chemist before accepting it. I would conclude that it does not materially alter. So, finally, **Answer (A) is the best answer** and **Answer (D) is incorrect**.

27.   **Answer (D) is the best answer.** The important fact to notice here is that unlike the previous questions, this question involves a *different* term, as opposed to an *additional* term — each party's form addresses the implied warranty of merchantability, but addresses it differently. Our analysis of § 2-207(1), however, would lead us to the same conclusion we came to with an additional term — there is an acceptance in spite of the different terms and therefore there is a contract formed by the writings of the parties.

We then go to subsection 2 to determine whose term is part of the contract and we discover a slight problem — § 2-207(2) tells us what to do with *additional* terms, but it does not tell us what to do with *different* terms. When there is a gap in a statute, courts have to try their best to fill that gap, and different courts have approached the problem differently.

Some courts have ruled that the offeror's term governs. For one thing, the offeror is the master of the offer and its terms should not be substantially altered by different language on a form that no one reads. For another, by affirmatively stating a term, the offeror has impliedly objected to a different term on the same subject. Therefore, **Answer (A) is correct, but (D) is a better answer**.

Other courts have read § 2-207(2) as if it applied to "additional or different terms." Applying that approach to our facts, the offeree's proposed term would undoubtedly be deemed rejected because it materially alters the contract. But under other facts, the offeree's proposed term might become part of the contract if it did not materially alter. Therefore, **Answer (B) is correct, but (D) is a better answer**.

The majority of courts have taken a simple, if thoughtless, approach. They "knock out" both terms and read in the default rule of the Code. Under our facts, the buyer would get a warranty of merchantability, not because its term governed, but because that is the default rule of the U.C.C. in § 2-314. Therefore, **Answer (C) is correct, but (D) is a better answer**.

28.   **Answer (B) is the best answer.** We looked at these facts in connection with offer and acceptance in Topic 2, Offer and Acceptance. We saw that an offer is a promise to do something conditional on getting something in return. Here, the uncle promised to pay the tuition if the niece went to a particular law school. This promise is an offer.

We also saw that the uncle bargained for a performance by the niece in return for his promise, and the niece rendered that performance. Her promise to go to the law school is irrelevant, since the uncle did not bargain for a promise. Therefore, **Answer (A) is incorrect.** A contract requires offer, acceptance, and consideration. So the elements of offer and acceptance are satisfied, and the remaining issue is whether there is consideration for. The requirements for consideration are spelled out in Restatement § 71:

§ 71 Requirement of Exchange; Types of Exchange

(1) To constitute consideration, a performance or a return promise must be bargained for.

(2) A performance or return promise is bargained for if it is sought by the promisor in exchange for his promise and is given by the promisee in exchange for that promise.

(3) The performance may consist of

   (a) an act other than a promise, or

   (b) a forbearance, or

   (c) the creation, modification, or destruction of a legal relation.

(4) The performance or return promise may be given to the promisor or to some other person. It may be given by the promisee or by some other person.

The first requirement is that the performance or return promise must be bargained for. Subsection (2) explains what this means:

(2) A performance or return promise is bargained for if it is sought by the promisor in exchange for his promise and is given by the promisee in exchange for that promise.

To find a bargain, look for a "reciprocal inducement" — did the promisor make the promise in order to get something from the promisee? Did the promisee give the thing in order to get what the promisor promised? In our facts, the promisor (the uncle) sought a performance (going to his alma mater) from the promisee (the niece). The promisee (the niece) gave the performance (went to the alma mater) in order to get what the promisor (the uncle) promised (tuition paid). Since the niece's performance was "given by the promisee in exchange for that promise," the element of bargain is satisfied and **Answer (D) is incorrect.** It does not matter that the promisee might have had mixed motives and went for other reasons as well, as long as the promised inducement was one reason. *See* RESTATEMENT § 81.

Therefore, there was a bargained-for exchange and the requirement of consideration is satisfied. As pointed out in subsection (4), it does not matter that the promisor did not materially benefit from the bargain. Although some cases talk about consideration in terms of "benefit to the promisor or detriment to the promisee," the Restatement looks only to whether there is a bargain. It is part of your freedom of contract to bargain for what you want, even if there is no benefit or if the benefit runs to someone else. Therefore, **Answer (C) is incorrect.**

29.   **Answer (A) is the best answer.** According to Restatement § 71(3)(b), the performance that is bargained for can be "the creation, modification, or destruction of a legal relation." Here, each party agreed to destroy their legal relation — a contract. **Answer (D) is incorrect** because the parties who form a contract have the freedom to terminate it, a process called mutual rescission. When the parties to a contract mutually agree to rescind it, they each give up their contractual rights against the other. That is the consideration. Therefore, **Answer (C) is incorrect** because each party bargained for something. **Answer (B) is incorrect** because it does not matter what they thought, or whether they enjoyed a benefit from the termination.

30.   **Answer (D) is the best answer.** A reward is an offer to be accepted by performance. The rancher gave the offeror the requested performance, but because she did not know about the reward, her performance was not induced by the offer. Therefore, it was not bargained-for. **Answer (B) and Answer (C) are incorrect.**

We can presume that as part of his contract with the county, the sheriff had an obligation to apprehend criminals. Therefore, he was not induced by the offer to render the performance since he was already obligated to do it. This rule, known as the "pre-existing duty rule," comes up in a number of contexts. In short, there is no consideration if a person merely does what the person already has a legal obligation to do. *See* RESTATEMENT § 73. Therefore, **Answers (A) and (C) are incorrect.**

31.   **Answer (C) is the best answer.** The innkeeper conferred a benefit on the son. The father, however, did not bargain for him to confer that benefit in exchange for the father's promise. The father could not have bargained for the innkeeper's services because they had already been rendered before the promise was made. This situation is sometimes described as "past consideration," but that expression is a bit misleading because past consideration is no consideration at all. Therefore, **Answer (A) is incorrect.**

In Topic 6, Obligations Enforceable Without Consideration, we will look at the concept of *restitution*, which may obligate a person to pay for a benefit conferred on them. Restitution, however, is not contract, and the call of the question was whether the promise was enforceable as a contractual obligation. Furthermore, because a parent has no legal obligation to a 25-year-old child, the benefit was conferred on the son and not on the father. Therefore, **Answer (B) is incorrect.**

Answer (D) is a red herring. Since this promise is not enforceable, it doesn't matter whether it was in writing or not.

32.   No. Most courts have held in this situation that the promise of the pension was an unenforceable gift promise because it was not bargained for by the woman. *See, e.g.,*

Feinberg v. Pfeiffer Co., 322 S.W.2d 163 (Mo. Ct. App. 1959). This is a logical but an outrageous result, and Congress addressed this kind of abuse when it enacted E.R.I.S.A., the Employees Retirement Income Security Act.

33.   Yes. A contract is illusory if one of the parties has an alternative that will result in the other party getting nothing. But if a party has a choice between two alternatives, either of which standing alone would be consideration, then there is consideration for the exchange. *See* Restatement § 77.

34.   **Answer (C) is the best answer.** The law is obviously conflicted here. As we saw in Question 30, under the "pre-existing duty rule," there is no consideration if a person merely promises to do what he is already obligated to do. It would appear that if the man is obligated to pay 5%, then he was doing no more than what he was already obligated to do when he agreed to pay 4%. But the law also favors the settlement of disputes, and creates an exception to the pre-existing duty rule in a case like this one. Therefore, **Answer (A) is incorrect**.

However, the law does not favor the settlement of *all* disputes, so **Answer (D) is incorrect** because it goes too far. It only favors the settlement of disputes where the person raises a claim or defense in *good faith*. Therefore, **Answer (B) is incorrect**. If the claim or defense is asserted in good faith, then there is consideration for the settlement even if in fact the claim or defense turns out to be invalid. *See* Restatement § 74.

35.   No. The law does not inquire into the adequacy of consideration. As long as there was a bargained-for exchange, contract formation does not require equivalency in the values exchanged. *See* Restatement § 79. Of course, an imbalance in the consideration may indicate that there is some other defense to contract formation. *See* Topic 4, Formation Defenses. Furthermore, if the man sought to enforce the contract by specific performance, principles of equity might bar his claim. *See, e.g.,* Cal. Civ. C. § 3391.

36.   **Answer (C) is the best answer.** These are, of course, the facts of the famous case of *Wood v. Lucy, Lady Duff-Gordon*, 118 N.E. 214 (N.Y. 1917). The lawyer's argument actually carried the day in the appeal to the intermediate appellate court. But in the Court of Appeals, the highest appellate court in New York, Judge Cardozo found that there was consideration. He looked beyond the literal language to the context of the deal and found that the parties meant to have a serious commercial deal, but that it was "imperfectly expressed." He then found what they meant to say was that the man did have an obligation, and that obligation was to make "reasonable efforts to bring profits and revenues into existence." **Answer (D) is incorrect** because it goes too far — he would be performing the contract if he made efforts to obtain endorsements even if he did not actually obtain any.

There are various ways to characterize the problem in this case, but it all comes down to consideration. It could also be called an "illusory contract," because it may initially look like there is not a contract, but once the implied promise is made part of the exchange, there is clearly a bargained-for consideration. **Answer (A) is incorrect** because if there is consideration, the rule of mutuality of obligation is satisfied; in fact, "mutuality of obligation" just means consideration. **Answer (B) in incorrect** because there is the commitment necessary for a promise once the implied promise is read into the contract.

37.   **Answer (C) is the best answer.** Just because a contract is subject to a condition does not mean it is illusory. The condition might be beyond the control of either of the parties. And

when it is within a party's control, that party has a good faith obligation not to hinder or prevent its occurrence. A condition only makes the contract illusory "if the promisor knows at the time of making the promise that the condition cannot occur." RESTATEMENT § 76(1). Therefore, **Answer (B) is incorrect**.

The particular condition this contract is subject to is called a "satisfaction clause." The argument that a person can get out of the contract just by claiming he or she is not satisfied has a superficial appeal. But the law divides satisfaction clauses into two kinds — objective and subjective. Objective satisfaction applies to things like mechanical utility or operative fitness. In that case, the person exercising satisfaction has to act reasonably. That constraint is enough of a commitment that the law says there is consideration.

Subjective satisfaction applies to situations requiring fancy, taste, or judgment. In that case, the person exercising satisfaction has to act in good faith, that is, honestly. That constraint is enough of a commitment to satisfy the consideration requirement. In either event, there is consideration even though there is a satisfaction clause. The person does not have a free out, so **Answer (A) is incorrect**.

Whether the subject of a portrait is satisfied with the portrait is clearly an example of subjective satisfaction. Therefore, **Answer (D) is incorrect**.

38. **Answer (D) is the best answer**. It is true that the contract lacks a specific quantity and there is no gap-filler for quantity. This contract might have failed for lack of consideration at common law, but the U.C.C. specifically provides that in a contract for the sale of goods, quantity may be measured by the output of the seller or the requirements of the buyer. Section 2-306(1) provides:

> **§ 2-306. Output, Requirements and Exclusive Dealings**.
>
> (1) A term which measures the quantity by the output of the seller or the requirements of the buyer means such actual output or requirements as may occur in good faith, except that no quantity unreasonably disproportionate to any stated estimate or in the absence of a stated estimate to any normal or otherwise comparable prior output or requirements may be tendered or demanded.

In this case, the quantity is measured by the output of the seller, so **Answer (C) is incorrect**. That quantity is measured in good faith. The seller, can't, for example, suddenly produce a larger quantity when the market price for the goods becomes unfavorable as compared to the contract price. Another restraint is the historical production, for "no quantity unreasonably disproportionate to any stated estimate or in the absence of a stated estimate to any normal or otherwise comparable prior output or requirements may be tendered or demanded." Output and requirements contracts are not illusory since the parties have a commitment that can be measured, so **Answer (A) and Answer (B) are incorrect**.

39. **Answer (A) is the best answer**. Let's first deal with the firm offer rule. The woman's offer to hold the offer open for a month fits the requirements of a firm offer under U.C.C. § 2-205. However, the man did not accept that offer. Instead, he proposed a six-month option for a consideration of one dollar and the woman accepted it. The statute states that the period of irrevocability under a firm offer may not exceed three months. But this rule only applies to an option that lacks consideration. The parties are free to create a longer option as long as there is consideration for it. Because the firm offer was taken off the table by the man's

counteroffer, **Answer (B) and Answer (C) are incorrect**.

The issue comes down to whether the consideration of $1 "to make it legal" makes the option contract enforceable. Sometimes a token consideration, such as the recital of $1, is referred to as a "nominal consideration." If that phrase means "small consideration," then it does not compute. Since the law does not inquire into the adequacy of consideration, there is no such thing in contract law as a "small" consideration — there either is a bargain or there isn't.

The real issue with "nominal consideration" is whether there is a bargain or whether the purported consideration is a sham cooked up to disguise what might otherwise be a gift promise. In the area of option contracts, contract law has been very tolerant of recitals of consideration, judging it more important that the parties agreed to a consideration than that they actually performed by tendering or paying it. Restatement § 87(1) provides that "[a]n offer is binding as an option contract if it . . . is in writing and signed by the offeror, recites a purported consideration for the making of the offer, and proposes an exchange on fair terms within a reasonable time."

Under our facts, there would seem to be no reason not to honor this exchange. When the man said he was offering the dollar "to make it legal," in fact, that is exactly what he was doing, showing that he was making a serious bargain, and the woman seemed to accept it in that light. The underlying exchange of the colt for $2,000 was on fair terms, and it was to be performed in a reasonable time under the circumstances. Therefore, **Answer (A) is correct** and **Answer (D) is incorrect**.

40.   Yes, according to the Restatement, but I have my doubts. The Restatement looks only at whether there has been a bargained-for exchange and does not seem to care about whether anything of value has been exchanged in that bargain. According to the "peppercorn theory" of consideration, we do not inquire into the adequacy of consideration, so even a trivial value like a peppercorn will support a bargain. Nevertheless, it would make sense to me that there be a requirement of some measurable economic value in the exchange. In any event, Restatement § 1 defines a *contract* as a set of promises "for which the law gives a remedy." Since it is impossible to give a remedy for breach of the promise of everlasting gratitude, this exchange would likely not count as a contract under the Restatement, even if it did pass the consideration requirement.

41.   **Answer (B) is the best answer.** An agreement that is *void* is unenforceable as a matter of law — that is, neither party can say or do anything that will make the agreement enforceable. For example, an agreement to murder someone is a void contract because it is illegal to make the contract. Contracts entered into by minors (those under the age of 18 in most jurisdictions) are not void, but they are *voidable* at the minor's option. *See Zelnick v. Adams*, 561 S.E.2d 711 (Va. 2002). Therefore, **Answer (A) is incorrect**.

        A *voidable* contract is one that a party has the power to avoid for one of several reasons. *See* RESTATEMENT § 7. One reason for avoiding a contract is that the party seeking to avoid it was a minor when he entered into the contract. While minors are permitted to enter into any contract an adult can, provided that the contract is not one the law prohibits for minors (*e.g.*, an agreement to purchase cigarettes or alcohol), they are also permitted to later avoid performance of the contract. *See* RESTATEMENT § 14 and *Nicholas v. People*, 973 P.2d 1213 (Colo. 1999).

        In order for a minor to avoid a contract, he need only manifest his intention not to be bound by it. The minor may manifest his intent to avoid (or "disaffirm") the contract by explicit or implicit words or actions. In general, a minor may disaffirm a contract at any time during his minority or for a reasonable time after he reaches the age of majority. A minor who fails to timely disaffirm will have constructively affirmed the contract. *See, e.g., Dixon v. American Buildings Co.*, 379 S.E.2d 533 (Ga. Ct. App. 1989). A minor may also affirmatively reaffirm or ratify a contract, but he cannot do so until after he turns 18. *See, e.g., Fletcher v. Marshall*, 632 N.E.2d 1105 (Ill. App. Ct. 1994). Here, the singer's refusal to perform unless he received more money would likely be interpreted as an implicit disaffirmance of the earlier contract. Therefore, **Answer (D) is incorrect**.

        An exception to the general rule is that a minor is not able to avoid a contract made when he or she is emancipated. Some states prohibit disaffirmance in cases where the minor has engaged in business as an adult. *See, e.g., Martin v. Stewart Motor Sales*, 73 N.W.2d 1 (Iowa 1955). However, most jurisdictions require that the minor go through a proceeding to have himself or herself declared emancipated. You may have heard stories of young actors and athletes going through such proceedings. In Washington State, for example, the emancipation statute is found at RCW 13.64. Because there are no facts indicating that the singer had gone through such a proceeding, **Answer (C) is incorrect**.

42.   **Answers (A), (B), and (C) are incorrect** for the same reasons given in the answer to Question 41.

        That brings us to Answer (D), which is based on actual events. Bob Dylan, at one time, the most famous living American musician, and still a legend in folk and rock music circles, entered into a recording contract with Columbia Records when he was 20 years old. At the time, the age of majority in New York (whose law governed the contract) was 21. When Dylan sought to disaffirm the contract shortly after turning 21, Columbia was able to thwart him because he had used Columbia's studio six or seven times after his 21st birthday. Thus, like Dylan, the singer should be barred from disaffirming his contract with the recording company because he used the studio and equipment after reaching the age of majority. Therefore, **Answer (D) is the best answer.**

43.   **Answer (A) is the best answer.** As a general rule, when a minor disaffirms a contract, the other party must return the consideration paid by the minor, and the other party has no remedy if the minor has dissipated the consideration she received. RESTATEMENT § 14 cmt. c. This rule supports the general policy that a person deals with a minor at his peril.

A minor who enters into a contract to purchase food, shelter, clothing, medical attention, or other goods or services necessary to maintain his well-being may, technically speaking, avoid the contract, but the minor will generally be liable in restitution for the reasonable value of the goods and services received. *See* RESTATEMENT § 12 cmt. f, *Williams v. Buckler*, 264 S.W.2d 279 (Ky. Ct. App. 1954), and *Zelnick v Adams, supra*. However, a car is generally not considered a necessary, so the restitution exception would not apply and **Answer (D) is incorrect.**

When the minor disaffirms, courts generally require the other party to restore to the minor the consideration he paid when he entered the contract. Therefore, **Answer (B) is incorrect** as a general rule. However, some jurisdictions may require the minor to restore the consideration received in certain circumstances. One such circumstance arises when a minor affirmatively misrepresents her age when she enters into a contract. Depending on the law of the applicable jurisdiction, the minor may not be able to avoid the contract or may be required to make restitution for the value of the goods returned. Some states permit disaffirmance even if the minor misrepresented her age when entering into the agreement. *See, e.g., Gillis v. Whitley's Discount Auto Sales, Inc.*, 319 S.E.2d 661 (N.C. Ct. App. 1984). Some states prohibit disaffirmance in all cases where the minor misrepresented her age. *See, e.g., Youngblood v. State*, 658 S.W.2d 598 (Tex. Crim. App. 1983). Some states permit disaffirmance, but subject the minor to tort liability for her misrepresentation. *See, e.g., Kiefer v. Fred Howe Motors, Inc.*, 158 N.W.2d 288 (Wis. 1968). There are no facts in this question suggesting that the young woman *affirmatively* misrepresented her age and *appearing* older is not enough to constitute misrepresentation. Therefore, **Answer (C) is incorrect.**

Another exception requiring the minor to restore the consideration when disaffirming the contract may arise if the minor paid cash for the goods and services instead of receiving credit. Some courts are less sympathetic to a minor who is a plaintiff using minority as a sword to get the cash back. But if the other party extended credit to the minor, the exception will not apply since the minor is a defendant using minority as a shield to resist the obligation to pay.

44.   No. The minor would be correct if he said that he could disaffirm the contract. But even if a minor is not liable on the contract, a minor is liable in restitution for the reasonable value of food, clothing, shelter, medical attention, or other goods or services necessary to maintain his well-being. This makes sense from a policy standpoint, because if this were not the rule, sellers might refuse to provide these goods and services to minors. Note that in restitution, a party is not liable for the contract price but for the reasonable value of the benefit conferred. This rule prevents the minor from being taken advantage of. Therefore, if the bill in this question was for $14, but the reasonable value for that meal was only $10, the minor

would be liable only for $10 in restitution and not for the $14 contract price.

45. **Answer (C) is the best answer.** Mental incapacity is grounds for avoiding a contract. *See* RESTATEMENT § 15. However, if a person has not been declared mentally incompetent as a matter of law, then the person seeking to avoid the contract must prove as a matter of fact that the mental illness led him to enter into the contract in order to be able to avoid it.

Different jurisdictions have different tests for the standard required to avoid a contract for mental illness. Some apply the "cognitive test," which asks whether the person understood the nature and consequences of the transaction. Here, the man did understand the nature and consequences of the transaction, so it is unlikely that he would be able to avoid the purchase under the cognitive test. Therefore, **Answer (A) is incorrect.**

Some jurisdictions apply the "motivational test," which recognizes that even if a person understands the nature and consequences of the transaction, the person may not be able to act in accordance with that understanding due to the mental illness. It would appear that the man was not able to act in accordance with his understanding of the business, and therefore should be able to avoid the contract under these facts. However, the motivational test disadvantages the other party to the transaction, who has no reason to know that the person is entering the contract because of a mental illness. Therefore, the motivational test is satisfied *only if* the other party knows or has reason to know of the condition. Under the facts, there is no indication that the seller of the business knew of the mental illness. Therefore, **Answer (B) is incorrect** because it contains an incomplete description of the motivational test.

California applies the cognitive test. See *Smalley v. Baker*, 262 Cal. App. 2d 824 (1968), from which the facts of this question were taken. New York applies the motivational test. *See Ortelere v. Teachers' Retirement Board of the City of New York*, 250 N.E.2d 460 (N.Y. 1969). Since under the facts of this question, the man would not be able to avoid the contract under either test, the outcome does not depend on the jurisdiction, and **Answer (D) is incorrect.**

46. **Answer (A) is the best answer.** The key to this question is that "the woman's family had her declared incompetent and a guardian appointed." Because she had been judicially declared incompetent, as a matter of law she was incapable of making a contract — any contract she entered was void. Therefore, the tests for mental incompetency as a matter of fact are irrelevant **and Answer (B) and Answer (C) are incorrect.** Likewise, it is irrelevant whether the choice was rational or not, so **Answer (D) is incorrect.**

Although the contracts entered into by a person who has been declared legally incompetent are void, the person is liable in restitution for the reasonable value of necessaries such as food, shelter, clothing, and medical care. *See* RESTATEMENT § 12 cmt. f. The policy here is the same as it is with minors: we would not want the suppliers of those goods and services to refuse to provide them out of fear that they would not be paid because the contract was void.

47. **Answer (D) is the best answer.** A promisor may avoid a contract on the ground of duress if his assent was induced by an *improper threat* that left him with *no reasonable alternative* but to assent. *See, e.g., Totem Marine Tug & Barge, Inc. v. Alyeska Pipeline Service Co.*, 584 P.2d 15 (Alaska 1978). Certain threats are improper *per se*: (1) a threat of crime or tort, including a threat that would itself be a crime or tort; (2) a threat of criminal prosecution; (3) a threat to bring a civil suit in bad faith; or (4) a threat that breaches the duty of good faith and fair dealing owed to the promisor. RESTATEMENT § 176(1). Other threats are improper

when coupled with an exchange on unfair terms. RESTATEMENT § 176(2). None of those apply here because the singer was only seeking to modify the contract to better reflect his current market value. The compensation he sought was not an exchange on unfair terms. Nor would the singer's threat not to perform unless the manager agreed to pay him more money fall within any of the categories identified by Restatement § 176(1). The only possibility is "a threat that breaches the duty of good faith and fair dealing owed to the victim," but these facts do not fit that claim because the singer was not demanding more money "without legitimate commercial reason." RESTATEMENT § 176 cmt. e. The singer's star was on the rise. He was no more guilty of breaching the duty of good faith and fair dealing than an athlete who demands more money or a trade despite having a contract in place. Therefore, **Answer (A) is incorrect**.

Undue influence involves taking unfair advantage of another's weakness of mind or taking an oppressive and unfair advantage of another's necessity or distress. *See, e.g., Odorizzi v. Bloomfield School District*, 246 Cal. App. 2d 123 (1966). Like duress, undue influence involves coercing a promisor into acting against his free will. Unlike duress, undue influence requires no threat, nor does it require that the party exercising the influence leave the promisor with no other reasonable alternative than that sought. *See* RESTATEMENT § 177. There is no evidence that the singer attempted to exercise any undue influence over the manager or that the manager was susceptible to undue influence. Therefore, **Answer (B) is incorrect**.

Unconscionability can arise where disparate bargaining power between the parties (1) deprives the party asserting unconscionability of any meaningful choice as to the terms of the agreement (procedural unconscionability) and (2) results in one or more terms that are so one-sided, under the circumstances existing at the time of the making of the contract, as to be oppressive or manifestly unfair (substantive unconscionability). RESTATEMENT § 208. Some courts seem willing to find a term unconscionable when only the substantive prong of the test has been satisfied. *See, e.g., Donovan v. RRL Corp.*, 27 P.3d 702 (Cal. 2001). Most courts, however, will require a showing of *both* procedural and substantive unconscionability. *See, e.g., Williams v. Walker-Thomas Furniture Co.*, 350 F.2d 445 (D.C. Cir. 1965). The facts of this question do not suggest that the hotel manager lacked bargaining power. Indeed, even having consented to forming a new contract, he still signed the singer for considerably less than the singer's going value. Nor are the terms of the deal so unfair as to deprive the manager of the benefit of his bargain. Therefore, **Answer (C) is incorrect**.

48.	**Answer (A) is the best answer.** Unlike the facts of Question 47, now the manager should be able to shield himself from liability by claiming duress. As explained in the previous answer, Restatement § 175 allows a party to avoid a contract if his assent was induced by, *inter alia*, a threat of crime or tort, including a threat that would itself be a crime or tort. RESTATEMENT § 176(1)(a). Brandishing a gun is both a crime and a tort and a threat of a greater crime or tort. The fact that the threat was made by someone other than the singer does not prevent the manager from avoiding the contract unless, *inter alia*, the singer had no reason to know of the threat. The singer was in the room at the time. So, even if he did not know that the threat *would* be made, he did know that the threat *was* made. As such, he should not be able to profit from it by holding the manager to the contract that the manager consented to only after the threat.

Answers (B) and (C) are incorrect for the same reasons discussed in the answer to Question 47. **Answer (D) is incorrect because Answer (A) is correct.**

49. **Answer (B) is the best answer.** If the manager was so drunk as to be legally incapable of forming a contract, then he may be excused from performing the June 8 contract. "Mere mental weakness" is not enough to excuse the manager on the ground of incapacity. RESTATEMENT § 16; *Estate of McGovern v. State Employees' Retirement Board*, 517 A.2d 523 (Pa. 1986). On the other hand, if the manager was unable, when he entered into the June 8 agreement, to understand in a reasonable manner the nature and consequences of the transaction, or to act in a reasonable manner in relation to the transaction, and the singer had reason to know of the manager's condition, then the manager may avoid the contract *even if his intoxication was purely voluntary*. Therefore, **Answer (A) is incorrect**.

A person lacking contractual capacity when he formed a contract may, upon (re)gaining the necessary capacity to do so, impliedly ratify the contract he made while lacking capacity by acting in a manner that is clearly inconsistent with disaffirmance or avoidance. Because the singer would have been bound to perform from July 1–7 under either the first contract or the second one, the fact that the manager allowed him to perform was not necessarily a ratification of the second contract. Therefore, **Answer (C) is incorrect**.

The facts suggest that the manager, while perhaps under the influence of alcohol, was not so drunk as to be incapacitated. First, he negotiated the singer down from his initial demand of $75,000 to $50,000. Second, he prepared the new contract. Third, he signed the new contract, and had the presence of mind to have the singer sign, too (in the event that the latter might try to bail out despite the increased compensation). Fourth, he tore up the original contract, suggesting that he understood that the new deal replaced the old deal. *Compare, e.g.*, *Lucy v. Zehmer*, 84 S.E.2d 516 (Va. 1954). Therefore, **Answer (D) is incorrect** and **Answer (B) is the best answer**.

Even if the court were to find the manager was incapacitated, Restatement § 15(2) precludes the manager from avoiding the contract "to the extent that the contract has been so performed in whole or in part or the circumstances have so changed that avoidance would be unjust. In such a case a court may grant relief as justice requires." The singer, believing that he had a contract to perform at the manager's hotel for $50,000, did so, only to learn after the fact that the manager did not intend to pay him more than $25,000. The singer has fully performed. The manager has only paid $25,000 of the $50,000 he promised to pay. If the court finds that the manager was incapacitated, it should exercise its equitable powers to decide what award — between $0 and $25,000 — would constitute "justice" for the singer.

50. **Answer (C) is correct.** The facts of the question indicate that the singer purchased the apartment in August, so he had reached the age of majority. There is nothing in the facts of this question to suggest that he was intoxicated or mentally incompetent when he signed the installment purchase contract. Therefore, **Answer (A) is incorrect**.

The singer was mistaken in his belief that Sharman had the right to sell the apartment. However, a contract is generally voidable on grounds of mistake *only if* the mistake is mutual, that is, shared by both parties. Here, Sharman was not under a mistaken belief, so the defense of mistake will not be successful. *See* RESTATEMENT § 152. Therefore, **Answer (B) is incorrect**.

The choice between Answers (C) and (D) boils down to whether the contract is voidable on grounds of fraudulent misrepresentation. One problem is that misrepresentation generally requires a false statement of fact. However, Sharman did not actually say that he could convey good title. The Restatement takes the position that non-disclosure of a fact known to a party is the equivalent of an affirmative misrepresentation if it concerns a material fact and if disclosing the material fact would correct a mistaken belief the other party had about a basic assumption on which the other party was making the contract. *See* RESTATEMENT §§ 159, 161–62. Whether or not a buyer of realty will receive clean title to the realty after satisfying the purchase contract is certainly a material fact, and the singer's assumption that Sharman had good title to convey was a basic assumption on which the singer made the contract. As such, the singer was entitled, *inter alia*, to avoid his contract with Sharman, cease making payments under the contract, and recover any monies paid to Sharman (although he may owe Owen for the use of the apartment during the time he occupied it). Therefore, **Answer (C) is correct** and **Answer (D) is incorrect**.

51.   **Answer (A) is the best answer.** The interest rate provided in the contract was usurious — and, therefore, illegal. A contract made illegally, or for an illegal purpose, is void. In case you are curious, under applicable New York law, any rate of interest over 16% is usurious (*see* N.Y. BANKING LAW § 14-a (McKinney 2001)), and any loan charging a usurious rate of interest is void, regardless of whether the lender knew or intended that the interest rate was usurious. *See, e.g., Babcock v. Berlin*, 123 Misc. 2d 1030 (N.Y. Sup. Ct. 1984).

While the interest term *might* be substantively unconscionable, there are no facts to suggest procedural unconscionability. (See the answer to Question 47 for more discussion of unconscionability.) Because most courts require both procedural and substantive unconscionability to avoid a contract, **Answer (B) is not the best answer**.

As discussed in greater depth in Topic 8, Terms Implied by Law, the implied duty of good faith and fair dealing only applies to the performance and enforcement of a contract, not to its formation. Therefore, **Answer (C) is incorrect**.

Answer (D) is not the best answer because there is no evidence that Sharman affirmatively misrepresented — knowingly (fraud) or not (negligent misrepresentation) — the contract interest rate or its legality. And, absent some duty to speak, Sharman's silence was not a misrepresentation. Generally, neither party to a contract has a duty to volunteer information unless the other party asks. The facts do not indicate that the singer asked Sharman about the contract interest rate. Nor do the facts clearly raise one of the exceptions found in Restatement § 161 in which common or statutory law would have required Sharman to disclose in the absence of a question by the singer.

52.   No. The agreement is void. In most cases of misrepresentation, the perpetrator of the fraud induces the person to enter a contract by affirmatively making false statements of fact or by failing to disclose required facts. An example is Sharman's inducing the singer to buy the apartment by either affirmatively representing that he had title or failing to disclose that he did not have title. We call this "fraud in the inducement." The person who was misled must prove the elements of misrepresentation in order to avoid the contract.

Under the facts of this question, the singer did not even know the contents of the agreement — in fact, he did not know that he was entering into an agreement at all. Therefore, he did not manifest assent to a contract. We call this rare event "fraud in the factum" ("fraud in the making"). In these circumstances, the agreement is void.

53.   **Answer (B) is the best answer.** The singer may be able to avoid the contract as unconscionable. As discussed in the answer to Question 47, unconscionability can arise where (1) the party asserting unconscionability is deprived of any meaningful choice as to the terms

of the agreement (procedural unconscionability) and (2) one or more terms that are so one-sided, under the circumstances existing at the time of the making of the contract, as to be oppressive or manifestly unfair (substantive unconscionability). RESTATEMENT § 208.

Unconscionability works best in the consumer context, where a party signs a contract of adhesion with non-negotiable terms dictated by the other party. Even though parties ought to read their contracts, they usually don't read beyond the "dickered" terms, especially where they could not have bargained for better terms anyway. Most courts will not hold the fact that a person did not read the contract against them, so **Answer (D) is not the best answer**. The singer had the opportunity to read the contract and bargain for better terms, but apparently passed up those opportunities. It is therefore hard to find procedural unconscionability under these facts.

However, some courts that are outraged by the substance of a contract may find it unconscionable solely on the basis of substantive unconscionability. A court may use a "sliding scale" approach whereby the magnitude of the contract's substantive unconscionability will require very little procedural unconscionability to satisfy the court that it should not enforce the contract. For example, one New York court stated, "While determinations of unconscionability are ordinarily based on the court's conclusion that both the procedural and substantive components are present, . . . there have been exceptional cases where a provision of the contract is so outrageous as to warrant holding it unenforceable on the ground of substantive unconscionability alone." *Gillman v. Chase Manhattan Bank, N.A.*, 534 N.E.2d 824, 829 (N.Y. 1988) (citations omitted). On the other hand, if the court considers procedural and substantive unconscionability as equally important and inquires into each prong without regard for its findings regarding the other, the singer may be out of luck.

Nevertheless, unconscionability is still the singer's *best* argument. For a case in which an English court found that contracts entered into by the rock group Fleetwood Mac were unconscionable, see *Clifford Davis Management, Ltd. v. WEA Records, Ltd.*, 1 ALL ER 237 (1975). The contract term is not illegal, so **Answer (C) is incorrect**. Although a party has a duty not to affirmatively misrepresent the terms of the contract (*i.e.*, "Don't worry. This contract is only for two years, so you can re-negotiate it at that time"), a party does not have a duty to inform the other of what the terms are, since the other is capable of finding out for itself. Therefore, **Answer (A) is incorrect**.

54.   **Answer (D) is the best answer.** When we say that a contract is *within* the statute of frauds, we mean that there is a statute that provides that the particular kind of transaction must be evidenced by a writing. When we refer to *the* statute of frauds, we mean any such statute. Of course, it is up to each state to enact these statutes, but historically there are certain transactions that are frequently found to be within a state's statute of frauds. Those transactions are enumerated in Restatement § 110. U.C.C. § 2-201(1) provides that a contract for the sale of goods for $500 or more is within the statute of frauds. This contract concerns a sale of goods, but it is for less than $500 and, therefore, it is not within the statute of frauds.

        Answer (A) is incorrect because one transaction that is frequently found within the statute of frauds is a contract to answer for the duty of another, sometimes called "the suretyship provision." *See* RESTATEMENT § 112. This transaction fits that description, because the friend is agreeing to pay the debt of the debtor.

        Answer (B) is incorrect because another transaction that is frequently found within the statute of frauds is a promise to transfer an interest in land. *See* RESTATEMENT § 125. Many jurisdictions have an exception for a lease of land for a term of a year or less, but here the lease is for two years, so this transaction is likely to be within the statute.

        Answer (C) is incorrect because another transaction that is frequently found within the statute of frauds is a contract that cannot be fully performed within a year from the time the contract was made. *See* RESTATEMENT § 130. Here, the promise was made on January 10 of one year, and it will not be fully performed until May 31 of the following year; therefore, it cannot be performed within a year from the date it was made, so it is within the statute.

55.   **Answer (A) is the best answer.** The contract was oral. It was made on January 10 and would not be performed until the end of May of the following year, which is a period of more than one year.

        Answer (B) is incorrect because contracts for the sale of goods for $500 or more must be evidenced by a writing, but this transaction is for services rather than goods. Therefore, it is not within the U.C.C. Article 2 statute of frauds.

        Answer (C) is incorrect. As we shall see, a promisee may be able to recover because of reliance on a contract that is within the statute of frauds. However, the issue here is not whether the professor can recover any money. The issue is whether the contract is within the statute of frauds, and it is.

        Answer (D) is incorrect. All of these events — her death, her quitting, or her being fired — might *terminate* the contract within a year. But the question is whether it can be *performed* within a year, and by its terms it cannot be.

A good approach to a statute of frauds problem is to first ask whether the contract is within the statute. If it is, then to be enforceable, it has to be evidenced by a writing. If there is no writing, then look for an exception to the statute.

56.   **Answer (D) is the correct answer.** Since the contract is within the statute of frauds, there must be a writing that evidences it. The requisites of the writing needed to satisfy the statute are stated in Restatement § 131:

> ### § 131 General Requisites of a Memorandum
>
> Unless additional requirements are prescribed by the particular statute, a contract within the Statute of Frauds is enforceable if it is evidenced by any writing, signed by or on behalf of the party to be charged, which
>
> (a) reasonably identifies the subject matter of the contract,
>
> (b) is sufficient to indicate that a contract with respect thereto has been made between the parties or offered by the signer to the other party, and
>
> (c) states with reasonable certainty the essential terms of the unperformed promises in the contract.

The rules are similar in U.C.C. § 2-201, which requires "some writing sufficient to indicate that a contract for sale has been made between the parties and signed by the party against whom enforcement is sought."

Answer (A) is incorrect because the writing does not have to *be* a contract; it just has to *evidence* a contract. Don't make the writing do too much work.

Answer (B) is incorrect because the writing must be signed only by "the party to be charged." That means it has to be signed by the party who is claiming that the contract is not enforceable. So if the law school claimed the contract was not enforceable on account of the statute of frauds, the professor would have to produce a writing signed by an authorized person, such as the dean; if the professor claimed the contract was not enforceable, the law school would have to produce a writing signed by the professor.

Answer (C) is incorrect because either one of these documents alone is probably not sufficient to evidence the contract. One issue is whether an email is a "writing." The U.C.C. (even though it is not applicable here, the definition can be useful) defines "writing" in § 1-201(b)(43) as follows: " 'Writing' includes printing, typewriting, or any other intentional reduction to tangible form." Some cases have held that since an email can be reduced to tangible form, it is a writing. Furthermore, Uniform Electronic Transactions Act (U.E.T.A.) § 7(c) provides that "[i]f a law requires a record to be in writing, an electronic record satisfies the law." So these records probably pass that test.

Another issue is whether, even if the documents are writings, are they "signed" writings? The definition of "signed" in U.C.C. § 1-201(b)(20) provides: " 'Signed' incudes using any symbol executed or adopted with present intention to adopt or accept a writing." And U.E.T.A. § 7(a) states that "[a] record or signature may not be denied legal effect or enforceability solely because it is in electronic form." The question to ask is whether these records were adopted by the dean with the intention of showing that they came from her. I think both the electronic signature on the email and the letterhead "From the desk of the

Dean" are sufficient to show this. You will also find that as a matter of policy, courts do not like to refuse enforcement to contracts that they think were really made yet are within the statute of frauds. Therefore, they are quite liberal in finding that the signed writing requirement is satisfied.

A final issue is whether the document reasonably identifies the subject matter of the contract. The dean's email indicates the parties and the term, but does not indicate the salary. The writing does not have to evidence all of the terms of the contract, but it has to contain the essential terms. The absence of the salary term could prove fatal. In a contract for the sale of goods, on the other hand, the absence of a price term would probably not be fatal because there is likely a way to supply the missing term through the default rules. There is, however, no default rule for a salary. Similarly, the dean's memo to the payroll department contains the salary but no other terms, so it might be insufficient.

On the other hand, several writings taken together may contain sufficient essential terms to satisfy the statute. Restatement § 132 provides:

§ 132 Several Writings

The memorandum may consist of several writings if one of the writings is signed and the writings in the circumstances clearly indicate that they relate to the same transaction.

Under this rule, sometimes called the "composite document rule," the writing requirement can be satisfied by several writings, and it likely was here.

57. Yes. This question shows how stupid the statute of frauds can be. Presumably one of the policies behind it is to keep people from trying to enforce promises that weren't really made. And the one-year statute supposedly makes the promise easier to prove when the evidence is still fresh. Yet in this case, the court will be asked to decide whether the promise was made some 51 years after it was made.

Will the statute of frauds keep the niece from offering the evidence? No, because this transaction is not within the statute of frauds. Since the time of performance is measured by the lifetime of the aunt, it could have been performed within a year. Therefore, the transaction is not within the statute and the niece does not have to show that it is evidenced by a writing. It then becomes a question of fact whether a court believes her testimony. Obviously it would have been preferable to get it in writing, so the statute of frauds can be said to perform a "channeling" function that encourages us to get agreements in writing and not have to face this issue.

58. **Answer (D) is the best answer.** This contract is within the Article 2 statute of frauds. Wheat is a good according to § 1-205(1) and the price is more than $500. There is, however, no writing signed by the farmer — the party "against whom enforcement is sought." So we look for an exception and we find one in § 2-201(2), which provides:

(2) Between merchants if within a reasonable time a writing in confirmation of the contract and sufficient against the sender is received and the party receiving it has reason to know its contents, it satisfies the requirements of subsection (1) against such party unless written notice of objection to its contents is given within 10 days after it is received.

Under this section, a contract can be enforceable against a party even though that party did not sign a writing that evidences the contract. Therefore, **Answer (A) is incorrect**.

The section only applies "between merchants." This means, according to § 2-104(3), that "[b]oth parties are chargeable with the knowledge or skill of merchants." The grain buyer is undoubtedly a merchant. Is the farmer? Some cases come to the aid of farmers in this situation and hold that even though a farmer regularly buys and sells a commodity, the farmer is not necessarily a merchant for that purpose. *See* David B. Harrison, *Farmers as "Merchants" Within Provisions of UCC Articles 2, Dealing With Sales*, 95 A.L.R.3d 484 (1979). This makes no sense to me. Nevertheless, even if there is some authority that would give the farmer this defense, **Answer (B) is incorrect** because you are instructed to choose the best answer, so you want to choose the one about which there is the least doubt.

The section makes the writing effective even if it is not signed by the party against whom enforcement is sought as long as it is "sufficient against the sender." In this case, we would ask if the confirmation is sufficient against the buyer. The confirmation is a writing signed by the buyer, but does it "indicate that a contract for sale has been made between the parties"? I think it does, because it describes the goods and has a quantity and price. Any other terms, such as delivery date, can be filled in by testimony as to the agreement or by the default rules. Therefore, since the writing is sufficiently definite and can be made even more definite, **Answer (C) is incorrect**.

The section only applies if the confirmation "is received and the party receiving it has reason to know its contents." The definition of "receives" is found in § 1-202(e), which provides that "a person 'receives' a notice or notification when: (1) it comes to that person's attention" or was delivered to their place of business. Neither of these conditions was satisfied here. Note that if the section had provided that it is sufficient if the sender "notifies" the other party, then the buyer would probably prevail because a person can be notified even if they never receive the notice. The definition of "notifies" in § 1-202(d) states:

> A person "notifies" or "gives" a notice or notification to another by taking such steps as may be reasonably required to inform the other in ordinary course, whether or not the other person actually comes to know of it.

Under that section, you *notify* a person if you send the letter to his address even if it does not reach him.

59. No. The transaction is for the sale of goods for $500 or more, so it is within the statute of frauds. It is not evidenced by a writing. But an interesting exception applies here. U.C.C. § 2-201(3)(b) provides:

> (3) A contract which does not satisfy the requirements of subsection (1) but which is valid in other respects is enforceable . . .
>
> (b) if the party against whom enforcement is sought admits in his pleading, testimony or otherwise in court that a contract for sale was made, but the contract is not enforceable under this provision beyond the quantity of goods admitted;

Under this exception, if you admit in your pleading (such as the answer to a complaint) or your testimony that you made the contract, then your defense of the statute of frauds will not be successful. Does this make sense? I think so. One policy behind the statute of frauds is to prevent people from being bound by agreements they did not make; it should not protect them from agreements they admit they made. Note that this exception applies only to contracts within the Article 2 statute of frauds (sale of goods for $500 or more) and even there it only applies to an admission in a pleading, deposition or testimony in court. This is probably because those admissions are made formally, often under oath. A casual admission in a conversation would not be sufficient.

60.   **Answer (D) is the best answer.** This is a transaction involving the conveyance of real property, so it is within the statute of frauds. The transaction is not evidenced by a writing. So we are looking for an exception to the statute of frauds that would make the contract enforceable. Reliance can create such an exception. Restatement § 129 states:

§ 129 Action in Reliance; Specific Performance

A contract for the transfer of an interest in land may be specifically enforced notwithstanding failure to comply with the Statute of Frauds if it is established that the party seeking enforcement, in reasonable reliance on the contract and on the continuing assent of the party against whom enforcement is sought, has so changed his position that injustice can be avoided only by specific enforcement.

Performance can be an exception to the statute of frauds. Once the agreement has been fully performed, it is too late for a party to claim the defense of the statute of frauds. This makes sense, for if a purpose of the statute is to protect people from agreements they did not actually make, a person who completes performance of the contract does not need that protection, for by the act of performing, the person has acknowledged making the contract. For this reason we do not say that agreements within the statute of frauds are *void* or *voidable*; if they were, then a party could avoid the contract after it was performed. Instead, we say they are *unenforceable*.

Part performance is more problematic. One issue is whether part performance is sufficient to prove the terms of the contract. If a buyer gives a seller $5,000, that may indicate that they had an agreement, but it does not sufficiently prove the terms of that agreement. Also, the remedy of restitution will be available to a party who confers a benefit on the other party under an unenforceable contract, so the party who partly performed is not deprived of a remedy. Therefore, because part performance is generally not enough to make the contract enforceable, **Answer (A) is incorrect.**

In this case there was more than a part performance; there was substantial reliance on the agreement, and the buyer's acts in reliance were undertaken with the knowledge and consent of the seller. This makes the reliance reasonable, and it would be unjust to deprive the buyer of a remedy. The question then becomes, what remedy? In cases of reliance, a party often recovers only the amount they are out of pocket because of the reliance. Recall that Restatement § 90 states that "[t]he remedy granted for breach may be limited as justice requires." In this case, however, the reliance also serves the evidentiary function of convincingly showing that there was an agreement between the parties. Therefore, the seller does not need the protection of the statute of frauds, and most courts will find it just to enforce the contract by specific performance. Therefore, **Answers (B) and (C) are incorrect under these facts.**

61.   **Answer (B) is the best answer.**

This is an agreement to convey real property, so it is clearly within the statute of frauds. Therefore, **Answer (A) is incorrect.** The question then becomes whether there is a writing sufficient to evidence the contract and signed by the party against whom enforcement is sought. The check tendered by the buyer said on it "DP on 500 Eddy $300,000." This would seem sufficient to indicate the transaction as it contains the essential terms of describing the property sold and the price. Other terms can be supplied by testimony of the parties' agreement along with default terms supplied by custom and usage. For example, the buyer said that title had to be "satisfactory." It could be argued that requiring satisfaction makes a contract illusory, but that is a losing argument. *See* Topic 3, Consideration. In this context, there would be sufficient standards to determine what makes a title satisfactory. Therefore, **Answer (C) is incorrect**. The writing must be signed by the party against whom enforcement is sought, which is the seller in this case. The buyer signed the front of the check, but the seller signed the back of it when he indorsed it. Therefore, there is a writing signed by the seller.

If we have a writing that sufficiently satisfies the statute of frauds, we don't have to go to the exceptions, but if we did, the performance exception would probably not be applicable. These facts show a part performance by the buyer in paying $30,000. The fact that one person gives another person $30,000 is certainly an indication that there is some transaction between them, but it is not enough to satisfy the statute because it does not prove the essential terms of what the property is or what the price is. Therefore, **Answer (D) is incorrect**.

62. **Answer (A) is the best answer**. This transaction is within the suretyship provision of the statute of frauds because the father's promise to answer for his daughter's debt is a promise to answer for the debt of another. *See* RESTATEMENT § 112.

   Answer (B) is an incorrect red herring, but it gives us a good opportunity to review an aspect of consideration discussed in Topic 3, Consideration. It looks like a good argument because it appears that the father did not get anything from the bank in exchange for his promise. But with consideration, we need to look for a bargain rather than benefit to the promisor, so the better question to ask is whether he bargained for something. We then see that his promise induced the bank to give the loan to his daughter, which is what he bargained for. Recall that the performance or return promise that is bargained for does not have to be given to the promisor; it can be given to some other person, such as the daughter in this case. *See* RESTATEMENT § 71(4). Therefore, **Answer (B) is incorrect**.

   Since we have a transaction within the statute of frauds and it is not evidenced by a writing, there would have to be an exception that makes it enforceable. In contracts for the sale of goods, a formal admission can be an exception. That exception does not apply here, however. This is not an Article 2 transaction. Furthermore, the admission was not made formally; for example, under oath. Therefore, **Answer (C) is incorrect**.

   Reliance can be an exception. *See* RESTATEMENT § 139. In considering whether reliance should be an exception here, it is worth considering again the policies behind the statute of frauds. One policy is evidentiary, and reliance is more likely to make the promise enforceable when the reliance evidences that the contract was made. That is not the case here. Another policy is to caution a party against ill-considered transactions; requiring them to assent in writing may make them think twice before entering into a transaction that requires a substantial commitment. In this case, allowing reliance as an exception would swallow up the rule. If the exception applied, a lender could always claim that it incurred the obligation because of the promise by the third party, even though it knew it was supposed to get the promise in writing. For these reasons, I think most courts would not find it just to apply the reliance exception under these facts and therefore, **Answer (D) is incorrect**.

63.   **Answer (C) is the best answer.** We looked at questions with similar facts in Topic 2, Offer and Acceptance, and in Topic 3, Consideration. We saw that an *offer* is a promise to do something conditional on getting something in return. Here, the niece was already planning to go to law school, so the uncle was not bargaining for anything in return. Because he was not seeking anything in return for his promise, there is no bargained-for consideration, and hence no bargained-for contract. His promise is merely a gift promise. Therefore, **Answer (A) is incorrect.**

In this chapter we will be looking at obligations that may be created even in the absence of bargained-for consideration. In this fact situation, the uncle may have an obligation because of the niece's *reliance* on his promise. Historically, courts have turned what would otherwise be gift promises into enforceable promises when the promise reasonably induced reliance by the promisee. Those cases became the basis for Restatement § 90. It provides:

> **§ 90 Promise Reasonably Inducing Action or Forbearance**
>
> (1) A promise which the promisor should reasonably expect to induce action or forbearance on the part of the promisee or a third person and which does induce such action or forbearance is binding if injustice can be avoided only by enforcement of the promise. The remedy granted for breach may be limited as justice requires.
>
> (2) A charitable subscription or a marriage settlement is binding under Subsection (1) without proof that the promise induced action or forbearance.

As you know, a Restatement section is not a statute but just a shorthand way of stating common law rules. Nevertheless, because of the widespread acceptance of the reliance doctrine, if the facts satisfy the elements of § 90, that can be a good predictor of whether a court will enforce the promise. Let's apply our facts to the elements:

Element 1: *A promise.* The definition of *promise* in Restatement § 2 is "a manifestation of intention to act or refrain from acting in a specified way, so made as to justify a promisee in understanding that a commitment has been made." Does the uncle saying "I promise to give you $500 to make things a little easier for you" satisfy this requirement? I think it does. He manifested that he would pay her $500 and she understood that he had made a commitment.

Element 2: *which the promisor should reasonably expect to induce action or forbearance on the part of the promisee or a third person.* Should the uncle have reasonably expected the niece to act on the promise? I think so. He made it in a serious context in which he knew extra money would be useful to her.

Element 3: *and which does induce such action or forbearance.* Did the niece commit some act because of the promise? Yes, she bought the study aids.

Element 4: *is binding if injustice can be avoided only by enforcement of the promise.* Unfortunately, Restatement § 90 does not give us much help on how to determine this matter of justice. Curiously, § 139(2), which addresses promises enforceable in spite of the statute of frauds, provides some suggestions:

§ 139 Enforcement by Virtue of Action in Reliance

(2) In determining whether injustice can be avoided only by enforcement of the promise, the following circumstances are significant:

(a) the availability and adequacy of other remedies, particularly cancellation and restitution;

(b) the definite and substantial character of the action or forbearance in relation to the remedy sought;

(c) the extent to which the action or forbearance corroborates evidence of the making and terms of the promise, or the making and terms are otherwise established by clear and convincing evidence;

(d) the reasonableness of the action or forbearance;

(e) the extent to which the action or forbearance was foreseeable by the promisor.

It seems to me that all of these circumstances support enforcement in this case. In short, it would be unjust if the uncle got away with it.

Element 5: *The remedy granted for breach may be limited as justice requires*. This limitation was not found in the First Restatement. It appears that the drafter of that section, Samuel Williston, thought that reliance was a consideration substitute. Therefore, the reliance made the promise enforceable just like consideration would. But the Restatement (Second) reflects the modern trend, which sees reliance as an alternative theory of enforcement. If there was a bargained-for contract, the promisee would be entitled to the expectancy — what she would have had if the contract had been performed. But in reliance, a modern court is more likely to restore the promisee to where she was before she relied on the promise. In other words, the promise will be enforced only to the extent of the reliance. Under our facts, $400 will restore the niece to where she was before she relied on the promise. Therefore, most courts will enforce the promise only to that extent, so **Answer (B) is incorrect**.

Because consideration is not required for a promise enforceable because of reliance, **Answer (D) is incorrect**. I suggest you think of reliance as a backup position. First, look for consideration for a promise. If you don't find it, then look to see if the promise is enforceable because of reliance. By the way, sometimes you will hear references to "promissory estoppel." That is the same thing as reliance. Because of the reasonable reliance by the promisee, the promisor is estopped from claiming that the promise is not enforceable. Hence, *promissory estoppel*.

64. **Answer (A) is the best answer.** Alpha offered $5 million to the museum if it would name the wing after his family. The museum accepted. There is clearly offer and acceptance, but is there consideration? In the view of Restatement § 71, Alpha got what he bargained for, and its value is irrelevant. If you insist on finding economic value, it is present. The museum has only one name to offer, and it may well be marketable. See *Wolford v. Powers*, 1882 Ind. LEXIS 551 (Nov. 1882), in which the court upheld a contract in which a consideration was paid for the naming of a child, stating that "[t]he value of all things contracted for is measured by the appetite of the contractors, and therefore the just value is that which they

be contented to give."

Because there is a bargained-for contract, we do not need to inquire into whether the promise is enforceable on a theory of reliance. Therefore, **Answers (B), (C), and (D) are not the best answers.** However, the following questions will explore the application of reliance to variations of this transaction.

65.   **Answer (B) is the best answer.** Unlike the previous question, there is no bargained-for consideration under the facts of this question. Therefore, **Answer (A) is incorrect.** The museum should have a reliance claim under Restatement § 90(1), which requires proof that (1) a promise was made, (2) the promisor could reasonably foresee the promise would induce action or forbearance by the promisee, (3) the promise did induce such action or forbearance, and (4) as a result of which, injustice can be avoided only by enforcing the promise. Many courts add that the promisee's reliance must be reasonable. *See, e.g., Chrysler Corp. v. Chaplake Holdings, Ltd.*, 822 A.2d 1024 (Del. 2003); *First National Bank of Logansport v. Logan Manufacturing Co.*, 577 N.E.2d 949 (Ind. 1991); *Pop's Cones, Inc. v. Resorts International Hotel, Inc.*, 704 A.2d 1321 (N.J. Super. Ct. App. Div. 1998); *Karnes v. Doctors Hospital*, 555 N.E.2d 280 (Ohio 1990); *Durkee v. Van Well*, 654 N.W.2d 807 (S.D. 2002). There is no reason why a charitable pledge should be treated differently from any other promise that induces reliance, so **Answer (C) is incorrect.**

Answer (D) is incorrect because there are facts here indicating reliance. The museum stopped the campaign and began construction because of the pledge. There might be issues as to whether injustice can be avoided only by enforcing the pledge and whether the remedy should be limited to the amount of reliance rather than the amount of the pledge. It is hard to estimate how much the museum lost. The museum would have continued seeking donations had Alpha not made the pledge. But, as things currently stand, the museum cannot build the new wing without the money Alpha pledged. One question is whether the museum can find one or more donors to make pledges to the campaign or pledge additional amounts to make up for the loss of Alpha's money. If so, then Alpha may be off the hook. If not, then injustice will certainly result if a court does not enforce Alpha's promise. Courts are hesitant to assume that there is a bottomless pit of charitable money out there that fundraisers can tap at will.

66.   **Answer (B) is the best answer according to the Restatement, but some case law suggests that Answer (D) is the best answer.**

The museum needed to give consideration if it was trying to enforce Alpha's pledge as a contract, rather than a promise, and there is no evidence of consideration in the facts. Therefore, **Answer (A) is incorrect.**

As we have seen in the previous two questions, a charitable pledge is an appropriate promise to subject to analysis under Restatement § 90(1), so **Answer (C) is incorrect.**

Some courts as a matter of policy have been sympathetic to the enforcement of charitable pledges, and have enforced them even if there was no actual reliance. These cases became the basis for Restatement § 90(2):

> (2) A charitable subscription or a marriage settlement is binding under Subsection (1) without proof that the promise induced action or forbearance.

Restatement § 90(2) eliminates the element of reliance from charitable pledge cases.

However, this may be a case where the drafters of the Restatement included a rule that has not been accepted as a majority rule; in other words, the drafters were being *prescriptive*, stating what they think the law ought to be, rather than *descriptive*, stating what the law is. Therefore, if we take the Restatement at its word, Answer (B) would appear to be correct.

But, according to Mary Frances Budig, Gordon T. Butler, and Lynn M. Murphy, *Pledges to Nonprofit Organizations: Are They Enforceable and Must They Be Enforced?*, 27 U.S.F. L. REV. 47 (1992), many jurisdictions have either not adopted Restatement § 90(2) or specifically rejected it. *See, e.g., Arrowsmith v. Mercantile-Safe Deposit & Trust Co.*, 545 A.2d 674 (Md. 1988); *Congregation Kadimah Toras-Moshe v. DeLeo*, 540 N.E.2d 691 (Mass. 1989). In those jurisdictions, the primary factor courts use to decide whether to enforce charitable pledges seems to be whether the pledge was for a sufficiently specific purpose — and, in some cases, of sufficiently significant value — to presume foreseeable reliance by the charity even if there was no actual reliance. This contrasts with situations where the court looked at whether the pledge was a general pledge on the basis of which the pledgor could not reasonably foresee specific, detrimental reliance by the charity. *See, e.g., Maryland National Bank v. United Jewish Appeal Federation of Greater Washington, Inc.*, 407 A.2d 1130 (Md. 1979) (denying charity the right to enforce a pledge made to its general purpose fund against the estate of the pledgor). Because Alpha's pledge was for the specific purpose of building the new wing, and because Alpha knew or should have known that his pledge accounted for a substantial part of the fundraising goal for the new wing, his pledge was both specific enough and significant enough to make the museum's detrimental reliance reasonable and reasonably foreseeable. So, it is likely that if the court either disregards the issue of actual reliance or presumes reliance, then the museum will be successful, which would make **Answer (B) the correct answer**.

67.   **Answer (B) is the best answer.** We looked at the facts of this question in Topic 3, Consideration, and concluded that the corporation's promise of the pension was an unenforceable gift promise because it was not bargained for by the woman. Therefore, **Answer (A) is incorrect.** *See Feinberg v. Pfeiffer Co.*, 322 S.W.2d 163 (Mo. Ct. App. 1959).

However, a gift promise becomes enforceable if the elements of reliance are satisfied. Let's look at Restatement § 90. The corporation promised her a pension and should reasonably have known that this would induce the woman to retire. She did in fact retire. Can injustice be avoided only be enforcement of the promise? The woman is now elderly and it would be difficult for her to return to the workforce. In the *Feinberg* case on which these facts are based, the court concluded that it was just to enforce the promise. Therefore, **Answer (C) is incorrect**.

The only remaining issue is whether the corporation should be required to pay the full amount of the promise or whether "the remedy for breach may be limited as justice requires," that is, limited to the extent of the reliance. The *Feinberg* court did not address this issue, probably because it was working with the text of the First Restatement, which did not include that language. It seems to me this is a case where it would be very difficult to determine how much the reliance cost her — she forbore from continuing her employment at a time when it would be difficult for her to obtain employment, and she may have changed her living arrangements in reliance on the pension. Therefore, it would be just to enforce the promise and **Answer (D) is incorrect**.

68.   **Answer (C) is the best answer.** We know from Topic 5, Statute of Frauds, that an oral

agreement that cannot be performed within a year from the making is within the statute of frauds, and is unenforceable. Therefore, **Answer (A) is incorrect**.

But just as courts sometimes dispense with the requirement of consideration under Restatement § 90 when the promisee has changed his or her position because of the promise, so too do they sometimes dispense with the requirements of the statute of frauds in the interest of justice. Restatement § 139(1) provides:

§ 139 Enforcement by Virtue of Action in Reliance

(1) A promise which the promisor should reasonably expect to induce action or forbearance on the part of the promisee or a third person and which does induce the action or forbearance is enforceable notwithstanding the Statute of Frauds if injustice can be avoided only by enforcement of the promise. The remedy granted for breach may be limited as justice requires.

The elements of this Restatement section will look familiar because it so closely tracks § 90. It seems to me that the elements are satisfied here: The school should have reasonably expected its promise of a two-year job contract to induce action on the part of the teacher. The promise did in fact induce such reliance — she moved to a new city because of the promise. She will suffer an injustice if the promise is not enforced and thus *some amount* of recovery should be available. Therefore, **Answer (D) is incorrect** as the teacher should obtain a recovery in reliance.

The only issue is the measure of her recovery. If there were an enforceable contract, then she would receive $80,000, the amount she would have received over the lifetime of the contract, subject to her duty to mitigate. *See* Topic 12, Remedies. But these facts strongly suggest that it would be just to limit the remedy to the extent of her reliance on the promise — the $5,000 she spent on moving and getting settled. This is the amount that will put her back to where she was before the promise was made, which is generally the goal of reliance damages. Therefore, **Answer (C) is a better answer than Answer (B)**.

69. We looked at this fact situation in Topic 3, Consideration. We saw that the father could not have bargained for the innkeeper's services because they had already been rendered before the promise was made. This situation is sometimes described as "past consideration," but that expression is a bit misleading because past consideration is no consideration at all. Therefore, **Answer (A) is incorrect**.

We might look at reliance here, but we would not get very far. Restatement § 90 requires reliance on a promise, and there was no promise that induced action by the innkeeper. Therefore, **Answer (C) is incorrect**.

We now look at another broad source of obligations, the concept of *restitution*, also known as unjust enrichment, quasi-contract, and implied-in-law contract. The last two names for it are somewhat misleading, however, because they employ the word "contract." But in restitution, recovery is not based on a bargained-for contract. Instead, the law implies an obligation to pay for a benefit received when the benefit was not a gift and was not rendered officiously, that is, without the consent of the person who was benefitted. In other words, the "contract" is a fiction. The concept is found in Restatement (Third) of Restitution and Unjust Enrichment § 1:

1. Restitution and Unjust Enrichment

A person who has been unjustly enriched at the expense of another is subject to liability in restitution.

Another way of thinking of restitution is to see the law as implying a promise to pay for a benefit received when it is just to do so and then enforcing that implied promise. We saw examples of this concept in Topic 4, Formation Defenses, where we saw that parties who are capable of making only voidable or void contracts, such as minors or those who have been declared legally incompetent, are nevertheless required to make restitution for the reasonable value of necessaries that they contract to purchase. Here, the innkeeper did not intend to confer the benefit on the son as a gift, but rather with the expectation of payment. It was reasonable for him to think that the son would have wanted the services to be rendered, so they were not officious. Because the benefit was conferred on the son and not the father, it is the son (or his estate if he is no longer alive) who is liable in restitution. Therefore, **Answer (B) is incorrect** and **Answer (D) is correct**.

70. **Answer (D) is the best answer.** There is no contract between the daughter and her father. The vague statements that he made to her are not enough to constitute bargained-for consideration and may well have been made after the fact. Therefore, **Answer (A) is incorrect**. The father made no promise that induced her to give up her job. Because there was no promise, she does not have a claim in reliance. Therefore, **Answer (C) is incorrect**.

Her best claim is to seek restitution for the value of the benefit she conferred on her father. But a party does not have a claim in restitution when they confer the benefit as a gift. After all, we don't expect to be compensated when we give a gift to someone. There is a presumption in the law that a benefit conferred by a close family member was made as a gift. *See Estate of Orr*, 60 P.3d 962 (Mont. 2002). The vague statements by the father would not be enough to overcome this presumption. It could only be rebutted by proof of an express contract between them. For example, if he had said to her, "I will pay you $10 per hour for every hour you take care of me," and she had then done so, she could claim performance of an express contract. In the absence of such proof, **Answer (B) is incorrect** and **Answer (D) is correct**.

71. **Answer (C) is the best answer.** Restatement (Third) of Restitution and Unjust Enrichment § 21 provides:

§ 21 Protection of Another's Property

(1) A person who takes effective action to protect another's property from threatened harm is entitled to restitution from the other as necessary to prevent unjust enrichment, if the circumstances justify the decision to intervene without request. Unrequested intervention is justified only when it is reasonable to assume the owner would wish the action performed.

(2) Unjust enrichment under this section is measured by the loss avoided or by a reasonable charge for the services provided, whichever is less.

While it appears that Glenn has satisfied these elements, the overriding principle is that a volunteer is presumed to have rendered the services without intending to be compensated for his or her efforts. Comment c states: "Gratuitous services. There is no claim in restitution for services, however valuable, that the provider has rendered without intent to charge." The sticking point here is that there is nothing to suggest that Glenn had money on his mind when he went after Nick's boat. Like a Good Samaritan who stops to aid a fellow motorist in distress, he acted gratuitously.

Therefore, **Answer (A) is incorrect** because a gift is presumed. Contrast these facts with those in Question 69, where the services were provided by an innkeeper. An innkeeper providing food and lodging in the course of his business would probably be presumed to be rendering the services in the expectation of payment. **Answer (B) is incorrect** because what a reasonable person would do is irrelevant in the absence of a legal obligation. The reasonable person standard only applies to negligence causes of action, and negligence causes of action can only be applied where there is a legal duty to act. The fact that most people — or a reasonable person — would do something is not enough to make it a duty.

The remedy for a claim in reliance is measured by the extent of the reliance, usually expenditures incurred. Here there is no claim for reliance since Nick did not make a promise to Glenn. If there were a claim for restitution, the absence of expenditures would not in itself bar the claim. According to Restatement (Third) of Restitution and Unjust Enrichment § 21(2), "Unjust enrichment under this section is measured by the loss avoided or by a reasonable charge for the services provided, whichever is less." According to that standard, a person who is eligible for restitution for providing services may recover the value of the services even if the person had incurred no expense. Because a claim in restitution does not require an out-of-pocket expense, **Answer (D) is incorrect**.

72.   No. Rescuers have it tough in our society. We honor them, but we do not require the person whose life or property is saved to compensate them, even if the rescuer is injured in the process. Restatement (Third) of Restitution and Unjust Enrichment § 20 states a rule regarding recovery by one who saves another's life:

> **§ 20 Protection of Another's Life or Health**
>
> (1) A person who performs, supplies, or obtains professional services required for the protection of another's life or health is entitled to restitution from the other as necessary to prevent unjust enrichment, if the circumstances justify the decision to intervene without request.
>
> (2) Unjust enrichment under this section is measured by a reasonable charge for the services in question.

Comment b underscores the point that this provision applies only to professionals, such as doctors, and not to volunteers who act without the expectation of being compensated:

> b. *Professional services*. Emergency assistance rendered by a nonprofessional, however valuable, does not give rise to a claim in restitution under existing law. The result is that professional providers of medical assistance are routinely given an enforceable claim to compensation; while the nonprofessional rescuer or good Samaritan enjoys only such rewards as others may choose to bestow. *See* Illustration 7. The claim by a rescuer to recover for injuries suffered in the course of the rescue is a particularly compelling one, but such a recovery reflects compensation and insurance principles, not principles of unjust enrichment.

73.   **Answer (C) is the best answer.** As a general rule, look for a bargained-for contract before turning to claims based on reliance or restitution. In order to prevail on a claim that Nick

breached his contract with Glenn, Glenn must establish offer ("If you fetch my boat and bring it back to me, I'll pay you $100."), acceptance (Glenn giving the requested performance — retrieval of the boat), and consideration (Nick sought Glenn's performance in exchange for his promise and Glenn performed in exchange for Nick's promise to pay him). Therefore, Glenn has a viable breach of contract claim against Nick.

To recover in reliance, a party must establish that the court can prevent injustice only by enforcing the promise. In determining whether only enforcement of the promise can prevent injustice, see the circumstances set forth in Restatement § 139(2) in Question 63 above. Subsection (a) points courts to the unavailability of any other remedy. Since Glenn can recover for breach of contract, the court need not consider his reliance claim. Therefore, **Answer (A) is incorrect** because a person does not have a reliance claim when he has a contract claim based on the same promise. But if the court were to find no contract, Glenn appears to have a valid reliance claim.

Similarly, Glenn doesn't have a restitution claim because, while he conferred a benefit on Nick, he conferred it in response to the offer that Nick made. While a rescuer frequently acts as a volunteer, here Glenn committed the act in order to accept the offer by performance. Therefore, **Answer (B) and Answer (D) are incorrect**.

74. **Answer (D) is the best answer.** The law has struggled to come up with a theory to support a claim based on a promise made *after* the promisor has received the benefit. In contract, this is a case of "past consideration," which means that there is no consideration since the performance was not bargained for. Therefore, because no bargained-for contract was formed between Glenn and Nick, **Answer (A) is incorrect**. Similarly, a claim under reliance must fail because Glenn could not have relied on Nick's promise at the time he recovered the boat, making **Answer (B) incorrect**.

As more fully explored in the answers to Questions 71 and 72, but for the promise, Glenn would be denied recovery under the rule of Restatement (Third) of Restitution and Unjust Enrichment §§ 20 and 21 because he did not act with the intent to be paid. Nor is this the type of case in which courts have implied a quasi-contract in order to keep Nick from being unjustly enriched. He was not, in fact, enriched. Therefore, **Answer (C) is incorrect**.

If there is no claim in restitution without the promise, what difference does it make that there was a promise after the fact? The promise seems to perform two functions: 1) the promise makes it look less like the benefit was conferred as a gift, because a person doesn't promise to pay for gifts, and 2) it puts a value on a benefit that would otherwise be difficult or impossible to value. This view has been supported by some court cases.

In *Glenn v. Savage*, 13 P. 442 (Or. 1887), from which the facts of these hypotheticals have been taken, the court held that in order for Glenn to recover for rescuing Nick's property, Nick must have either asked for Glenn's assistance or, after learning of Glenn's actions, promised to pay Glenn after the fact. You may be familiar with the case of *Webb v. McGowin*, 168 So. 196 (Ala. Ct. App. 1935), in which the rescuer was injured in the process of saving the life of another person, and sought to enforce a promise made after the fact by that person. The rescuer did recover, and the case became the basis for Restatement § 86:

§ 86 Promise for Benefit Received

(1) A promise made in recognition of a benefit previously received by the promisor from the promisee is binding to the extent necessary to prevent injustice.

(2) A promise is not binding under Subsection (1)

(a) if the promisee conferred the benefit as a gift or for other reasons the promisor has not been unjustly enriched; or

(b) to the extent that its value is disproportionate to the benefit.

This notion of "promissory restitution" provides that a promise, made in recognition of a benefit already received, is binding to the extent necessary to prevent injustice, if (1) the promisee did not render the benefit as a gift, (2) not enforcing the promise would unjustly enrich the promisor, and (3) the promise is not disproportionate to the benefit the promisor received. Note that there are likely to be few occasions in which this rule will be invoked.

75. **Answer (C) is the correct answer.** At one time, the buyer had a legal obligation to pay $1,200, subject to any claims and defenses by the buyer. This obligation became unenforceable because of the statute of limitations, which is four years for the sale of goods. *See* § 2-725. For historical reasons that are too complicated to go into, the law has determined that a subsequent promise, made after the statute of limitations has run, revives the obligation, but only to the extent of the promise. The cases distinguish this from the unenforceable "moral obligation" cases on the basis that there was at one time a legal obligation and it is revived by the promise. Therefore, **Answers (A), (B), and (D) are incorrect**.

Authority for this rule can be found in Restatement § 82(1):

§ 82. Promise to Pay Indebtedness; Effect on the Statute of Limitations

(1) A promise to pay all or part of an antecedent contractual or quasi-contractual indebtedness owed by the promisor is binding if the indebtedness is still enforceable or would be except for the effect of a statute of limitations.

In most jurisdictions, the statute of frauds requires that the promisor make the new promise to pay the indebtedness in writing. Restatement § 110(4) provides:

§ 110. Classes of Contracts Covered

(4) Statutes in most states provide that no acknowledgment or promise is sufficient evidence of a new or continuing contract to take a case out of the operation of a statute of limitations unless made in some writing signed by the party to be charged, but that the statute does not alter the effect of any payment of principal or interest.

At one time a similar rule applied to obligations discharged in bankruptcy, but the Bankruptcy Code has changed that rule, so a subsequent promise does not revive a debt discharged in bankruptcy.

76.   **Answer (C) is the best answer**. This question introduces us to the Parol Evidence Rule. If we look at the way an agreement emerges from the process of negotiation, the parties usually discuss terms or exchange drafts, and then arrive at a point at which they say negotiations are over and it is time to finalize their agreement. They usually do this by signing a writing, or, to encompass electronic transactions, we might more broadly say by authenticating a record. Once the agreement is final, the negotiations are no longer part of it, so **Answer (D) is incorrect**. In the language of Restatement § 209, a final agreement is an "integrated agreement."

However, the fact that the parties have signed a writing does not necessarily mean that the writing is the *exclusive* source of the parties' understandings. Restatement § 210 refers to a *partially integrated* agreement as one that has both oral and written components, while a *completely integrated* agreement is one that has only a written component.

The key to distinguishing between a partially integrated agreement and a completely integrated agreement is the intent of the parties. Therefore, **Answer (A) and Answer (B) are incorrect** because they are incomplete.

77.   **Answer (A) is the best answer**. Recall that if an agreement is partially integrated, it represents the *final* agreement of the parties, but not necessarily their *complete* agreement. In the facts of Answer (A), the parties apparently discussed and agreed to a number of terms, but did not set them all out in the writing. For example, they might have agreed to such terms as the delivery date and the payment arrangement in the oral part of their agreement rather than in the written part.

Answer (B) is incorrect because the fact that the parties used a form to set down their terms comprehensively is a good — but not determinative — indication that they intended the writing to be a complete integration.

Answer (C) is incorrect because the fact that the parties included a *merger clause* (also called an *integration clause*) in their agreement is a good indication that they intended the writing to be a complete integration. In a commercial contract, the presence of that clause is likely determinative. But if the clause is buried in a contract of adhesion with a consumer who never knew it was there, some courts may say that it is not a good indication of the parties' intent. *See* Restatement § 216 cmt. e.

Answer (D) is incorrect because even if it does not contain a merger clause, a written agreement negotiated between two commercial parties that appears to cover all topics thoroughly is likely to be a complete integration.

78.   **Answer (D) is the best answer**. This is a classic parol evidence rule situation. The buyer wants to introduce evidence of oral promises that it claims are part of the agreement. The seller claims that evidence of the oral promises should be excluded. Note that the issue is not

one of fact — even if the seller in fact made the promises, the parol evidence rule can exclude them from evidence as a matter of law.

These facts involve the sale of goods, so the parol evidence rule from the UCC applies. It is found in § 2-202:

§ 2-202. Final Written Expression: Parol or Extrinsic Evidence.

Terms with respect to which the confirmatory memoranda of the parties agree or which are otherwise set forth in a writing intended by the parties as a final expression of their agreement with respect to such terms as are included therein may not be contradicted by evidence of any prior agreement or of a contemporaneous oral agreement but may be explained or supplemented

(a) by course of dealing or usage of trade (Section 1-205) or by course of performance (Section 2-208); and

(b) by evidence of consistent additional terms unless the court finds the writing to have been intended also as a complete and exclusive statement of the terms of the agreement.

Is this a writing that is intended by the parties "as a final expression of their agreement with respect to such terms as are included therein"? Because it is a signed agreement between two commercial parties, most courts will say that it is. Therefore, according to this statute, it "may not be contradicted by evidence of any prior agreement." Here, because the evidence of the salesman's representations contradicts the terms of the writing, the evidence will be excluded.

The terms would be express warranties if they were part of the contract, but the parol evidence rule excludes them, so **Answer (A) is incorrect**. The statute goes on to say that the writing may be supplemented by evidence of consistent additional terms. To resolve this problem, it is not necessary to reach this provision, since the terms contradict. The theory is that even if the writing is not a complete integration, it is nevertheless a partial integration, with the result that the written terms govern over contradictory oral terms, so **Answer (C) is incorrect**. The buyer might claim that the false statements amounted to fraud, a topic we will explore shortly. But the remedy for fraud is that the agreement is voided. Since the call of the question asked whether the buyer had a claim for breach of warranty rather than avoidance of the contract, **Answer (B) is incorrect**.

79. **Answer (C) is the best answer.** Like Question 78, this question provides another example in which the buyer wants to introduce extrinsic evidence to prove that oral promises were intended to be part of the agreement. Here, however, the oral terms do not *contradict* the terms of the written agreement as they did in the last question because the written agreement mentions nothing about the number of copies per minute or collating. Therefore, **Answer (D) is incorrect**.

The terms would be express warranties if they were part of the contract, but the parol evidence rule excludes them, so **Answer (A) is incorrect**. The statute goes on to say that the writing may be "supplemented . . . by evidence of consistent additional terms unless the court finds the writing to have been intended also as a complete and exclusive statement of the terms of the agreement." Here, the buyer is attempting to introduce terms that supplement the writing. They will be admissible if the writing is not the complete and exclusive statement of the terms of the agreement, but they will not be admissible if the writing is the complete and exclusive statement of the terms of the agreement. Because of the merger clause, we would conclude that the parties intended the writing to contain all the terms of the agreement, and therefore **Answer (C) is correct**.

The buyer might claim that the false statements amounted to fraud, a topic we will explore shortly. But the remedy for fraud is that the agreement is voided. Since the call of the question asked whether the buyer had a claim for breach of warranty rather than avoidance of the contract, **Answer (B) is incorrect**.

80.   **Answer (C) is the best answer.** The parol evidence rule applies when a party claims that there are additional terms that are not found in the writing. In that case, a court must determine whether the agreement is a complete integration or not. In this case, however, the party is not offering extrinsic evidence to prove that a term is part of the contract, but is offering the evidence to prove that no contract was formed. (*See* Topic 4, Formation Defenses.) If there is no contract, then it doesn't matter what the agreement says. So this evidence comes in as an exception to the parol evidence rule. Therefore, **Answer (A), Answer (B), and Answer (C) are incorrect** because when the extrinsic evidence is being offered to prove that there is a defense to contract formation, it is irrelevant whether the agreement is integrated or not.

81.   Yes. The parol evidence rule applies when a party is trying to prove that an oral term is part of the agreement after it has been reduced to writing. This fact situation exemplifies another exception, for the buyer is not trying to prove that the refrigerator is part of the *house sale* agreement. He is trying to prove that there are *two* agreements — a written agreement for the sale of a house, and an oral agreement for the sale of the refrigerator.

82.   Yes, in most jurisdictions but not in all. As indicated in the previous question, formation defenses are generally an exception to the parol evidence rule; that is, evidence of a formation defense will not be excluded by the parol evidence *even if* the writing is a complete and exclusive statement of the parties' agreement. But fraud may be an exception to the exception – some jurisdictions will allow evidence of other formations defenses, but will exclude evidence of fraud. The reasons become clear when we look at the elements of fraud. One of the elements is that the accused party knowingly made a false statement of fact. That element is probably satisfied under these facts.

But another element is that the accusing party's reliance on the statement was reasonable. Some courts hold that if the writing addressed the subject matter of the fraud with particularity, then it was not reasonable for a party to have relied on the oral statement. Here, the merger clause states that "no representations about the specifications of the copier have been made." In light of such a statement in the writing, it may not have been reasonable for the buyer to rely on the oral representation. Other courts, however, hold that because of the fraud, the party lacked the ability to assent to the agreement, so it doesn't matter what the writing says. In 2013, the California Supreme Court reversed its prior holdings and held that the parol evidence rule does not bar evidence of fraudulent promises that are at variance with the terms of the writing. *See Riverisland Cold Storage, Inc. v. Fresno-Madera Production Credit Ass'n*, 291 P.3d 316 (Cal. 2013).

83.   **Answer (D) is the best answer.** Restatement § 217 contains another exception to the parol evidence rule. The transaction involves the sale of goods, so the Article 2 parol evidence rule

would apply, but this exception would likely supplement the Code under § 1-103(b). That Restatement section provides:

§ 217. Integrated Agreement Subject to Oral Requirement of a Condition

Where the parties to a written agreement agree orally that performance of the agreement is subject to the occurrence of a stated condition, the agreement is not integrated with respect to the oral condition.

This exception applies even if the writing is a complete integration, so **Answer (A) is incorrect**. It is not a formation defense, because the manufacturer is not claiming that there is no agreement, but only that performance of the agreement is subject to a condition. Therefore, **Answer (C) is incorrect**.

If an oral understanding contradicts the terms of the writing, then the writing will govern. A good test for whether the terms contradict is to imagine they were both in the agreement and then determine whether they can live together there in reasonable harmony. For example, if the manufacturer had tried to get in evidence that the parties had an oral understanding that delivery would be on June 10, then the agreement would say:

The delivery date is June 1. The delivery date is June 10.

Those terms cannot live together, so the oral understanding would not be admissible. But under our facts, the manufacturer claims the agreement says something like this:

The delivery date is June 1. Delivery will be accepted only if the new storage unit is completed.

Those terms can live in harmony, so the oral understanding does not contradict the writing, and **Answer (B) is incorrect**.

84.   **Answer (D) is the best answer.** The writing is a final and complete agreement between the parties. But § 2-202(a) provides that even if the writing is final and complete, evidence of course of performance, course of dealing, or usage of trade can supplement it. Therefore, **Answer (A) is incorrect**.

But does the evidence supplement the agreement or does it contradict it? This is a close question, as discussed in the famous case of *Columbia Nitrogen Corp. v. Royster Co.*, 451 F.2d 3 (4th Cir. 1971). In the hierarchy of interpretation, express terms govern over trade usage. *See* § 1-303. Therefore, **Answer (C) is incorrect**. Accordingly, it could be argued that the express price term of $100,000 governs over the seller's claimed price of $103,000. But as discussed in the previous question, this issue is not so easily resolved. The seller is not claiming that the parties agreed on a price of $103,000, which would contradict the $100,000 price in the writing. The seller is claiming that when the trade usage is supplied, the price term in the contract looks something like this:

The price is $100,000. This price is an estimate, and if the price of a raw material goes up, a seller may pass along that increase to the buyer.

When stated that way, the trade usage appears to supplement rather than contradict the writing. Therefore, **Answer (B) is incorrect**.

85.   **Answer (B) is the best answer.** U.C.C. § 1-303 defines *course of performance, course of dealing,* and *trade usage,* and establishes a hierarchy when they conflict. At the top of the hierarchy is the express terms of the agreement, followed by course of performance, course

of dealing, and trade usage. It makes sense that if the parties agree on an express term, then it is their intention to displace these other ways of interpreting their expressions and conduct. The express term used in this agreement, "regularly," is a vague term that has no intrinsic meaning. Therefore, the other concepts will be examined to see if they give meaning to the term, so **Answer (A) is incorrect**.

Section 1-303(a) defines "course of performance" as follows:

> (a) A "course of performance" is a sequence of conduct between the parties to a particular transaction that exists if:

>> (1) the agreement of the parties with respect to the transaction involves repeated occasions for performance by a party; and

>> (2) the other party, with knowledge of the nature of the performance and opportunity for objection to it, accepts the performance or acquiesces in it without objection.

Under the facts, the parties' course of performance established that "regularly" meant every week under the contract for the first machine. However, there is no course of performance under the contract for the third machine, so **Answer (C) is incorrect**.

Section 1-303(b) defines "course of dealing" as follows:

> (b) A "course of dealing" is a sequence of conduct concerning previous transactions between the parties to a particular transaction that is fairly to be regarded as establishing a common basis of understanding for interpreting their expressions and other conduct.

When the parties entered into the third contract, it is reasonable to assume that their conduct under the previous transactions established a course of dealing that carried over into the interpretation of that contract. Therefore, when they entered the third contract, the term "regularly" is interpreted as servicing every week.

Section 1-303(c) defines "usage of trade" as follows:

> (c) A "usage of trade" is any practice or method of dealing having such regularity of observance in a place, vocation, or trade as to justify an expectation that it will be observed with respect to the transaction in question. The existence and scope of such a usage are to be proved as facts. If it is established that such a usage is embodied in a trade code or similar record, the interpretation of the record is a question of law.

Under this agreement, there is an applicable usage of trade, which is monthly servicing. If there were no established course of dealing, the usage of trade would apply. But when there is both a course of dealing and a usage of trade, § 1-303(e) provides that course of dealing prevails over usage of trade. Therefore, **Answer (D) is incorrect**.

86. **Answer (D) is the best answer.** The insurance company's obligation is ambiguous – does it mean an obligation to pay all the damages incurred, or just the damages for the bodily injury? When an issue of interpretation arises, courts often look to the ancient "maxims of interpretation," four of which are enumerated here, to help resolve the issue.

Expressio unius est exclusio alterius is helpful when there is a list of enumerated items; the maxim captures the common sense meaning that anything not on the list was excluded on purpose. So if a restriction is placed on an "automobile, truck, or motorcycle," the interpretation is that it does not include a snowmobile, since snowmobile was not listed. This maxim is not applicable here, so **Answer (A) is incorrect.**

Ejusdem generis is helpful when there is a non-exclusive list in order to determine whether something else should be included. So if a restriction is placed on "a vehicle, including but not limited to an automobile, truck, or motorcycle," a snowmobile may well be included because it is also a motorized land vehicle, but a boat might be excluded because it is not a vehicle of that kind. This maxim is not applicable here, so **Answer (B) is incorrect.**

Noscitur a sociis is helpful when looking at the context in which the words are used. For example, where a contract requires that "floors, steps, stairs, passageways and gangways" are to be kept free from obstruction, a floor used exclusively for storage would not be included because all the other words are used to indicate passage. This maxim is not applicable here, so **Answer (C) is incorrect.**

The rule of *contra proferentem* is best used as a tie-breaker when all other attempts at ascertaining the meaning fail. It holds the drafter to be at fault for creating the ambiguity and therefore resolves it in a manner unfavorable to that party. Courts find this rule particularly useful when the issue arises in a contract of adhesion between a little guy and a big guy, like the insurance company in this example. *See Fitzgerald v. Western Fire Insurance Co.*, 679 P.2d 790 (Mont. 1984), from which this example is taken.

87. **Answer (D) is the best answer.** Note that this question does not invoke the parol evidence rule, because it has already been determined whether the agreement is found in the writing alone or in the writing plus oral understandings. Now the issue is the meaning of the language used by the parties in their agreement. Nevertheless, the inquiry is similar because there is a conflict about how much extrinsic evidence (often called parol evidence, just to confuse us) should be admitted to help resolve these issues.

It is difficult to state a general rule for what evidence will be admissible on an issue of interpretation, because different jurisdictions have different views, and those views are more like points along a spectrum than opposing views. At one end of the spectrum is the "four corners" approach that would look only at the document itself to determine whether the language is ambiguous. This approach is less restrictive than it sounds, because of course the judge is going to look at the document in its legal context, and will apply tools such as the maxims of interpretation discussed in the previous question to try to make sense of the language. Therefore, **Answer (A) is correct, but (D) is a better answer.**

The "four corners" approach was rejected by the famous case of *Pacific Gas & Electric Co. v. G.W. Thomas Dryage & Rigging Co.*, 442 P.2d 641 (Cal. 1968), in which Judge Traynor treated with scorn the idea that a judge can discern meaning merely from the face of the agreement. Therefore, **Answer (B) is correct, but (D) is a better answer.**

Once the court allows in extrinsic evidence to prove the meaning of the written agreement, the question then becomes whether there is any limit to that evidence. Courts have come down at many points on the spectrum of admissible evidence. The "context rule" expressed in *Berg v. Hudesman*, 801 P.2d 222 (Wash. 1990), is of the view that a very wide range of evidence should be allowed. The view that only objective evidence from disinterested third parties should be allowed is found in Judge Posner's opinion in *AM International, Inc. v. Graphic Management Associates, Inc.*, 44 F.3d 572 (7th Cir. 1995). Therefore, **Answer (C) is correct, but (D) is a better answer.**

88.   **Answer (D) is the best answer.** Contract interpretation is a two-step process. First, the court must determine whether the language is ambiguous, and then, if it finds that it is ambiguous, the court must determine the meaning. The first step is discussed in Question 87. With this question, we reach the second step, so the court has to go beyond the writing itself, but, again, jurisdictions will differ on how wide they will cast the net.

Testimony by the lawyer who drafted the contract is evidence that most courts will not admit. What a person had in mind is subjective, and there is a great risk that it could be conveniently generated after the fact. Moreover, most courts see the goal of contract interpretation as discovering the meaning the *parties* intended, not what the lawyers or even a reasonable party intended.

Most courts will look at the relevant circumstances surrounding the transaction, which would likely include prior drafts of the document. This approach is sometimes called the "plain meaning" approach to interpretation. Therefore, **Answer (A) is incorrect**. Many courts will also look at objective evidence, such as the testimony of a person in the trade or business as to the meaning of the language in that trade. Therefore, **Answer (C) is incorrect**. Technically, the conduct of the parties is not objective evidence because it is evidence of how the parties themselves interpreted the contract, rather than how a reasonable person would have interpreted it. Nevertheless, the conduct objectifies the meaning, so many courts will look at it as providing a good indication of how the parties intended the contract to be interpreted. Therefore, **Answer (B) is incorrect**.

89.   **Answer (D) is the best answer.** This question describes the situation called "misunderstanding." *See* Restatement § 20. The classic misunderstanding case is *Raffles v. Wichelhaus*, 159 Eng. Rep. 375 (Ex. 1864), where the contract called for the goods to arrive on the good ship *Peerless*, but it turned out there were two ships named *Peerless*. The buyer was thinking of the one scheduled to arrive in October, while the seller was thinking of the one scheduled to arrive in December. The court held that there was no contract because each party had a different meaning in mind.

The problem is not just that each party has something different in mind — that would not matter most of the time, because the law is not concerned with their subjective thoughts. It only matters when the language they objectively manifested (like "Peerless" in the *Raffles* case) has two meanings, and they each ascribe a different meaning to the language. Proving that each party ascribed a different meaning to the language is necessary to establish misunderstanding, but it is not sufficient. It is also necessary to prove that each party did not know the meaning of the other, and that each party had no reason to know the meaning of the other.

One party can prove that the other party had reason to know its meaning by proving that that meaning is more reasonable; in other words, the party can prove imputed knowledge rather than actual knowledge. The rules of interpretation are applied to determine whether one of those meanings is more reasonable than the other. That is what Judge Friendly did in *Frigaliment Importing Co. v. B.N.S. International Sales Corp.*, 190 F. Supp. 116 (S.D.N.Y. 1960), where the ambiguous word was "chicken." He found for the defendant because the plaintiff had not sustained the burden of proving that its meaning was more reasonable, but he later realized he might have better decided the case as a matter of misunderstanding. Therefore, **Answer (B) is incorrect**. If each meaning is equally reasonable, a court could break the tie by applying the maxim of *contra proferentem*, but that concept is better reserved for cases where the drafter could have done a better job. In a true misunderstanding case, the drafter could not have done better because the drafter did not know there was a problem. Therefore, **Answer (A) is incorrect.**

It is hard for the instructor in a Contracts course to figure out where to put the concept of misunderstanding. It is sometimes lumped with the topic of mistake, but it rests uncomfortably there. According to Restatement § 151, a mistake is "a belief that is not in accord with the facts," but in a misunderstanding, there may well be no mistake; for example, there really was an October *Peerless* and a December *Peerless*. Furthermore, mutual mistake makes a contract voidable rather than void, so **Answer (C) is incorrect.** On the other hand, the topic of mutual assent is usually confined to offer and acceptance, and other assent issues don't fit in. I think the topic makes the most sense as an interpretation issue, for misunderstanding only occurs when all attempts at resolving the ambiguous language fail.

90.   **Answer (B) is the best answer.** The facts of this hypothetical are loosely drawn from *Konic International Corp. v. Spokane Computer Services, Inc.*, 708 P.2d 932 (Idaho Ct. App. 1985). Although it initially appears to be unreadable, Restatement § 20 does a good job of laying out the permutations that can arise in a case of misunderstanding:

> **§ 20 Effect of Misunderstanding**
>
> (1) There is no manifestation of mutual assent to an exchange if the parties attach materially different meanings to their manifestations and
>
> > (a) neither party knows or has reason to know the meaning attached by the other; or
> >
> > (b) each party knows or each party has reason to know the meaning attached by the other.
>
> (2) The manifestations of the parties are operative in accordance with the meaning attached to them by one of the parties if
>
> > (a) that party does not know of any different meaning attached by the other, and the other knows the meaning attached by the first party; or
> >
> > (b) that party has no reason to know of any different meaning attached by the other, and the other has reason to know the meaning attached by the first party.

The first step in our analysis is to determine if each party attached a different meaning to the manifestation. The answer is yes — the language "thirty-two-fifty" is ambiguous and the seller thought it meant $3,250 while the buyer thought it meant $32.50. Section (1) describes two situations — one where *neither party* knows or has reason to know of the other's meaning, and one where *both parties* know or have reason to know of the other's meaning. It makes sense for a court to say there is no contract in these situations, because in both cases, it is impossible to say which meaning prevails. Unable to declare the meaning of a material term of the contract, the court would have to conclude that there was no contract.

However, our facts say that the buyer "knew that this model should be worth around $3,000." Subsection (2)(a) makes one party's meaning operative when "that party has no reason to know of any different meaning attached by the other, and the other has reason to know the meaning attached by the first party." Here, the seller did not have reason to know the $32.50

meaning attached by the buyer, and the buyer had reason to know the $3,250 meaning attached by the seller. Therefore, **Answer (D) is incorrect** because a court would find under these facts that there is not a misunderstanding but a contract on seller's terms.

Answer (A) is incorrect because the maxim of *contra proferentem* should be applied to resolve an ambiguity only as a last resort. *See* RESTATEMENT § 206. Here, the issue is better resolved by applying a reasonable meaning over an unreasonable meaning, especially when one of the parties had reason to know that its meaning was unreasonable.

Answer (C) is incorrect because this is not a case where the parties entered into a contract for the sale of goods without settling on a price. If that were the case, U.C.C. § 2-305 would supply a reasonable price. Under these facts, the parties did settle on a price — they just stated it ambiguously.

91.   **Answer (C) is the best answer.** A party that grants an exclusive right, the exercise of which will benefit another, impliedly promises to use "reasonable efforts" on the other's behalf. *Wood v. Lucy, Lady Duff-Gordon*, 118 N.E. 214 (N.Y. 1917); *see also* RESTATEMENT § 77 cmt. d and illus. 9. Here, the broker agreed to be the owner's exclusive broker. This created an implied obligation on the part of the broker to do *something*. Therefore, **Answer (D) is incorrect.**

As Justice Cardozo famously said in *Wood*, the contract was "instinct with an obligation, imperfectly expressed." As in that case, the court would likely supply the term the parties failed to express. What is a fair obligation to place on the broker? To require the broker to find a buyer goes beyond the reasonable expectation of the owner. If that were the obligation, then the broker would be in breach if she did not find a buyer. Therefore, **Answer (A) is incorrect.** A court would also be unlikely to try to particularize exactly what the broker had to do, for the goal of finding a buyer could be achieved in a number of ways. Therefore, **Answer (B) is incorrect.** Instead, the court would employ the vague standard that the broker had to make "reasonable efforts," and in order to prove breach, the owner would have to prove that the broker's efforts fell short of that standard.

Article 2 places a similar obligation on one who contracts for exclusive dealings in goods. Section 2-306(2) provides:

> A lawful agreement by either the seller or the buyer for exclusive dealing in the kind of goods concerned imposes, unless otherwise agreed, an obligation by the seller to use best efforts to supply the goods and by the buyer to use best efforts to promote their sale.

92.   **Answer (A) is the best answer.** In a case in which a student challenged the LSAT contract provisions as unconscionable, the court found that the contract was indeed a contract of adhesion. But you will recall from Topic 4, Formation Defenses, that procedural unconscionability alone is not usually enough to establish unconscionability. The plaintiff must also prove substantive unconscionability — that the defendant used its bargaining power to impose unfair terms on the plaintiff. In *K.D. v. Educational Testing Service*, 87 Misc. 2d 657 (N.Y. Sup. Ct. 1976), the court concluded that the contract terms were reasonable in the light of the organization's need to protect the integrity of its exam. Therefore, **Answer (D) is incorrect.**

Answer (B) is incorrect because the organization did seem to follow its own rules and regulations; it just did not properly exercise its discretion when following them. What would have been the proper standard to measure its exercise of discretion? **Answer (C) is incorrect** because reasonable efforts is generally reserved for occasions when a court needs to supply a standard of measurement that the parties have omitted, as in the previous question. Here, we are measuring the exercise of discretion. For that purpose, a court would likely look to the standard of good faith.

Restatement § 205 imposes on each party to a contract "a duty of good faith and fair dealing in its performance and enforcement." Similarly, U.C.C. § 1-304 provides that "[e]very contract or duty within [the Uniform Commercial Code] imposes an obligation of good faith in its performance and enforcement." The facts of this question are drawn from *Dalton v. Educational Testing Service*, 663 N.E.2d 289 (N.Y. 1995), in which the court found that "[e]ncompassed within the implied obligation of each promisor to exercise good faith are 'any promises which a reasonable person in the position of the promisee would be justified in understanding were included.'" This included an obligation to *actually consider* any relevant material that the student supplied to the organization. By not considering that material, ETS breached its obligation of good faith and fair dealing.

93.   **Answer (C) is the correct answer**, although Answer (D) is the rule in a number of jurisdictions. Recall that Article 1 governs the other Articles of the UCC, including Article 2, which governs the sale of goods. Former Article 1 defined "good faith" as only "honesty in fact," but when that provision governed, § 2-103(1)(b) provided:

> "Good faith," in the case of a merchant, means honesty in fact and the observance of reasonable commercial standards of fair dealing in the trade.

So when former Article 1 governs the transaction, the answer depends on whether the seller was a merchant or not. However, Revised Article 1 changed the general definition of *good faith* in § 1-201(b)(20) to the definition that was formerly found in § 2-103(1)(b). It now encompasses both "honesty in fact" *and* "the observance of reasonable commercial standards." Therefore, because the Article 2 definition is redundant in a state that enacts Revised Article 1, that section is repealed when Revised Article 1 is enacted. In this book, we are assuming that Revised Article 1 is the governing law, so **Answers (A), (B), and (D) are incorrect**.

As a practical matter, when you are working with the law of a particular jurisdiction, you will have to find out whether Revised Article 1 has been enacted in your jurisdiction. Just to complicate matters, a number of jurisdictions that enacted Revised Article 1 nevertheless retained the old definition of "good faith," so in any jurisdiction you will have to look carefully at the enacted definitions in order to determine the applicable standard for good faith.

You may wonder why the distinction between the two definitions is such a big deal. "Honesty in fact" is generally subjective, inquiring into the party's motives, while "the observance of reasonable commercial standards," is objective, inquiring into custom and usage. It is usually easier for the plaintiff to prove violation of the objective standard. The issue comes up often with the conduct of banks. The case of *Reid v. Key Bank of Southern Maine, Inc.*, 821 F.2d 9 (1st Cir. 1987) is instructive. The bank pulled Reid's line of credit and demanded repayment of his outstanding loans, which it had a right to do if it acted in good faith. The bank wanted the "honesty in fact" definition to govern, because then Reid would have the difficult burden of proving that the bank did not act honestly when it pulled his loan; that is, it had some motive other than protecting its financial interests. Reid wanted the "observance of reasonable commercial standards" definition to govern, because then he could prove that a reasonable banker would not have had to pull the loan in order to protect its financial interests — something easier to prove than proving that the bank acted dishonestly.

94. It doesn't. A claim for breach of the covenant of good faith and fair dealing does not stand alone. The plaintiff has to prove that the defendant did not perform some obligation in good faith. If the plaintiff is successful, then it just has a claim for breach of contract for the defendant's breach of that obligation. There are no enhanced remedies such as punitive damages or attorney's fees.

Incidentally, in the case of *Dalton v. ETS*, discussed in Question 92, the court decided the appropriate remedy was specific performance. Since ETS had breached its obligation to examine the material that Dalton supplied in good faith, it ordered the organization to look at the material again in good faith. It did, and you can imagine the result.

95. **Answer (C) is the correct answer**, and **Answers (A), (B), and (D) are incorrect**. The warranty of good title (U.C.C. § 2-312), the implied warranty of merchantability (U.C.C. § 2-314), and the implied warranty of fitness for a particular purpose (U.C.C. § 2-315) all relate to goods sold subject to Article 2. The implied warranty of habitability relates to contracts for the sale of real estate or improvements to real estate, not goods. Article 2 governs the sales of goods, not real estate.

96. **Answer (B) is the best answer.** "Satisfaction" contracts require one party to perform to the satisfaction of the other. Satisfaction contracts come in two basic varieties: 1) those in which function dominates, and 2) those in which personal taste or aesthetics dominate. In the former, satisfaction is judged objectively, by asking whether a reasonable person in the position of the party whose satisfaction the contract required would be satisfied with the other party's performance. *See, e.g., Morin Building Products Co. v. Baystone Construction, Inc.*, 717 F.2d 413 (7th Cir. 1983). In the latter, satisfaction is judged subjectively, by asking whether the party whose satisfaction the contract required was, in fact, honestly satisfied with the other party's performance. *See, e.g., David Tunick, Inc. v. Kornfeld*, 838 F. Supp. 848 (S.D.N.Y. 1993).

Though subjective, satisfaction in the latter case is subject to the duty of good faith and fair dealing. Therefore, the party whose satisfaction is called for in the contract must be *honestly* dissatisfied with the other party's performance in order to avoid her performance obligations. *See* RESTATEMENT § 205. The facts of this question are far more like those of *Morin Building Products* (satisfactory exterior finishing of warehouse) than *Kornfeld* (forged Picasso). Absent some idiosyncrasy in the transaction that would cause a court to consider the aesthetic value of industrial painting to be more important in this transaction than its functional value, the court should apply the objective satisfaction test here, rather than the subjective test. Therefore, **Answer (A) is not the best answer**.

Neither Answer (C) nor Answer (D) is the best answer. Answer (D) could be true, yet that would not affect the outcome of this case since the satisfaction is not measured by good faith. Similarly Answer (C) could also be true, but it is only relevant to the extent that the "industry standard" would satisfy a reasonable person in the manufacturer's position.

97. **Answer (A) is the best answer.** According to U.C.C. § 2-314(1), "a warranty that the goods shall be merchantable is implied in a contract for their sale if the seller is a merchant with respect to goods of that kind." Here, the seller was a seller of paint, and the paint would not likely "pass without objection in the trade," nor would it be "fit for the ordinary purposes for which such goods are used," in the language that describes what it means for goods to be merchantable in U.C.C. § 2-314(2)(a) and (c). As such, the seller would have violated the

implied warranty of merchantability found in U.C.C. § 2-314(1).

The implied warranty of fitness for a particular purpose would not apply in this case because there are no facts to indicate that the seller knew any particular purpose for which the painter would use the paint and that the painter relied on the seller's skill or judgment to select the paint. *See* U.C.C. § 2-315. Therefore, **Answer (B) is incorrect**.

Section 2-314 states that the *seller* is liable for breach of the implied warranty of merchantability. The statute imposes strict liability on the seller, and it does not matter that, as here, the seller was innocent. Therefore, **Answer (C) is incorrect**. Note that even though the seller (the paint store) is liable to the buyer (the painter), the seller of the paint can go after *its* seller (the distributor or manufacturer), which likewise gave an implied warranty of merchantability when it sold the paint. The claim will thereby work its way up the chain until it reaches the responsible party.

Because Answer (A) is correct, **Answer (D) is incorrect**.

98.   Technically no. Article 2 applies to "transactions in goods." Section § 2-102. The definition of "goods" in § 2-105(1) is "all things . . . which are movable at the time of identification to the contract." Software is an intangible, in spite of some early cases that said it was a good because it came on a disk that was movable. *See, e.g., Advent Systems Ltd. v. Unisys Corp.*, 925 F.2d 670 (3d Cir. 1991). Nevertheless, in the absence of a body of law governing software (The Uniform Computer Information Transactions Act was adopted in two states, Maryland and Virginia, but has been withdrawn from consideration by the Uniform Law Commission), many courts have applied Article 2 to software transactions by analogy. *See, e.g., ProCD v. Zeidenberg*, 105 F.3d 1147 (7th Cir. 1997). This makes sense, especially since most software companies, like the company in this question, have modeled the language of their warranties after the UCC model. A sophisticated analysis of the law applicable to computer software can be found in the Principles of the Law of Software Contracts, promulgated by the American Law Institute. Unlike the Restatements, which describe the law as decided by the courts, the Principles prescribes what the law ought to be in these transactions.

99.   **Answer (B) is the best answer.** We are assuming that Article 2 applies to this transaction by analogy. Unless explicitly waived, disclaimed, or otherwise limited, every contract for the sale of goods by a merchant who deals in goods of the kind includes an implied warranty that the goods, *inter alia*, are fit for the ordinary purpose for which such goods are used. U.C.C. § 2-314(2)(b). Because the business purchased the software from a software manufacturer, the fact pattern deals with a merchant who deals in goods of the kind. The facts tell us that there was a glitch in the software. While not every glitch would be a breach of the warranty, the facts tell us that the glitch makes the software unusable. [Parenthetically, Principles of the Law of Software Contracts § 3.03 suggests that one cannot expect something as complicated as graphics software to be glitch-free.] Therefore, if the warranty were not disclaimed, there would likely be a breach of the implied warranty of merchantability because the software is not "fit for the ordinary purposes" for which it would be used.

Implied warranties can be disclaimed under either § 2-316(2) or (3). This company has elected to use § 2-316(2), which requires that disclaimer of the implied warranty of merchantability "must mention merchantability and in case of a writing must be conspicuous." Here, the disclaimer specifically states "**including but not limited to the implied warranty of merchantability**" and it has bolded the disclaimer language, which is probably sufficient to make it conspicuous under the definition in § 1-201(b)(10). Because there is no claim for breach of the implied warranty of merchantability, **Answer (A) and Answer (C) are incorrect.**

According to § 2-313, an express warranty is "any affirmation of fact or promise made by the seller to the buyer which relates to the goods and becomes part of the basis of the bargain." The promise by the software company that "this software will operate free of any errors for a period of one year" would seem to qualify as an express warranty unless it was effectively disclaimed. In fact, the company also stated that **"there are no warranties, express or implied."** Does this language effectively disclaim the express warranty that was given? No. Section 2-316(1) states that words creating an express warranty and words negating an express warranty "shall be construed wherever reasonable as consistent with each other; but . . . negation or limitation is inoperative to the extent that such construction is unreasonable." In other words, if an express warranty is both given and taken away, it is deemed given. If you think about it, this makes sense. Most sellers, like this software company, in effect wipe the slate clean by disclaiming all warranties. They then give an express warranty that they intend to apply to the transaction. In their disclaimer, they are in effect saying "there are no *other* warranties, express or implied." Because the software company gave only an express warranty, **Answer (D) is incorrect** and **Answer (B) is correct**.

100.   **Answer (C) is the best answer.** Unless explicitly waived, disclaimed, or otherwise limited, where the seller, at the time of contracting, has reason to know (1) the particular purpose for which the goods are sought and (2) that the buyer is relying on the seller's skill or judgment to select or furnish suitable goods, the seller warrants that the goods shall be fit for the buyer's particular purpose. U.C.C. § 2-315. Under the facts, the software company knew the particular purpose for which the business wanted the software and the software company knew that the business was relying on their expertise to select or furnish the appropriate software. Therefore, the statutory requirements of U.C.C. § 2-315 appear to have been satisfied. *See, e.g., Lewis v. Mobil Oil Corp.*, 438 F.2d 500 (8th Cir. 1971) (seller recommended lubricating oil for use on buyer's saw mill equipment); *Valley Iron & Steel Co. v. Thorin*, 562 P.2d 1212 (Or. 1977) (seller selected the grade of metal to use in making hoedad collars for buyer). Therefore, **Answer (D) is incorrect**.

Answer (A) is incorrect because, unlike the implied warranty of merchantability (discussed in the answers to Questions 98 and 99), a seller does not have to be a merchant who deals in goods of the kind in order to create the implied warranty of fitness for a particular purpose. But was the implied warranty of fitness for a particular purpose effectively disclaimed? Implied warranties can be disclaimed under either § 2-316(2) or (3). This company has elected to use § 2-316(2), which requires that disclaimer of the implied warranty of fitness for a particular purpose "must be by a writing and conspicuous." Here, the disclaimer is in writing and states, **"there are no warranties, express or implied."** Unlike the disclaimer of the implied warranty of merchantability, no magic words are required to disclaim the implied warranty of fitness for a particular purpose. The software company has bolded the disclaimer language, which is probably sufficient to make it conspicuous under the definition in § 1-201(b)(10). Because the implied warranty of fitness for a particular purpose was created but was also effectively disclaimed, **Answer (B) is incorrect and Answer (C) is correct**.

101. **Answer (A) is probably the best answer**, though it may be a close question in some jurisdictions. The problem of modification has proved difficult for contract law. On the one hand, the parties should be free to change today the agreement they made yesterday. Parties often insert a No Oral Modification clause in a contract, requiring modifications to be in writing, but in the absence of such a clause and in the absence of a statute of frauds issue, there is no reason why a written agreement cannot be modified by an oral agreement. Therefore, **Answer (C) is incorrect**.

On the other hand, while parties should be free to alter their contractual obligations, one party should not be free to coerce the other party into making a change. Thus, in the case of *Alaska Packers' Association v. Domenico*, 117 F. 99 (9th Cir. 1902), the court held that a modification in which an employer agreed to pay employees a higher wage was not enforceable because of economic duress. In that case, however, because the workers were on a ship in Alaska, the employer had no reasonable alternative but to agree to the higher wage. Under our facts, in contrast, Sam could have refused Betty's demand and hired another painter. Because Betty's behavior probably does not rise to the level of duress, **Answer (B) is incorrect**.

In the modified agreement, Betty did not promise to do anything that she was not already bound to do, so there was no consideration for Sam's agreement to pay $600 more. The "pre-existing duty" rule is found in Restatement § 73, which provides that "[p]erformance of a legal duty owed to a promisor which is neither doubtful nor the subject of honest dispute is not consideration." However, many modern courts do not follow this rule when the parties make a good-faith modification, even though that modification lacks consideration. This rule is found in Restatement § 89:

§ 89 Modification of Executory Contract

A promise modifying a duty under a contract not fully performed on either side is binding

(a) if the modification is fair and equitable in view of circumstances not anticipated by the parties when the contract was made; or

(b) to the extent provided by statute; or

(c) to the extent that justice requires enforcement in view of material change of position in reliance on the promise.

This rule only applies when the modification is executory; that is, it has not been fully performed on either side. Furthermore, it only applies when there is a statute, reliance, or a change in circumstances not anticipated by the parties. Here, there is no applicable statute or reliance. It could be argued that the demand for Betty's services is a circumstance that would justify her charging more. But it does not seem fair and equitable that Sam should have to pay her more for the same services just because of that. Therefore, since the situations described in this Restatement section are unlikely to be found in our facts, **Answer (D) is incorrect**, and we revert to the pre-existing rule to conclude that the modification is not binding.

102. Probably not. Recall from our discussion of consideration in Topic 3, Consideration, that formalistically this modification should be enforceable. In theory, there are three contracts, each with consideration. The first is the original contract to do the work for $6,000. The second is the agreement to rescind the first contract. The third is the agreement to do the work for $6,600.

The case of *Schwartzreich v. Bauman-Basch, Inc.*, 131 N.E. 887 (N.Y. 1921) arose on similar facts. An employee was hired at a salary of $90 per week. The employee got a better offer from another employer and induced his present employer to tear up the old contract and then enter a new one at a salary of $100 per week. The court held that the modification was enforceable, stating that "[t]here is no reason that we can see why the parties to a contract may not come together and agree to cancel and rescind an existing contract, making a new one in its place." Williston, however, criticizes this view as elevating form over substance:

> But calling an agreement an agreement for rescission does not do away with the common law requirement of consideration, and when the agreement for rescission is coupled with a further agreement that the work provided for in the earlier contract shall be completed and that the other party shall give more than it originally promised, the total effect of the second agreement is that one party promises to do exactly what it had previously bound itself to do, and the other party promises to give an additional compensation for that same performance.

Williston on Contracts 4th ed. § 7:37. So, a formalistic judge might say that the modification is now enforceable, but most courts do not think the result should turn on whether the parties in fact rescinded their old contract before they made the modification. Therefore, it is likely that the outcome would not differ from the outcome under the original facts and Betty would still be required to do the work for $6,000.

103. **Answer (D) is the best answer.** In this case there is no threat by Betty, so **Answer (B) is incorrect.**

There is no consideration for the modification under these facts. Betty was obligated to replace the boards, so she did not do anything under the modification that she was not required to do under the original contract. Therefore, **Answer (C) is incorrect.**

The issue then comes down to whether a modification will be enforceable if there is no consideration. While some courts might not honor the modification, the modern view is that under these circumstances it is likely to be enforced because, in the words of Restatement § 89, "the modification is fair and equitable in view of circumstances not anticipated by the parties when the contract was made." Therefore, **Answer (D) is a better answer than Answer (A).**

104. **Answer (C) is the correct answer.** This contract involves the sale of goods (recall that according to § 2-105(1), the definition of "goods" includes specially manufactured goods). Therefore, U.C.C. Article 2 applies. Section 2-209(1) changes the common-law rule:

> (1) An article modifying a contract within this Article needs no consideration to be

binding.

Because there is no evidence of duress under these facts, **Answer (B) is incorrect**. Because the statute changes the common law pre-existing duty rule, **Answer (A) is incorrect**. And because we are dealing with a statute, we do not need the rationale for the change in the common law rule found in Restatement § 89(a). Note also that the Article 2 rule is broader than the Restatement rule; it makes a modification enforceable whether or not there are circumstances not anticipated by the parties. Therefore, **Answer (D) is incorrect**.

105.   No. The Code did away with the requirement of consideration for a modification, but it did not do away with the other requirements of contract formation, such as duress, and the requirement that the parties act in good faith. Official Comment 2 to § 2-209 states in part:

> However, modifications made thereunder must meet the test of good faith imposed by this Act. The effective use of bad faith to escape performance on the original contract terms is barred, and the extortion of a "modification" without legitimate commercial reason is ineffective as a violation of the duty of good faith.

See, e.g., Skinner v. Tober Foreign Motors, Inc., 187 N.E.2d 669 (Mass. 1963). In a sense, the common law courts and the U.C.C. have arrived at a similar solution to the problem of modification from different directions. According to Restatement § 89, the common law requires consideration, except where the modification is fair and equitable; the Code does not require consideration, except where the modification is unfair and inequitable.

106.   **Answer (C) is the best answer.** Let's first dispose of the consideration issue. This is a contract for the sale of goods, so it is governed by Article 2. Section 2-209(1) provides that a modification of a contract within Article 2 needs no consideration. As discussed in Question 105, the modification might not be enforceable if a party did not act in good faith, but there is no evidence under the facts that the seller acted in bad faith. Therefore, **Answer (A) and Answer (D) are incorrect**.

The parties included a no oral modification (NOM) clause in their contract. According to § 2-209(2), "[a] signed agreement which excludes modification or rescission except by a signed writing cannot be otherwise modified or rescinded," so it looks like this provision is an enforceable term of the contract. The problem is that a NOM is found in just about every contract, and it is almost a certainty that it will be ignored. The drafters of the Code were aware of the propensity of parties to make oral modifications in spite of the NOM clause, so they added § 2-209(4): "Although an attempt at modification or rescission does not satisfy the requirements of subsection (2) or (3) it can operate as a waiver." In other words, as happened here, the parties by their conduct agreed to waive the NOM clause and then made an enforceable oral modification. The buyer has no right to mislead the seller by agreeing to the modification and then trying to take advantage of it. Therefore, **Answer (B) is incorrect and Answer (C) is correct**.

If courts routinely find that the parties have waived their right to enforce NOM clauses, why do drafters nevertheless regularly put them in their contracts? I would venture that the drafters do so to encourage the parties to get everything in writing, which is the better practice. But failure to follow that practice is not fatal to their modification.

107.   **Answer (C) is the best answer.** A novation is an agreement in which a party (or parties) to the original agreement is replaced, with the consent of the other parties, with a new party

(or parties) who bears the rights and obligations of the original party. A party who is replaced no longer has any rights or obligations under the new agreement. RESTATEMENT § 280. In a suretyship agreement, one person (the surety) agrees to be responsible for the debt of another, but the surety is an additional debtor and does not take the place of the original debtor. Here, the contractor agreed to make a new agreement with the parents. Because the contractor agreed that the parents would assume the obligations of the son, and he would no longer be liable for the debt, this agreement is a novation. Because the contractor can no longer look to the son for payment, the parents are not sureties. Therefore, **Answer (A) is incorrect**.

Modifications and substituted agreements, by contrast, change the terms but involve the same parties as the contract they modify or replace. *See* RESTATEMENT §§ 89 and 279. Therefore, **Answer (B) and Answer (D) are incorrect** since this agreement involved new parties.

108.   No. A novation discharges the original agreement and any breach of the novation would not give the contractor the right to revive and enforce the original contract against the son. *See* RESTATEMENT § 280 and cmt. b.

109.   No. If no price had been agreed upon, then Sam would have to pay the reasonable price for the job. But since the parties agreed on a price of $6,000, the contract price governs and it doesn't matter whether the price is reasonable or not.

110.   **Answer (D) is the best answer.** Let's first revisit modification. Notice that the facts here differ from the facts of Question 103 because in that question, Betty requested the modification during performance of the contract; in the words of Restatement § 89, this was a modification of an "executory contract," one that neither side had finished performing. During that time, there is something for each party to give and take. RESTATEMENT § 89 cmt. a says that "[t]his Section relates primarily to adjustments in on-going transactions." But once one party has completed performance, the other party is a debtor, and we are now talking about discharge of a debt rather than modification of a contract. Here, when Betty completes performance, Sam is indebted to her in the amount of $6,000. Therefore, **Answer (B) is incorrect** because modification is no longer possible.

As we have seen, once Betty completes performance, it is too late for the parties to modify the contract, but they can now make an accord. An *accord* is an agreement in which the creditor agrees to discharge the debt in return for payment of less than the amount of the debt. They key here is that an accord is an *agreement*, so the same rules of formation apply that apply to other contracts – offer, acceptance, consideration, and no defenses to formation. An offer to enter into an accord puts a creditor between a rock and a hard place — the creditor must either accept the terms of the offer or reject it, perhaps jeopardizing the possibility of being paid. Nevertheless, the creditor has a reasonable alternative — reject the offer and make a claim for the full amount of the debt. Because an offer to enter into an accord does not rise to the level of coercive behavior, **Answer (C) is incorrect**.

An offer to enter into an accord, however, must be accompanied by consideration. Sam owes Betty $6,000. He is offering her $600 less than that amount, but there is no consideration for her agreement to give up the $600 she is owed. By paying $5,400 of the $6,000 debt, he is just doing what he is already obligated to do. Therefore, an enforceable accord was not formed and Betty can recover the $600. **Answer (A) is incorrect**. Incidentally, U.C.C. § 3-311 technically governs when the parties use a check to effectuate their accord and satisfaction. Because we would look to the common law of accord and satisfaction to determine whether the elements of that statute are satisfied, I am not alluding to it in this analysis.

111. **Answer (A) is the best answer**. Under these facts, all the elements of an enforceable accord are satisfied. There is offer and acceptance, and the consideration is the resolution of a disputed debt. In other words, if Sam had made a claim against Betty, she might have ended up getting some amount less than $6,000. Therefore, it is not clear how much she was entitled to and she got something for her giving up the $600 — the resolution of a claim against her. Of course, the dispute must be raised in good faith to constitute consideration. There is no evidence of bad faith here. Because there is consideration for the accord, **Answer (D) is incorrect**.

Just as resolution of a dispute can be consideration for an accord, so can liquidation of an unliquidated debt. If Betty had agreed to paint the house with no agreed price, then the price would be unliquidated — not determined by the parties or a court. If she then billed Sam for $6,000 and he claimed he owned her only $5,400, then the liquidation of the debt at that amount is the consideration. A third form of consideration for an accord is for the debtor to give the creditor something additional or different that was not in the original agreement. If Betty had agreed that Sam had until January 1 to pay the $6,000 and they agreed that he could pay $5,400 on December 1 to discharge the debt, then there is consideration — Betty is giving up $600 in return for early payment. You can see why courts favor accord and satisfaction. This quick and dirty dispute resolution mechanism allows parties to resolve their disputes out of court. Note that there is no requirement that an accord be evidenced by a writing, so **Answer (C) is incorrect**.

A substituted contract rarely arises, but let's work through this difficult concept. In an accord, the parties agree that the debt will be discharged on the debtor's *payment* of the lesser amount. In a substituted contract, the parties agree that the debt will be discharged on the debtor's *promise* of the lesser amount. This is obviously a trap for the creditor, for in that case, the unliquidated or disputed debt is discharged the moment the promise is accepted. Was there consideration? Yes – the creditor got the promise of a liquidated and undisputed amount instead of a claim for an unliquidated or disputed amount.

Under our facts, Betty agreed that Sam's payment would discharge the debt. This clearly creates an accord. If he did not make payment, then he would be in breach of the accord and she could sue either on the accord or on the underlying debt. Therefore, **Answer (B) is incorrect**. Assume, alternatively, that Sam had said, "I promise you $5,400 if you agree to discharge the debt," and she agreed. Would that be a substituted contract? If it is, the debt is discharged the moment she accepts the offer, whether Sam pays or not. This is obviously bad news for a creditor. Fortunately for them, most courts say that if the language is ambiguous, since most reasonable creditors would not agree to a substituted contract, it is interpreted as creating an accord. So to create a substituted contract, the parties have to go out of their way to unambiguously agree to discharge the debt in return for a promise to pay.

112. **Answer (D) is the best answer**. The supplier will claim that it was unable to perform due to commercial impracticability. *See* U.C.C. § 2-615 for the rule in Code cases, such as this one, and Restatement § 261 when the common law applies. Hundreds of years ago, the default rule may have been that an obligation was unconditional unless the parties stated otherwise

in the contract, but that rule was changed by the case of *Taylor v. Caldwell*, 122 Eng. Rep. 309 (1863). Therefore, **Answer (A) is incorrect**.

The modern rule is that it is not breach if, in the words of § 2-615(a), "performance as agreed has been made impracticable by a contingency the non-occurrence of which was a basic assumption on which the contract was made." This is sometimes characterized as the "foreseeability" test, but that characterization is probably too broad. Most events are foreseeable, especially by flinty-eyed attorneys who often take a dim view of future events. The real question is whether, if reasonable parties at the time they formed the contract had discussed the possibility of this event arising, they would have agreed it excused nonperformance. In fact, § U.C.C. § 2-615(a) expressly mentions "compliance in good faith with any applicable foreign or domestic government regulation" as an excusing event. Therefore, an embargo would likely qualify as such an event, so **Answer (B) is incorrect**.

It looks, therefore, as though the supplier should be excused. However, if you look carefully at the facts, the supplier did not promise "100,000 wallboard sheets from China" — he promised "100,000 wallboard sheets." Therefore, it could be argued that he can still perform even though he does not have wallboards from China. For this reason, a party who is relying on an exclusive source of supply should make that clear in the contract, and should take all reasonable steps to contract with that source. *See* Official Comment 5 to § 2-615. Therefore, **Answer (C) is incorrect and Answer (D) is the best answer**.

113.   No. A party's performance is not excused by the occurrence of a foreseeable event that makes a contract unprofitable for that party. *See, e.g., Karl Wendt Farm Equipment Co. v. International Harvester Co.*, 931 F.2d 1112 (6th Cir. 1991). Furthermore, even if the event were unforeseeable, a mere increase in price did not make performance "impracticable." When it agreed to provide the wallboard at a fixed price, the supplier assumed the risk of price increases. Official Comment 4 to § 2-615 states in part:

> Increased cost alone does not excuse performance unless the rise in cost is due to some unforeseen contingency which alters the essential nature of the performance. Neither is a rise or a collapse in the market in itself a justification, for that is exactly the type of business risk which business contracts made at fixed prices are intended to cover.

114.   **Answer (D) is the best answer.** When a party claims excuse because of impracticability or frustration, the party is really asking contract law to supply a condition precedent to their performance. A party is always free to list the events that condition their performance, and they often do so by means of a Force Majeure clause. However, the facts do not indicate that the contractor did so in this case. Therefore, **Answer (A) is incorrect**.

As discussed in the answers to the previous questions, impracticability requires the occurrence of an event the non-occurrence of which was a basic assumption on which the parties made their contract. However, impracticability makes the most sense when claimed by a seller. After all, the obligation of a buyer is to *pay*, and the event does not prevent the buyer from being able to do so. Therefore, **Answer (C) is incorrect**.

A buyer is usually claiming to be excused not because it cannot perform, but because the value has gone out of that performance. Here, for example, the buyer can still perform by paying, but it would be paying for wallboard that it no longer needs because it has no houses to build. This doctrine is called *frustration of purpose*. *See Krell v. Henry*, [1903] 2 K.B. 740

(C.A. 1903). Restatement § 265 states that a party's duty to perform may be discharged if (1) an event occurs the non-occurrence of which was a basic assumption on which the contract was made, and (2) as a result, the party's principal purpose was substantially frustrated. We have the same problem with the first element that we have with impracticability. Is a collapse in the market in which the goods would be used such an event? Official Comment 4 to § 2-615 states in part:

> Neither is a rise or a collapse in the market in itself a justification, for that is exactly the type of business risk which business contracts made at fixed prices are intended to cover.

Furthermore, the purpose may be frustrated, but the buyer can still sell the wallboard or store it for later use. Why should the seller have taken the risk that the buyer would not be able to use the goods? While this may be a close question, I think most courts would not excuse the buyer. Therefore, **Answer (D) is a better answer than Answer (B)**.

115. Yes. The provision "if the Red Sox win the World Series" is an express condition. It is worth memorizing the definition of *condition* found in Restatement § 224:

> A condition is an event, not certain to occur, unless its non-occurrence is excused, before performance under a contract becomes due.

The Red Sox winning the World Series is an event. It is not certain to occur. And the event must occur before the performances under the contract are due. Therefore it is a condition. It is an express condition, because it is stated in the contract.

Notice that the email exchange does not include that condition. Is it nevertheless a term of the contract? Yes. A bit of review from Topic 7, Parol Evidence and Interpretation, may be helpful. To apply the parol evidence rule, we must determine whether the parties intended the writing to be their complete and exclusive agreement. Here, it is unlikely that they intended this informal exchange to be their complete agreement on a $500,000 contract. And even if they did, Restatement § 217 states that an agreement is not integrated when there is an oral condition to its performance. Therefore, the condition is part of the agreement.

116. **Answer (B) is the correct answer.** The rule is found in Restatement § 234:

§ 234 Order of Performances

(1) Where all or part of the performances to be exchanged under an exchange of promises can be rendered simultaneously, they are to that extent due simultaneously, unless the language or the circumstances indicate the contrary.

(2) Except to the extent stated in Subsection (1), where the performance of only one party under such an exchange requires a period of time, his performance is due at an earlier time than that of the other party, unless the language or the circumstances indicate the contrary.

According to subsection (1), where the performances "can be rendered simultaneously, they are to that extent due simultaneously." Here, payment cannot be simultaneous with building since building takes time. Therefore, we go to subsection (2), which provides that "where the performance of only one party under such an exchange requires a period of time, his performance is due at an earlier time than that of the other party." Here, only the building requires a period of time, so that performance is due first. Therefore, **Answer (B) is correct and Answers (A), (C), and (D) are incorrect**.

117. Yes. The rule stated in Restatement § 234 is a default rule. It is the rule "unless the language or the circumstances indicate the contrary." The contractor could use language that expressly changes the rule, such as demanding payment before he performs. Of course, that language would disadvantage the woman, who would then have no leverage to get the contractor to perform. So it is likely that the parties would reach a compromise calling for

progress payments to be made as work progresses. The contractor could argue that provision for progress payments is so common that the term would be supplied by custom and usage. This would likely be a losing argument. Restatement § 234 cmt. e states that "it is not feasible for courts to devise such formulas for the wide variety of such cases that come before them in which the parties have made no provision."

118. **Answer (C) is the best answer**. The woman clearly committed a breach when she did not do what she promised to do. The issue is: What is the consequence of that breach? Does the man still have to perform? Prior to Lord Mansfield's historic decision in *Kingston v. Preston*, 99 Eng. Rep. 437 (K.B. 1773), English courts found that unconditional promises had to be performed even if the other party had not performed. That case set things right, and found that simultaneous performances were implied conditions of each other, or "constructive conditions of exchange." Therefore, while it would have been the correct answer before 1773, today **Answer (A) is incorrect**.

Under the modern view, even if the parties do not expressly state in the contract that the simultaneous performances are conditional, it is implied that they are. *See* Restatement § 238. Therefore, **Answer (B) is incorrect**. Even though the woman's breach was material, the man's contractual duties were not necessarily discharged. According to Restatement § 242 cmt. a: "Ordinarily there is some period of time between suspension and discharge, and during this period a party may cure his failure." Here, the woman said she would pay later. While her failure to tender the money on delivery clearly establishes the man's right to suspend his performance, his duties are probably not discharged. If she pays within a reasonable period of time, and offers damages for the delay, then she has cured the breach. Therefore, **Answer (D) is incorrect**.

119. **Answer (C) is the best answer**. The woman breached the contract when she did not pay. As you already know, but we will emphasize in Topic 12, Remedies, the basic remedy for breach of contract is expectancy damages — damages that put the non-breaching party where he would have been had the contract been performed. Here, the man's expectancy was to receive $10,000, so he has a claim for $10,000 in damages.

The man has no basis for rescission. The woman materially breached, and a material breach would relieve him of his obligation to perform. But since he has already performed, it is too late to withhold his performance. Therefore, **Answer (B) is incorrect**. By extending credit, the man gave up the right to make his performance a condition of performance by the other party. This demonstrates the power of conditions — they are good leverage to get the other party to perform.

When a party negotiating a contract realizes that their own performance is not conditional on performance by the other party, they need to regain some leverage. They might think about building other remedies into the contract. In the construction contract in Questions 115–17, for example, we saw that the contractor who has given up the right to make his performance conditional by going first can remedy the situation by requiring that the owner make progress payments. The lawyer who has to perform services before getting paid can require that the client pay a retainer before the lawyer performs the services. In this case, the man could take a security interest in the car, which would give him the right to repossess it when the buyer did not pay. But without jumping through the right hoops to create a security interest (all of which is explained in U.C.C. Article 9, which you can look forward to studying in a course called Secured Transactions), a seller does not have that right. Therefore, **Answer (A) is incorrect.** Since other answers are incorrect, **Answer (D) is incorrect.**

120. **Answer (C) is the best answer.** There is no express condition in the contract, so **Answer (A) is incorrect.** On the other hand, it is accurate to say that the woman's performance was conditional on the contractor's performance and he did not satisfy the condition. This problem with the rule of constructive conditions of exchange arose shortly after the case of *Kingston v. Preston*, discussed in Question 118, was decided. In *Boone v. Eyre*, 126 Eng. Rep. 160(a) (K.B. 1777), Lord Mansfield again saved the day, coming up with what came to be called the rule of "substantial performance" – if one party's performance is a constructive condition of the other party's duty, the condition is satisfied if the party *substantially* performs. We will shortly explore what it means to substantially perform, but it is fair to conclude that in this case the contractor can be said to have substantially performed. Even though the condition was not literally satisfied, the contractor came close enough to deem the condition satisfied, and the woman has to perform. Therefore, **Answer (B) is incorrect.**

An immaterial breach of a promise amounts to substantial performance, so we could say in this case that the contractor's breach was only immaterial. However, **Answer (D) is incorrect** because an immaterial breach is still a breach. Because it is a breach, the other party is entitled to damages. Putting those two concepts together, because the contractor substantially performed, the condition that had to occur before the woman had to perform is deemed satisfied. Therefore the woman has to pay the $500,000, but because the contractor breached his promise, she can deduct as damages the losses caused by the breach — the cost of putting in the molding and sodding the lawn.

121. **Answer (B) is the best answer.** While it is not possible to stop a lawyer from arguing public policy, it would be a good idea to identify the relevant policy. I can't think of what policy might be applicable here. On the other hand, the insurer needs to have the information about the loss quickly so that it can investigate the claim while the evidence is still fresh. Therefore, **Answer (C) is incorrect.**

The insurance company took advantage of good drafting techniques here and made the provision a condition instead of a promise. If the homeowner had merely *promised* to report a loss within 30 days, then the homeowner would be in breach of that promise and could argue that the breach was immaterial. But the homeowner did not make a promise. Therefore, **Answer (D) is incorrect.** The homeowner had no obligation to report the loss, but if it did not do so, then the condition to the insurer's duty was not satisfied. An express condition can't be substantially performed – the event either occurs or it doesn't. Courts often say that express conditions will be strictly enforced. Therefore, **Answer (A) is incorrect.**

Because the express condition was not satisfied, the only out for the homeowner is to ask a court for relief from the harsh effect of the condition. Restatement § 229 provides:

§ 229 Excuse of a Condition to Avoid Forfeiture

To the extent that the non-occurrence of a condition would cause disproportionate forfeiture, a court may excuse the non-occurrence of that condition unless its occurrence was a material part of the agreed exchange.

A forfeiture is the loss of an out-of-pocket expense, not a lost opportunity; failure to obtain the insurance proceeds is not a forfeiture, but payment of the insurance premiums could be. The homeowner would have to claim that payment of the premiums every month and getting nothing in return caused a forfeiture. To prove that the occurrence of the condition was not a material part of the exchange, the homeowner would probably have to show that the late notice did not prejudice the insurance company.

122. **Answer (D) is the best answer.** A *promise* is "a manifestation of intention to act or refrain from acting in a specified way, so made as to justify a promisee in understanding that a commitment has been made." RESTATEMENT § 2(1). A "condition" is "an event, not certain to occur, which must occur, unless its nonoccurrence is excused, before performance under a contract becomes due." RESTATEMENT § 224. The parties to a contract can agree to specifically condition one or both parties' performance on the occurrence of some event. *See* RESTATEMENT § 226.

Conditions may be either express or implied (constructive). An express condition is set forth explicitly in the parties' agreement. A constructive condition is implied into the agreement as a matter of fact, law, or equity. The lawyer and Beta expressed the condition in their agreement; therefore, the condition must have occurred before Beta could enforce the lawyer's obligation to pay rent. RESTATEMENT § 225(1). The non-occurrence of the condition, unless the lawyer is responsible for it failing to occur, technically deprives Beta of the expected performance, but does not give him a remedy against the lawyer. RESTATEMENT § 225(3). Beta, having been willing to make his contract with the lawyer conditional on her (hopefully early) release from the lease with Alpha, could not treat the contract as unconditional and begin charging rent. Therefore, **Answer (A) is incorrect**.

Although the occurrence of the condition is out of the lawyer's control, there is an implied promise on her part to try to bring it about or at least not to hinder its coming about. But the facts do not indicate that the lawyer promised to induce Alpha to let her out of their lease agreement. She may have promised to try. But, having tried and failed, she is not liable for the non-occurrence of the condition. Therefore, **Answer (B) is incorrect**.

While the law generally abhors a forfeiture, see *UNUM Life Insurance Co. v. Ward*, 526 U.S. 358 (1999), any loss Beta suffered after September 1 was pursuant to the terms of the agreement into which he freely entered. Therefore, **Answer (C) is incorrect**.

123. **Answer (D) is the best answer.** A "material breach" deprives the non-breaching party of its reasonable contractual expectations. It "is so dominant or pervasive as . . . to frustrate the purpose of the contract." *Jacobs & Young, Inc. v. Kent*, 129 N.E. 889 (N.Y. 1921). Factors to consider in determining whether a breach is material include: (1) the extent to which the non-breaching party can be adequately compensated for the part of the benefit of which she is deprived; (2) the extent to which the breaching party will suffer forfeiture if the non-breaching party is excused from her contractual obligations due to the breach; (3) the likelihood that the breaching party will cure, taking into account all of the circumstances, including any reasonable assurances by the breaching party; and (4) the extent to which the breaching party's behavior comports with standards of good faith and fair dealing.

RESTATEMENT § 241.

Similar to the builder's substitution of "Cohoes Pipe" for "Reading Pipe" in *Jacobs & Young*, the contractor's use of Brown bricks was not a material breach, in light of the unavailability of Acme bricks; therefore, the contractor substantially performed.

If the contractor did its best to match the color and texture of Acme No. 63 bricks when it chose Brown No. F-17 bricks, the contractor's use of Brown No. F-17 bricks to supplement the inadequate supply of Acme No. 63 bricks did not substantially deprive the woman of the benefit of the bargain. Therefore, **Answer (A) is incorrect**.

As in *Jacobs & Young*, to the extent that there was some diminution in the value of the house because the contractor was forced to use Brown No. F-17 bricks to supplement the inadequate supply of Acme No. 63 bricks, the contractor could compensate the woman for that diminution by paying monetary damages, which would likely be little to none. Therefore, **Answer (B) is incorrect**.

Answer (C) is incorrect because the contractor's use of Brown No. F-17 bricks to supplement the inadequate supply of Acme No. 63 bricks rather than halting work until an adequate supply of the specified brick could be secured was entirely consistent with its duty of good faith and fair dealing.

124. **Answer (D) is the best answer.** This Question pursues the "What's the big deal about 'Reading pipe'?" query that nearly every Contracts professor asks some poor student each year while discussing *Jacobs & Young, Inc. v. Kent*, 129 N.E. 889 (N.Y. 1921). Unless the contractor knew the woman's particular purpose, *and* the contractor purposefully laid the brick to thwart the woman's particular purpose, then the contractor substantially performed and the woman would be entitled only to the diminution in value (if any) caused by the contractor's use of both Acme No. 63 bricks and Brown No. F-17 bricks, rather than Acme No. 63 bricks throughout.

Answers (A) and (C) are incorrect because the contractor substantially performed.

Answer (B) is precisely the relief that Judge Cardozo refused to award the party in the woman's position in *Jacobs & Young*, and there is arguably less reason to award it under the facts of this Question than in *Jacobs & Young*. In either case, it would be an astounding waste. In *Jacobs & Young*, Judge Cardozo found that the wrong pipe had been used inadvertently, so the contractor was not at fault. The dissent disagreed, concluding that at best the contractor had failed to supervise properly. Here, the contractor knowingly used the wrong bricks, but did not do so with a dishonest intent. The contractor had to use the Brown No. F-17 bricks or some other brick because there simply were not enough Acme No. 63 bricks available given the construction schedule. Therefore, **Answer (B) is not the best answer**.

125. No. It is true that the contractor is barred from recovery *on the contract* because the condition that had to occur before he would be paid under the contract was not satisfied. However, he did confer a benefit on the woman — the value of the work completed, less the cost of repair. Most courts will allow a party who has materially breached to recover *off the contract* in restitution for the value of the benefit conferred. Restatement § 374(1) provides:

§ 374 Restitution in Favor of Party in Breach

(1) Subject to the rule stated in Subsection (2), if a party justifiably refuses to perform on the ground that his remaining duties of performance have been discharged by the other party's breach, the party in breach is entitled to restitution for any benefit that he has conferred by way of part performance or reliance in excess of the loss that he has caused by his own breach.

126. **Answer (C) is the best answer.** A repudiation is a definite and unconditional refusal to perform, given prior to the time for performance. Think of it as "breach by anticipatory repudiation." *See* RESTATEMENT § 250 and Keith A. Rowley, *A Brief History of Anticipatory Repudiation in American Contract Law*, 69 U. CIN. L. REV. 565 (2001). Only in Answer (C) did the buyer definitely and unconditionally manifest to the seller that he would not perform as promised.

Answer (A) is incorrect because the buyer's statement to the seller ("I am not sure . . .") was equivocal. **Answer (B) is incorrect** because, while the buyer's statement was clear, unequivocal, and unconditional, he did not make it to the seller or to anyone acting as the seller's agent so as to give the seller constructive notice of the buyer's repudiation. **Answer (D) is incorrect** because merely requesting more favorable terms or suggesting a modification to the terms of a contract does not repudiate the contract. *See Truman L. Flatt & Sons Co. v. Schupf*, 649 N.E.2d 990 (Ill. App. Ct. 1995). On the other hand, refusing to perform unless the other party agrees to the requested terms is a repudiation.

127. Yes. When one party affirmatively states unequivocally that he will not perform, this is often described as an "express" repudiation. If the party does not say anything, but puts it out of his power to perform, this is often described as an "implied" repudiation. That is what happened under these facts. Note that an implied repudiation *is* a repudiation; it is a repudiation by conduct rather than by words. If a party makes an equivocal statement such as "I'm not sure I am going to perform," the issue is whether those words constitute an express repudiation. It is not an implied repudiation.

128. No. Assuming that time is not of the essence of this contract, the buyer is only saying that he will perform a day late, not that he won't perform at all. When you are faced with this issue, ask if the statement would be a total breach if it occurred at the time for performance instead of in advance. If on July 1, the buyer said, "I am not going to pay you ever," that would be a total breach, so it is an anticipatory repudiation if he says it prior to July 1. If on July 1, the buyer said, "I am not going to pay you until tomorrow," that would only be a partial breach that would entitle the seller to damages but would not entitle the seller to cancel the contract. Therefore, the statement has the same effect if made prior to July 1.

129. **Answer (D) is the best answer.** After a promisor has repudiated, a promisee may (1) do nothing, subject to the promisee's obligation to mitigate damages, and await the promisor's performance at the appointed time, (2) cancel the contract, (3) act in reliance on the repudiation, or (4) immediately bring suit against the promisor. Likewise, a promisee may, without prejudicing his right to any other remedy for the promisor's repudiation, urge the promisor to retract his repudiation or perform in spite of it. *See* RESTATEMENT § 257 and *Mobil Oil Exploration & Producing S.E., Inc. v. United States*, 530 U.S. 604 (2000).

If the seller chose to sell the house to another buyer after the original buyer's repudiation, the seller could sue the buyer for the difference between the contract price ($250,000) and the price at which the seller was able to sell to the new buyer ($245,000), plus any incidental and consequential damages (more on those in Topic 12, Remedies) that the seller could prove. Therefore, **Answers (A), (B), and (C) are correct, but (D) is a better answer.**

130. **Answer (D) is the best answer.** A repudiating promisor may retract his repudiation, as long as the retraction comes to the other party's attention before the latter materially changes his position in reliance on the repudiation or indicates to the promisor that he considers the repudiation to be final. RESTATEMENT § 256(1). If the seller did not act on the buyer's repudiation before the buyer retracted his repudiation, the seller would have lost the right to cancel, bring suit, resell the house, or otherwise act in reliance on the buyer's repudiation.

    The seller was entitled, but not required, to urge the buyer to retract his repudiation. RESTATEMENT § 257. Whether the buyer retracted in response to the seller's urging or of his own volition, the effect of the retraction is the same — if the seller acted in reliance on the buyer's repudiation prior to the buyer's retraction, the buyer's retraction would be ineffective. If the buyer retracted prior to any act by the seller in reliance on the buyer's repudiation, the buyer's retraction would restore the contract. Therefore, **Answer (A) is incorrect.**

    Had the buyer not retracted, Answer (B) would be correct, because the buyer's anticipatory repudiation entitled the seller, *inter alia*, to resell the house (see the answer to Question 129.) However, an effective retraction nullifies a prior repudiation. The buyer's repudiation prior to the seller's resale was a necessary, but not necessarily sufficient, condition to the seller being entitled to resell the house. Therefore, **Answer (B) is not the best answer.**

    Even though the deadline for the buyer's performance (July 1) has not yet come, that date served only as a date beyond which the seller would have a claim for breach at the time for performance was due — as opposed to anticipatory breach — and is therefore irrelevant to the call of the question. The seller could act in reliance on the buyer's repudiation prior to the deadline, and be completely entitled to do so. Retracting the repudiation before July 1 is necessary for the buyer to avoid liability for his prior repudiation; however, retracting a repudiation before performance is due is not always sufficient to absolve the breaching party of liability. Therefore, **Answer (C) is not the best answer.**

131. No. The buyer's repudiation allowed the seller to suspend his own performance, including any preparatory actions the seller had to take in order to perform his end of the contract to sell the house to the buyer. RESTATEMENT § 253(2).

132. **Answer (D) is the best answer.** Because this transaction involves the sale of goods, Article 2 of the U.C.C. applies. Section 2-609 provides:

    § 2-609. Right to Adequate Assurance of Performance.

    (1) A contract for sale imposes an obligation on each party that the other's expectation of receiving due performance will not be impaired. When reasonable grounds for insecurity arise with respect to the performance of either party the other may in writing demand adequate assurance of due performance and until he receives such assurance may if commercially reasonable suspend any performance for which he has not already received the agreed return.

(2) Between merchants the reasonableness of grounds for insecurity and the adequacy of any assurance offered shall be determined according to commercial standards.

(3) Acceptance of any improper delivery or payment does not prejudice the aggrieved party's right to demand adequate assurance of future performance.

(4) After receipt of a justified demand failure to provide within a reasonable time not exceeding thirty days such assurance of due performance as is adequate under the circumstances of the particular case is a repudiation of the contract.

The Code rules for anticipatory repudiation are found in § 2-610, but the Code does not define anticipatory repudiation. Therefore, according to § 1-103(b), the Code incorporates the common law rule for repudiation. As discussed above, at common law, a repudiation must be a definite and unequivocal refusal to perform. Here, the seller whined and complained, but did not refuse to perform, so there is no anticipatory repudiation. Therefore, **Answer (A) is incorrect**.

Nevertheless, the seller's statement puts the buyer between a rock and a hard place. If the buyer treats it as a repudiation and cancels the contract, and he then refuses the seller's performance on the date of delivery, he is the breaching party. But if he doesn't treat it as a repudiation, and the seller doesn't deliver, then he won't have the goods and will have to scramble to find them. If he then claims damages against the seller, the seller can argue that he should have known that the language constituted a repudiation.

The Code in § 2-609 (and the common law in Restatement § 251) have a nice solution to the problem of uncertainty regarding performance. A party who has "reasonable grounds for insecurity" may demand assurances from the other party and suspend his performance until he gets them. If he gets adequate assurances, then the contract is back on track. If he doesn't get adequate assurances, then he can conclude that there has been a repudiation and can proceed accordingly.

In the Code provision, there is a *right* to demand assurances, not a requirement. Therefore, **Answer (B) is incorrect**. Although the Restatement rule does not require the demand to be made in writing, the Code does, so **Answer (C) is incorrect** and **Answer (D) is the best answer**.

133.   **Answer (B) is the best answer.** As discussed in Questions 126 and 132, this statement would not constitute an anticipatory repudiation because it was not a clear and unequivocal refusal to perform. Therefore, **Answer (A) is incorrect**. Nevertheless, the statement would give the seller reasonable grounds for insecurity. Therefore, **Answer (D) is incorrect**.

A party who has reasonable grounds to believe the other party might breach, can make only *reasonable* demands for assurance. A party can't use the demand for assurances as an excuse to rewrite the contract with favorable terms that he did not originally request. The buyer had no right under the contract to payment on June 15, and can't require it as an assurance. He is only entitled to assurance that he will be paid on July 1. Therefore, **Answer (C) is incorrect** and **Answer (B) is correct**.

134.   **Answer (B) is the best answer.** The bank's letter provided a timely assurance that the buyer would have the $250,000 at the time of the closing.

Answer (A) is incorrect because promising to "do everything I can to make sure that I have the money by July 1" is no more than the buyer had promised under the contract.

Answer (C) is not the best answer. This was probably an adequate assurance but it was not timely because the seller asked for assurances by June 10, and the buyer did not provide them until June 14. The fact that the buyer's delay was due to his financial adviser being out of town should not excuse his delay. If the buyer had a sufficient portfolio to enable him to satisfy the seller by selling off part of the portfolio, the buyer could easily have formulated another strategy for providing assurances that did not require letting the seller's deadline pass. Of course, this reasoning is premised on it being reasonable for the seller to expect the assurances by June 10. This seems reasonable, for the seller will need to make other arrangements as soon as possible if the buyer is deemed to have repudiated. Note that this is in the buyer's interest, for timely action by the seller may well mitigate damages. On the other hand, I can't say for sure that this answer is incorrect. If my client was the seller and he had not taken any action in reliance before receiving this assurance, I might recommend that he treat it as an adequate assurance rather than risk litigating the issue. But since there is another answer that is free of doubt, this is not the best answer.

Answer (D) is incorrect because, while a certified check for the full amount might have assured the seller under other circumstances, because the buyer waited until the day before performance was due, the buyer failed to "provide within a reasonable time such assurance of due performance as is adequate in the circumstances," in the language of Restatement § 251(2). The fact that the buyer's payment of $250,000 by certified check on June 30 would have constituted full performance of his contractual obligation to the seller in the absence of the seller's reasonable grounds for insecurity ignores the fact that the seller properly requested assurances and that the buyer did not give them in a timely fashion. Even if a court were to find that the seller's demand for assurances in 10 days was unreasonable, the court should not find that the buyer's last minute assurance was adequate.

135. No. Recall that the demand for assurances arises in a situation where a party does not actually repudiate, but gives the other party reasonable concern that he might repudiate. Having provided the seller with adequate assurances of due performance, the buyer should have addressed those concerns and the contract is back on track for performance. Therefore, if the seller sold the house to a third party or otherwise disposed of it before July 1, *the seller* would be the repudiating party, entitling the buyer to the same remedies (discussed in Question 129) the seller would have if the buyer repudiated.

What if the party who gave what appeared to be adequate assurances nevertheless did not come through and repudiated at the time for performance? Are things any worse for him? They are not. He may be a double dirty contract breaker, but as we will see in Topic 12, Remedies, the remedies for breach are designed to compensate the nonbreaching party rather than to punish the breaching party, so he would be faced with no extra penalty.

136. **Answer (D) is the best answer.** A promisor's failure to timely provide adequate assurances of due performance, following a proper request for assurances, is deemed to be an anticipatory repudiation. *See* RESTATEMENT § 251(2). As discussed in the answer to Question 129, a promisee whose promisor has repudiated may (1) do nothing, subject to the promisee's obligation to mitigate damages, and await the promisor's performance at the appointed time, (2) cancel the contract, (3) act in reliance on the repudiation, or (4) immediately bring suit against the promisor. Likewise, a party who does not receive adequate assurances after a reasonable demand may, without prejudicing his right to any other remedy for the

promisor's repudiation, urge the promisor to retract his repudiation or perform in spite of it. Therefore, because the seller could have done any or all of the foregoing, **Answers (A), (B), and (C) are correct, but (D) is a better answer.**

137.   **Answer (D) is the best answer.** As you will learn if you take a course in Sales, although we frequently say that Article 2 applies to transactions in goods, it is not always that easy to figure out whether a transaction involves goods. The Code defines "goods" in § 2-105(1) as things which are "movable," which might on its face exclude electricity. Some courts have nevertheless found that electricity is a good, while others have found that even if it is not a good, it makes sense to treat it as analogous to a good because it is a commodity that is bought and sold very much like goods. *See* Gary D. Spivey, *Electricity, Gas, or Water Furnished by Public Utility as "Goods" Within Provisions of Uniform Commercial Code, Article 2 on Sales*, 48 A.L.R.3d 1060 (1973). Other courts have held that a demand for assurances can be made in common law transactions outside of Article 2. *See* RESTATEMENT § 251. Therefore, **Answers (A), (B), and (C) are correct, but (D) is a better answer.**

Of course, the Restatement is not a statute, so a state is free to find that there is no common law demand for assurances in that jurisdiction. In a very annoying decision, *Norcon Power Partners, L.P. v. Niagara Mohawk Power Corp.*, 705 N.E.2d 656 (N.Y. 1998), the New York Court of Appeals seems to end up rejecting all of these approaches and ends up allowing a demand for assurances only on the limited facts of the case, because it wants the common law to grow only incrementally.

138. In Topic 6, Obligations Enforceable Without Consideration, we looked at reliance and restitution as claims in the absence of a bargained-for contract. Now the concepts return, but we are looking at them as remedies for breach when there is a contract. As these facts indicate, often the expectancy will give the non-breaching party the greatest recovery. However, there may be times when he or she cannot claim the expectancy, so relying on restitution and reliance damages may provide a better alternative for the nonbreaching party to recover the greatest amount.

One way to measure expectation damages is to use this formula from E. ALLAN FARNSWORTH, CONTRACTS § 12.9:

Loss in Value + Other Loss - Cost Avoided - Loss Avoided

Here, the "Loss in Value" is the $100,000 the contractor would have had. "Other Loss" includes incidental and consequential damages, of which there are none under these facts. "Cost Avoided" is the $30,000 the contractor did not need to spend because of the breach. "Cost Saved" is savings caused by the breach, for example through mitigation, of which there are none under these facts.

So, plugging the numbers from our problem into this formula, we get $100,000 + $0 - $30,000 - $0 = $70,000. Another way to look at it is to ask what the contractor would have had if the contract had been performed, which is always the measure of the expectancy. He would have had a profit of $10,000. Since he has spent $60,000, it will take an award of $70,000 to bring him from being out $60,000 to being ahead $10,000.

The contractor's reliance damages are $60,000, the amount he is out of pocket without reimbursement. Remember, reliance damages seek to restore the promisee to where he or she would have been had they not relied on the promise. The contractor's claim in restitution is not clear. The measure of restitution is always the value of the benefit conferred. However, there are different ways to measure that amount. The owner will claim it is $40,000, *i.e.*, the value of the benefit conferred to her. But the contractor might well demonstrate that a reasonable contractor would have charged $66,000 (his expenses plus profit) to do the work that he performed, so he conferred a benefit worth that much on the owner. As a rule of thumb, a court is more likely to measure restitution from the point of view of the non-breaching party, which in this case would be the contractor, and thus the restitution damages would likely be $66,000.

139. **Answer (B) is the best answer.** The builder is in breach and it would probably be regarded as a material breach. Therefore, the owner owes the builder nothing on the contract. However, the modern view is that even a party who materially breaches can recover in restitution. *See* RESTATEMENT § 374. Therefore, **Answer (A) is incorrect.**

Let's look at it from the point of view of the non-breaching party, the owner. The owner is entitled to the expectancy — to have the house built at a cost of $200,000. When the first builder breached, the owner mitigated by finding another builder to complete the job at a reasonable price, which was $75,000. To get the house built for $200,000, the owner cannot pay the first builder more than $125,000 ($125,000 + $75,000 = $200,000). Therefore, **Answer (C) and Answer (D) are incorrect** because payment of these amounts would overcompensate the builder and would not compensate the owner for the breach.

140. $150,000. The builder's remedy is in restitution, and restitution is always measured by the value of the benefit conferred. The benefit conferred was 75% of a $200,000 contract, so the builder cannot recover more than 75% of $200,000, which is $150,000. Another way to look at it is that since the owner was able to save money when having the building completed, the benefit of that savings should not go to the breaching party. See *Kreyer v. Driscoll*, 159 N.W.2d 680, 683 (Wis. 1968), where the court stated:

> [W]here a defendant justifiably refuses to perform his contract because of the plaintiff's breach but the plaintiff has rendered part performance which is of a net benefit to the defendant, the plaintiff can get judgment with some exceptions for the amount of such benefit in excess of the harm he has caused the defendant by his breach *but in no case exceeding a ratable proportion of the agreed compensation.* (Emphasis added.)

141.   **Restitution.** According to Restatement § 344(c), a party's restitution interest is "his interest in having restored to him any benefit that he has conferred on the other party." Restitution seeks to ensure that a party is not unjustly enriched, and puts that party back where they were by making them restore the benefit conferred by another. When the seller breaches, the seller must disgorge any benefits conferred by the buyer, which would include an amount paid as a down payment.

142.   **Reliance damages.** According to Restatement § 344(b), a party's reliance interest is "his interest in being reimbursed for loss caused by reliance on the contract by being put in as good a position as he would have been in had the contract not been made." Reliance damages reimburse the non-breaching party for any expenses actually incurred, *inter alia*, in reliance on the breaching party's promise to perform. Reliance damages seek to put the non-breaching party in as good a position as he would have been in had he never entered into the contract.

Here, the restaurant had the base built in preparation for performance and the seller knew that this expense had to be incurred. Some authorities say that reliance damages can only be recovered as an alternative remedy rather than an additional remedy. I don't think there is doubt that this amount could be recovered, for because of the breach, the buyer had to have two bases built instead of one. So the only issue is how to characterize it. Perhaps it could be characterized as part of the expectation interest, which is defined in Restatement § 344(a) as "his interest in having the benefit of his bargain by being put in as good a position as he would have been in had the contract been performed." In order to be put in that position, the buyer will have to be compensated for the cost of one of the bases. Perhaps the cost of the second base could be characterized as part of consequential damages, for it was reasonably foreseeable that if the seller breached, the buyer would have to get another oven, which could include a new base.

143.   **Incidental damages.** Incidental damages are costs incurred in a reasonable effort to avoid

or mitigate damages caused by the other party's breach. *See* RESTATEMENT § 347. Under the Code, it often includes things like insurance, transportation, and costs of obtaining cover. *See* §§ 2-710 and 2-715(1). Here, the buyer reasonably incurred the cost of hiring a broker to help it find a replacement oven.

144. **Expectancy damages.** Expectation damages seek to put the non-breaching party in as good a position as he would have been in had the breaching party fully performed by awarding the non-breaching party the difference between the value of the performance promised and the performance, if any, actually received. Direct or "cover" damages are the most common form of expectancy damages. If the original party did not perform, then the other party can have the job done by someone else and recover the difference between what it actually cost and what it would have cost under the contract. Since this question involves an oven, which is a good, the rule would be found in U.C.C. § 2-712, which describes the damages as "the difference between the cost of cover and the contract price." In pleading, these losses would be called "general damages." They don't have to be spelled out in a complaint because a defendant would know the plaintiff is claiming them.

145. **Consequential damages.** At common law, these are the damages permitted under the *Hadley* Rule — the losses which a reasonable party in the shoes of the breaching party at the time they entered the contract would have reasonably known would result from the breach. They are not the loss of the thing itself that was promised, but losses that were set in motion by that loss. As with other avoidable consequences, the non-breaching party has a duty to take reasonable steps to mitigate consequential damages. RESTATEMENT § 350(1).

Here, the facts state that the seller knew that the restaurant would not be able to sell pizzas without the oven, so it is responsible for the consequences of failing to deliver the oven — the profit the restaurant lost because it could not operate without an oven. Under the Code, these damages are described in § 2-715(2). In pleading, these losses would be called "special damages." *See* FRCP Rule 9(g). They have to be spelled out with particularity in the complaint because a defendant would not necessarily know the plaintiff is claiming them.

146. **Answer (D) is the best answer.** The student has a claim for breach of an express warranty. We are accustomed to manufacturers and sellers promising to "repair or replace" defective parts for a certain period of time. Such a "remedial promise" is a limited remedy under § 2-719(1)(a), for it limits the remedy for breach of warranty found in § 2-714(2). Since no such limited remedy was part of these facts, **Answer (A) is incorrect**.

The remedy for breach of warranty set forth in § 2-714(2) is "the difference at the time and place of acceptance between the value of the goods accepted and the value they would have had if they had been as warranted." The $200 difference in the price between the seller's computer like the one accepted ($1,800) and the seller's computer as promised ($2,000) is one measure of the difference in value. But in fact, many courts use the cost of repair or replacement as a handy objective measure of the difference in value. Therefore, **Answer (B) and Answer (C) are incorrect** because they are insufficient.

147. $6,000. If this answer surprises you, it shouldn't. It is simply a matter of plugging the numbers into the § 2-714(2) formula for damages for breach of warranty: the difference between the value of the goods as promised and the value of the goods as accepted. Here, that is $12,000 - $6,000 = $6,000. But, you protest, that is more than the customer paid for

the computer. To which contract law replies, "So what?" The buyer is entitled to the benefit of the bargain, and if she bargained to pay $5,000 for something worth $12,000, contract law will honor the bargain.

148.   **Answer (C) is the best answer.** The increase in price is not the kind of event that will excuse nonperformance. There is nothing keeping the seller from performing. The seller will not make as much money as she hoped by performing, but each party took the risk that the value would go up or down prior to closing. Therefore, **Answer (D) is incorrect.**

The buyer has the option to sue for $100,000 in damages, measured by her expectancy — had the contract been performed, she would have had a house worth $400,000 at a cost of $300,000, so the increase in her wealth would have been $100,000. However, she has the alternative of seeking the equitable remedy of specific performance. Equitable remedies are only available if the remedy at law (money damages) is inadequate. Money damages are not adequate to put the buyer where the buyer would have been when there is no similar property on the market to purchase. With real estate, every parcel is unique, so specific performance will usually be granted. Therefore, **Answer (A) and Answer (B) are incorrect** because they are insufficient.

149.   **Answer (D) is the best answer.** Historically, courts of equity jealously guarded their powers. While in most jurisdictions, the courts of law and courts of equity have merged, the rules restricting access to equity remain in place. Because of the historical restrictions on access to equitable remedies, parties cannot compel the court to use its equity powers. Therefore, **Answer (C) is incorrect**. On the other hand, the remedy at law is probably not adequate. There used to be cases in which the issue of whether a particular player was unique was litigated. *See, e.g., Dallas Cowboys Football Club, Inc. v. Harris*, 348 S.W.2d 37 (Tex. Civ. App. 1961). But today it is pretty much settled that professional athletes are unique — even if an athlete is not "one of a kind," it is still burdensome to find a replacement. Because a court is likely to find that the remedy at law is not adequate, **Answer (A) is incorrect**.

On the other hand, a court is unlikely to grant the equitable remedy of specific performance, compelling the player to play for the club. This sounds uncomfortably similar to involuntary servitude and involves problems of supervision that the court does not want to have to deal with. Therefore, **Answer (B) is incorrect.** The court is, however, likely to grant an injunction, enjoining the player from playing for any other team. If this has the effect of specific performance, forcing him back to the club he was under contract with, so be it.

150.   **Answer (D) is the best answer.** The default rule (called the "American Rule") on attorney's fees is that each side pays its own attorney's fees whether it wins or it loses. There are two major exceptions and one minor exception. One major one is that the parties may provide in their contract that the prevailing party recovers attorney's fees. The other is if the claim is brought under a statute that provides for attorney's fees. U.C.C. Article 2 does not provide for attorney's fees, but many federal and state consumer protection statutes do provide for attorney's fees, so if you have a consumer plaintiff, be sure to check for appropriate statutes. Also, in rare cases a court may award attorney's fees when the plaintiff brings a frivolous claim.

Punitive damages are never awarded for breach of contract. Well, this is law, so there are always exceptions, but I think the only exception to this one arises when an insurance company denies a claim in bad faith and requires the insured to sue to recover. For the plaintiff to recover punitive damages, normally the claim will have to be brought as an intentional tort claim rather than as a contract claim.

Therefore, **Answer (A) and Answer (B) are incorrect**, and because they are incorrect, **Answer (C) is incorrect**.

151. Because glass tubing is a good, we look to Article 2 for the applicable law. Section 2-703 contains a handy overview of the seller's remedies when the buyer is in breach:

§ 2-703. Seller's Remedies in General.

Where the buyer wrongfully rejects or revokes acceptance of goods or fails to make a payment due on or before delivery or repudiates with respect to a part or the whole, then with respect to any goods directly affected and, if the breach is of the whole contract (Section 2-612), then also with respect to the whole undelivered balance, the aggrieved seller may

(a) withhold delivery of such goods;

(b) stop delivery by any bailee as hereafter provided (Section 2-705);

(c) proceed under the next section respecting goods still unidentified to the contract;

(d) resell and recover damages as hereafter provided (Section 2-706);

(e) recover damages for non-acceptance (Section 2-708) or in a proper case the price (Section 2-709);

(f) cancel.

Under these facts, it is obviously too late for Tubular to exercise the remedies found in subsections (a)-(c). Therefore, in addition to canceling the contract, Tubular could (1) sell the goods to another buyer and recover contract-resale damages under U.C.C. § 2-706; (2) recover contract-market damages under U.C.C. § 2-708(1); (3) recover for lost profits under U.C.C. § 2-708(2); or (4) recover the price under U.C.C. § 2-709. We will now look at each of these remedies in the following questions.

152. **Answer (A) is the best answer.** U.C.C. § 2-706 entitled Tubular to resell the goods in good faith and in a commercially reasonable manner, and having done so, to recover from Mercury the difference between the contract price (KP) and the resale price (RP), plus any incidental damages (ID) permitted by U.C.C. § 2-710, minus expenses saved (ES) by Tubular as a result of Mercury's nonperformance. The § 2-706 formula is:

$$(KP - RP) + ID - ES$$

Here, KP = $25,000 (5,000 x $5.00); RP = $24,000 (4,000 x $6.00); ID = $500 (the cost of transporting the glass from Mercury's plant back to Tubular's plant) + $250 (the cost of storing all 5,000 ft. of tubing for the month of May); and ES = $0 (Tubular had already manufactured and shipped the tubing before Mercury breached, so it saved nothing as a result of the breach). So, Tubular's § 2-706 damages are:

($25,000 - $24,000) + $750 - $0 = $1,750.

Note, incidentally, that while the Code contains these formulas for damages, they are just a way of arriving at the expectancy measure of damages. Had the contract been performed, Tubular would have been paid $25,000 by Mercury. As a result of the breach, Tubular has $24,000 from the resale, but to obtain that $24,000 it had to spend $500 in shipping and $250 in storage, so its net gain from the resale is $23,250. To bring Tubular from where it is as a result of the breach (ahead $23,250) to where it would have been if the contract had been performed (ahead $25,000) will require a payment of $1,750.

However, in order to recover the above-described resale damages, a seller must notify the buyer of its intent to resell the goods prior to its resale. U.C.C. § 2-706(3). Tubular failed to satisfy this requirement. While the Code is silent on the consequences of noncompliance, case law provides that it bars a seller from recovery under § 2-706. White & Summers state that "[f]ailure to comply deprives the seller of the measure of damages stated in 2-706 and relegates the seller to the measure provided in 2-708." Therefore, while Answer (C) reflects a proper calculation of Tubular's resale damages as of June 1, because Tubular did not provide Mercury with proper notice of resale, **Answer (C) is incorrect**.

Answer (B) is incorrect because, even if Tubular were entitled to recover under U.C.C. § 2-706, Answer (B) fails to include Tubular's incidental damages — the cost of storing the glass tubing until the new buyer picks up 4,000 of the 5,000 feet of tubing. **Answer (D) is incorrect** because, even if Tubular were entitled to recover under U.C.C. § 2-706, Answer (D) includes in Tubular's incidental damages the cost of transporting the 4,000 feet of glass tubing that the new buyer bought. However, the facts indicate that the new buyer, not Tubular, bore that cost.

153.   **Answer (A) is the best answer.** Under U.C.C. § 2-708(1), Tubular may recover the difference between the contract price (KP) and the market price *at the time and place for tender* (MP), plus any incidental damages permitted by U.C.C. § 2-710 (ID), minus expenses saved by Tubular as a result of Mercury's nonperformance (ES). So, the § 2-708(1) formula is:

$$(KP - MP) + ID - ES$$

Here, KP = $25,000 (5,000 x $5.00); MP = (5,000 x $5.50) = $27,500; ID = $750 (the cost of transporting the glass from Mercury back to Tubular, plus the cost of storing all 5,000 ft. of tubing for the month of May); and ES = 0. So,

($25,000 - $27,500) + $750 - $0 = -$1,750.

Because the market price was greater at the time and place of tender (May 1) than the contract price, Tubular will not have any recoverable damages. In other words, it was a losing contract for Tubular since it agreed to sell for less than the market price. In any event, the net result is $0 damages.

Answer (D) is incorrect because it makes the mistake of assuming that the difference between KP and MP is always a positive number generated by subtracting the smaller number from the larger number. KP - MP means just that — it is a positive number if the market price is lower than the contract price and a negative number if the market price is higher than the contract price. **Answer (C) is incorrect** because it measures MP as of the date Mercury breached — April 15, when MP = $5.00 per foot — instead of the date of tender — May 1, when MP = $5.50 per foot. **Answer (B) is incorrect** because it conflates the two errors of Answers (C) and (D), measuring MP on the wrong date — here, the date Tubular and Mercury formed their contract, April 2, when MP = $5.25 per foot — and treating KP - MP as a positive number.

154. **Answer (D) is the best answer.** Section 2-708(2) provides:

> (2) If the measure of damages provided in subsection (1) is inadequate to put the seller in as good a position as performance would have done then the measure of damages is the profit (including reasonable overhead) which the seller would have made from full performance by the buyer, together with any incidental damages provided in this Article (Section 2-710), due allowance for costs reasonably incurred and due credit for payments or proceeds of resale.

The recovery permitted Tubular under U.C.C. § 2-708(1) appears to be inadequate to put Tubular in as good a position as it would have been absent Mercury's breach, since it provides for no damages. The UCC allows an alternate remedy if the seller is a "volume seller" whose capacity to sell the subject goods is sufficiently large to meet the demands of all customers who seek to buy those goods. Thus, the sale to the second buyer is not necessarily a resale of the goods if the seller could have sold to both buyers. In that event, the aggrieved seller can recover the lost profit that the seller would have made had the buyer not breached.

Here, the facts say that "Tubular has the manufacturing capacity to produce orders on demand." Thus, it is a "volume seller" who could have supplied tubes to both Mercury and the new buyer. Section § 2-708(2) allows Tubular to recover any profits (B) that Tubular would have realized had Mercury performed, plus any incidental damages (ID) permitted by § 2-710, minus expenses saved (ES) by Tubular as a result of Mercury's nonperformance, minus any credit due Mercury for partial payment (PP), and minus any resale profit (RP) Tubular made on the resale to the new buyer. So the § 2-708(2) formula is:

$$\pi + ID - ES - PP - RP$$

Here, π = KP - MC (manufacturing cost), which is $25,000 (5000 x $5.00) - $22,500 (5,000 x $4.50) = $2,500; ID = $750 (the cost of transporting the glass from Mercury back to Tubular, plus the cost of storing all 5,000 ft. of tubing for the month of May); ES = $0; and PP = $0. What is the value of RP? Recall that Tubular lost money on the sale to the new buyer, so RP = $0. Plugging these values into the formula, we get:

$$\$2,500 + \$750 - \$0 - \$0 - \$0 = \$3,250.$$

Answer (A) is incorrect because it assumes Tubular is not a volume seller. **Answer (B) is incorrect** because it calculates (KP - DC) using only the 1,000 feet of tubing not resold. **Answer (C) is incorrect** because it fails to account for Tubular's incidental damages.

155. No. It is unlikely that Tubular will be able to recover the contract price under § 2-709. That section first provides that if the buyer fails to pay when due, a seller § 2-709 may recover the price of accepted goods. Here, Mercury did not accept the goods, so Tubular should not be able to recover the price. This rule makes sense, because otherwise the seller would get a double recovery — one from the new resale buyer and the other from the original buyer. The

exception to the rule also makes sense — the seller can recover the contract price under subsection (1) "if the seller is unable after reasonable effort to resell them at a reasonable price or the circumstances reasonably indicate that such effort will be unavailing."

Here, because Tubular was able to resell 4,000 feet of the tubing originally identified to its contract with Mercury, the issue arises only with respect to the unsold 1,000 feet. Since there is a market for these goods, it is premature to conclude that Tubular would be unable to sell them. Therefore, Tubular should not be able to recover the contract price. Note also that under § 2-709(2), the seller claiming the price under this section must hold the goods for the buyer. Again the Code is concerned about a double recovery. If the buyer pays the contract price, the buyer should get the goods.

156.   **Answer (C) is the best answer.** Okay, so this question doesn't really belong here. But it is good review of the formation issues in Topic 2, Offer and Acceptance, and you have to make sure the parties have a contract before you can talk about remedies for breach of contract.

Monica made an offer on July 14. Note that all exchanges in this problem were in writing, so we don't have any statute of frauds issues. She then revoked the offer on July 17. Chandler sent his expression of acceptance on July 19. At that time, he had received neither the letter of revocation nor the fax, so the attempt at revocation is ineffective. *See* RESTATEMENT § 42. Therefore, **Answer (B) is incorrect**.

Chandler's expression of acceptance contained an additional term — that delivery would be no later than September 1. According to § 2-207(1), a contract is formed even if there are additional or different terms in the acceptance. According to § 2-207(2), the additional term is a proposal, and between merchants it becomes part of the contract. We can assume that both parties are merchants, since they deal in fruit sales, so the term is presumptively part of the contract. But it is not part of the contract if one of the three enumerated exceptions applies. The exceptions in subsections (a) and (c) are not applicable, so the only issue is whether the additional term materially alters the contract under subsection (b). The default rule under § 2-309 is that delivery is to be within a reasonable time, so as long as "no later than September 1" is within that reasonable time, the additional term does not materially alter the contract. Therefore, the term becomes part of the contract and **Answer (A) is incorrect**.

Under our old friend the Mailbox Rule, an acceptance is effective on dispatch rather than on receipt. *See* RESTATEMENT § 63. Therefore, Chandler's acceptance is effective on July 19 when he sent it, not on July 21, when Monica received it. Since a contract was formed on July 19, **Answer (D) is incorrect**.

157.   **Answer (A) is the correct answer.** As discussed in the previous question, a contract for the sale of goods was formed and the seller breached it. An overview of the buyer's remedies when the seller is in breach is found in U.C.C. § 2-711:

§ 2-711. Buyer's Remedies in General

(1) Where the seller fails to make delivery or repudiates or the buyer rightfully rejects or justifiably revokes acceptance then with respect to any goods involved, and with respect to the whole if the breach goes to the whole contract (Section 2-612), the buyer may cancel and whether or not he has done so may in addition to recovering so much of the price as has been paid

(a) "cover" and have damages under the next section as to all the goods affected whether or not they have been identified to the contract; or

(b) recover damages for non-delivery as provided in this Article (Section 2-713).

(2) Where the seller fails to deliver or repudiates the buyer may also

(a) if the goods have been identified recover them as provided in this Article (Section 2-502); or

(b) in a proper case obtain specific performance or replevy the goods as provided in this Article (Section 2-716).

Chandler may cancel the contract. Under subsection 1, Chandler may purchase replacement mangoes from another supplier, per U.C.C. § 2-712, and recover the difference between the cover price and the contract price, plus any incidental and consequential damages or he may recover the difference between the market price when he learned of the breach and the contract price, per U.C.C. § 2-713, plus any incidental and consequential damages, less any expenses saved by Monica's breach. Alternatively, he may seek specific performance, per U.C.C. § 2-716. Damages for nonconformity under U.C.C. § 2-714 is not available to Chandler because that section only applies to accepted, nonconforming goods. Because he never accepted the goods, **Answer (C) is incorrect**.

Most of the time, an aggrieved buyer will "cover" by buying the goods from another seller and recover under § 2-712. The formula for cover damages under that section is:

$$(CP - KP) + ID + CD - ES$$

CP = the price of the cover goods, KP = the contract price, ID = incidental damages under UCC § 2-715(1), CD = consequential damages permitted by UCC § 2-715(2), and ES = expenses saved as a result of the breach.

Here, Chandler had no consequential damages because he obtained replacement mangoes by the date he needed them. Likewise, Chandler does not appear to have incurred any expenses mitigating the effects of, or to have saved any expenses due to, Monica's repudiation. So, Chandler's cover damages = $700 - $600 + $0 + $0 - $0 = $100.

U.C.C. § 2-713 allows the nonbreaching buyer to recover for the difference in the current market price and the contract price. The formula for calculating contract-market differential damages under that section is:

$$(MP - KP) + ID + CD - ES$$

MP = the market price of mangoes *when the buyer learned of the seller's repudiation*, and the other variables are the same as in U.C.C. § 2-712. Since Chandler learned of the repudiation on July 21, we would calculate market price as of that date. Chandler's contract-market differential damages = $650 - $600 + $0 + $0 - $0 = $50. Therefore, **Answer (B) is not the best answer**.

Chandler is unlikely to convince a court to award him specific performance under U.C.C. § 2-716, because there is no evidence that Monica's mangoes are unique and it is clear that other suppliers exist. *See* U.C.C. § 2-716(1) and Official Comment 2. Therefore, **Answer (D) is not the best answer**.

158.   **Answer (D) is the best answer.** Because this question involves a contract for software, we

must first determine the applicable law. In most states, there is no body of statutory law directly applicable to software contracts. However, most courts apply Article 2 by analogy. The warranty rules work especially well since most providers of software model their warranty language after goods contracts, as the software provider did in this question. *See* PRINCIPLES OF THE LAW OF SOFTWARE CONTRACTS §§ 3.02–3.06. Therefore, we will apply Article 2 in answering this question.

Because the design business did not discover the problem until after accepting the software, its remedy is limited to damages for breach of warranty under U.C.C. § 2-714. Before determining the remedies, we must first determine what warranties were given and which were breached. The software company effectively disclaimed the implied warranty of merchantability and the implied warranty of fitness for a particular purpose under § 2-316(2). That leaves only the express warranties that were created when the company promised that the software would perform certain specified functions. Note that the software company attempted to disclaim express warranties, but § 2-316(1) provides that express warranties that are both given and disclaimed are deemed to have been given. Therefore, the software company breached an express warranty when it provided software that did not perform the promised functions.

The remedy for breach of warranty is found in § 2-714(2) and (3):

§ 2-714. Buyer's Damages for Breach in Regard to Accepted Goods.

(2) The measure of damages for breach of warranty is the difference at the time and place of acceptance between the value of the goods accepted and the value they would have had if they had been as warranted, unless special circumstances show proximate damages of a different amount.

(3) In a proper case any incidental and consequential damages under the next section may also be recovered.

Under this formula, the buyer may recover its direct damages — the difference, at the time and place of acceptance, between the value of the (nonconforming) goods accepted and the value the goods would have had if they performed as warranted. There are many different measures of this difference in value. However, if we assume that the value of the nonconforming software was its price ($3,000), and that the value of the replacement software that performed the required functions was also its price ($4,000), then it would be fair to conclude that $1,000 represents the difference in value.

The aggrieved buyer is also entitled to recover any incidental and consequential damages recoverable under U.C.C. § 2-715. That section provides:

§ 2-715. Buyer's Incidental and Consequential Damages.

(1) Incidental damages resulting from the seller's breach include expenses reasonably incurred in inspection, receipt, transportation and care and custody of goods rightfully rejected, any commercially reasonable charges, expenses or commissions in connection with effecting cover and any other reasonable expense incident to the delay or other breach.

(2) Consequential damages resulting from the seller's breach include

(a) any loss resulting from general or particular requirements and needs of which the seller at the time of contracting had reason to know and which could not reasonably be prevented by cover or otherwise; and

(b) injury to person or property proximately resulting from any breach of warranty.

The design business does not appear to have incurred any incidental damages under these facts. As a consequence of the breach, however, the design business lost the advertising contract. One issue is whether that loss could have been prevented "by cover or otherwise." Under the facts, it would not have made sense for the design business to have covered by purchasing other software while the software company was still trying to solve the problem. Another issue is whether the software company had "reason to know" that the loss was likely. Here, the facts indicate that the design business told the software company that it needed the software for that purpose, so it had reason to know the loss was likely to result if the software did not perform. Note also that the software company did not disclaim liability for consequential damages, as it is permitted to do under § 2-719.

What is the measure of the consequential damages? The design business lost the profit of $1,000 it would have made on the advertising contract. Furthermore, when the business breached its contract with the advertising company, it had to pay $600 in damages to the advertising company. Would a reasonable seller in the shoes of the software company have known that if it did not provide the promised software, the buyer was likely to incur this loss? I think the answer is yes. Furthermore, would the seller have known that the business might have to pay a lawyer to defend itself? Again, the answer is yes. Notice an important distinction here. Absent an agreement to that effect, the seller is not liable for attorney's fees incurred in the buyer's litigation with the seller. But the seller is liable for attorney's fees that it reasonably knew would likely be incurred because of a third party's claim that was caused by the breach.

The software company is liable for the $1,000 in direct damages plus the $2,100 in consequential damages ($1,000 for the lost profit, $600 for the damages paid to the third party, and $500 for the attorney's fees incurred in defending the claim by the third party), for a total of $3,100. **Answers (A), (B), and (C) are incorrect** because each of those responses omits at least one of these items of damages.

159.   **Answer (A) is the best answer.** Magdalena is not a party to the contract. A fancy way of saying this is that she is not "in privity of contract" with the insurance company. Nevertheless, a person who is not a party to the contract can sue to enforce it if the person is a third-party beneficiary of the contract. Restatement § 302 provides a test for determining whether a person is a third-party beneficiary:

§ 302 Intended and Incidental Beneficiaries

(1) Unless otherwise agreed between promisor and promisee, a beneficiary of a promise is an intended beneficiary if recognition of a right to performance in the beneficiary is appropriate to effectuate the intention of the parties and either

(a) the performance of the promise will satisfy an obligation of the promisee to pay money to the beneficiary; or

(b) the circumstances indicate that the promisee intends to give the beneficiary the benefit of the promised performance.

(2) An incidental beneficiary is a beneficiary who is not an intended beneficiary.

Like many thorny issues in contract law, this one turns on the intention of the parties — did they intend to confer on this third person the right to enforce the contract? I suggest looking at these factors in order to answer this question:

1. Identify the promise the third party is seeking to enforce.

2. Determine whether the third party is named in the contract.

3. Determine whether performance of the promise runs to the third party.

4. Ask whether the promisee extracted that promise from the promisor with the intention of benefitting the third party.

Applying those factors in this case:

1. The insurance company's promise to pay $100,000 to the Magdalena.

2. Yes.

3. Yes.

4. Yes. As indicated in Restatement § 302(1)(b), the promisee (the man) bought the policy with the intention of giving the benefit to his wife. She is what is sometimes called a "donee" beneficiary because the promisee intended to give her the benefit as a gift.

This is the simplest example of a third-party beneficiary. Because Magdalena is a third-party beneficiary, **Answer (C) is incorrect** and she can recover even though she is not in privity of contract. **Answer (B) is incorrect** because she did not acquire her rights by assignment. **Answer (D) is incorrect** because she is not enforcing the promise as a representative of the man; she is enforcing it in her own right as a third-party beneficiary.

160. **Answer (A) is the best answer.** Let's apply our tests to see if the friend qualifies as a third-party beneficiary:

   1. Identify the promise the third party is seeking to enforce.

   2. Determine whether the third party is named in the contract.

   3. Determine whether performance of the promise runs to the third party.

   4. Ask whether the promisee extracted that promise from the promisor with the intention of benefitting the third party.

Applying those factors in this case:

   1. The buyer's promise to make the loan payments to the friend.

   2. Yes.

   3. Yes.

   4. Yes. As indicated in Restatement § 302(1)(a), the performance of the promise will satisfy an obligation of the woman to pay money to the beneficiary. The friend is sometimes called a "creditor" beneficiary because the promisee is indebted to her.

This is another simple example of a third-party beneficiary. Since the friend is a third-party beneficiary, **Answer (C) is incorrect** and she can recover even though she is not in privity of contract. **Answer (B) is incorrect** because the facts do not indicate that there was a novation. In a novation, the friend would agree to give up her claim against the woman as a debtor in return for the buyer becoming a new debtor; that did not happen here. **Answer (D) is incorrect** because a party who is an intended beneficiary is not an incidental beneficiary.

Incidentally, you may wonder why the facts don't say a bank made this loan, since that is usually how home purchases are financed. The answer is that the transaction would then be unrealistic because banks do not generally permit the borrower under a mortgage loan to transfer the loan to a third party. So the friend is trying to enforce a contract to which the friend is not a party.

161. No, the neighbor is out of luck. He is not a party to the contract. Under our factors, he is not named in the contract, performance of the promise does not run to him, and the man did not extract the promise from the painters with the intention of benefitting him. Therefore, we would conclude that he does not qualify as a third party beneficiary who could enforce Peter's Painting's promise to paint the neighbor's house. Note that the neighbor would have benefitted had the contract been performed, for the value of his property would likely have increased. This does not make him a third-party beneficiary, however. It makes him what Restatement § 302(2) calls an "incidental beneficiary," but in my view "incidental beneficiary" is another name for "loser."

162. **Answer (C) is the best answer.** This question introduces us to the topics of assignment and delegation. When dealing with this topic, it is useful to first break the contract down into the respective rights and duties of the parties. Note that each right has a corresponding duty:

Company has the right to receive 100,000 bushels of corn.

FirstCo has the right to receive payment.

Company has the duty to pay for the corn.

FirstCo has the duty to tender the corn.

Next we analyze what has happened under the facts, using the correct vocabulary: rights are *assigned* and duties are *delegated*. We see that:

FirstCo has delegated to SecondCo its duty to tender the corn.

FirstCo has assigned to SecondCo its right to payment.

Because it is a transaction in goods, this contract is governed by Article 2, so we find the rules for assignment and delegation in U.C.C. § 2-210. The rules for assignment and delegation in common law transactions are very similar; they are found in Restatement §§ 317 and 318.

Let's look first at delegation of duty. U.C.C. § 2-210(1) provides:

> (1) A party may perform his duty through a delegate unless otherwise agreed or unless the other party has a substantial interest in having his original promisor perform or control the acts required by the contract. No delegation of performance relieves the party delegating of any duty to perform or any liability for breach.

There is a strong policy in favor of delegation. Other than agreement of the parties, the only restriction on delegation is when "the other party has a substantial interest in having his original promisor perform or control the acts required by the contract." This is sometimes referred to as "choice of person," meaning that the duty is personal. Here, you are told that the company chose FirstCo because it had found it to be a very reliable supplier. That is not enough to involve choice of person, however, because the contract is to buy No. 2 yellow corn, and that commodity is the same whether delivered by FirstCo or by SecondCo.

With respect to assignment of rights, U.C.C. § 2-210(2) provides in pertinent part:

> (2) Unless otherwise agreed all rights of either seller or buyer can be assigned except where the assignment would materially change the duty of the other party, or increase materially the burden or risk imposed on him by his contract, or impair materially his chance of obtaining return performance.

There is a strong policy in favor of assignment of rights; it is even stronger in the case of the right to receive money, for much of our economy involves receivables financing – the use of the right to receive money as an asset. Here it does not change the duty of the company if it pays SecondCo instead of FirstCo and there is no way it would "increase materially the burden or risk imposed on him by his contract, or impair materially his chance of obtaining return performance."

Therefore, **Answers (A) and (B) are incorrect**, since the company has to accept the assignment and the delegation.

Answer (D) is also incorrect. The last sentence of U.C.C. § 2-210(1) states: "No delegation of performance relieves the party delegating of any duty to perform or any liability for breach." Delegation is favored in part because delegation does not relieve the delegating party of liability. Therefore, if SecondCo breaches the contract, the company has a remedy against both FirstCo and SecondCo.

163.   Those facts are probably not enough to make the delegation ineffective, for the performance is still not of a personal nature. However, U.C.C. § 2-210(6) provides:

> (6) The other party may treat any assignment which delegates performance as creating reasonable grounds for insecurity and may without prejudice to his rights against the assignor demand assurances from the assignee (Section 2-609).

Recall from Topic 9, Discharge of Duties, that a party who has reasonable grounds for insecurity because of a possible repudiation by the other party may demand assurances. Similarly, if the delegation causes the obligee (the one to whom the delegating party is obligated) to have reasonable grounds for insecurity, the obligee can demand assurances from the delegate (the one to whom the duty has been delegated) and if the obligee does not get those assurances, presumably the delegation is ineffective. Under these facts, it would appear that the past experiences with SecondCo give the company reasonable grounds for insecurity, so it could proceed under that section.

164.   **Answer (B) is the best answer.** First, put the right labels on what happened. The President had the *right* to have her portrait painted by Murphy and she *assigned* that right; Murphy had the *duty* to paint the President's portrait and she *delegated* that duty.

Next, you must determine whether the President's right was assignable. A right is assignable unless it "would materially change the duty of the obligor." RESTATEMENT § 317(2)(a). Recall that the *obligor* is the one obligated to perform, here Murphy. In this scenario, I think we would agree that this right was personal, and even though it is probably not more burdensome for Murphy, painting the portrait of the Vice-President is not the same as painting the portrait of the Vice-President. Therefore, the right is not assignable.

Third, you must determine whether Murphy's duty was delegable. According to Restatement § 318(2), "a promise requires performance by a particular person only to the extent that the obligee has a substantial interest in having the person perform or control the acts promised." Here, I think we would agree that the President (the *obligee* — the one to whom the duty is owed) has a substantial interest in having her painter of choice perform this personal service. Painting a portrait is not the same as delivering a commodity like corn. Therefore, the duty is not delegable.

Therefore, **Answers (A), (C), and (D) must be incorrect.**

165.   **Answer (A) is the best answer.** Recall the general rule of § 1-302(a) that the parties are free to vary the Code provisions. This concept is reinforced by the language "unless otherwise agreed" that appears in §§ 2-210(a) and (b).

Answer (B) is incorrect because there is no statutory requirement that the provision be conspicuous and case law has imposed no such requirement.

Answers (C) and (D) are incorrect because they refer to exceptions that we will address shortly, but there are no facts in this question that would invoke these exceptions.

166.   No. Notice that the provisions on assignment of rights in § 2-210(2) are prefaced by the language "[e]xcept as otherwise provided in Section 9-406." Article 9 kicks in when there is a security agreement. [You can look forward to studying Article 9 in the course called Secured Transactions.] Section 9-406 provides in part that "a term in an agreement between an account debtor and an assignor . . . is ineffective to the extent that it . . . prohibits . . .

the assignment or transfer of . . . the account."

Therefore, the restriction on assignment between the company and FirstCo is not effective and the lender can enforce the obligation against the company. Note that § 9-406 does not affect the prohibition on assignment in Question 165. Article 9 only applies when there is a *secured* transaction, and Question 165 involved only a *sales* transaction.

167. **Answer (D) is the best answer.** The drafter for the company obviously did not use this book, or s/he would have realized that the language creates an ambiguity. We know that rights are assigned and duties are delegated. So what does it mean to say that a *contract* may not be assigned? Whatever the parties may have intended, this happens often enough that the Code actually has a provision giving us the answer. Section 2-210(4) provides:

> (4) Unless the circumstances indicate the contrary a prohibition of assignment of "the contract" is to be construed as barring only the delegation to the assignee of the assignor's performance.

Although the use of the terms "assignee" and "assignor" makes the provision more difficult to understand, the provision is trying to state that this broad language bars the delegation of duties but not the assignment of rights. Therefore, **Answer (A) is incorrect** because while the parties have the freedom to bar both assignment and delegation, they did not effectively do so when they used this language.

Answer (B) is incorrect because that is not how the language is interpreted under the statute. Does this interpretation seem to get it backwards, since the parties appeared to bar assignment? Maybe, but in resolving ambiguities, we try to carry out the intent of the parties. Parties are usually more concerned with the delegation of duties than with the assignment of rights, since who does the performing is usually more important than who gets the performance. And if that doesn't appear to be the case, then the provision provides wiggle room to decide otherwise if "the circumstances indicate the contrary."

So the lesson is to get it right when you draft a contract. To get it right, you must understand the terminology. If you mean to prohibit the assignment of rights, then clearly say, "rights may not be assigned." If you mean to prohibit the delegation of duties, then clearly say, "duties may not be delegated."

Answer (C) is incorrect because a provision restricting assignment is ineffective only in an Article 9 transaction and here the transaction is not within the scope of Article 9.

168. **Answer (C) is the best answer.** There is a split of authority on this point, but the majority rule is that the prohibition affects only the *right* of the parties to delegate and does not deprive them of the *power* to delegate. Therefore, the delegation is effective and the homeowner's remedy is damages. This is an important distinction.

In *Bel-Ray Co., Inc. v. Chemrite (Pty) Ltd.*, 181 F.3d 435, 441–42 (3d Cir. 1999), the Circuit Court of Appeals looked at how the Appellate Division in New Jersey had analyzed this issue:

> To resolve this claim, the Appellate Division looked to § 322 of the Restatement (Second) of Contracts, which provides in relevant part:
>
> > (2) A contract term prohibiting assignment of rights under the contract, unless a different intention is manifested . . . .

(b) gives the obligor a right to damages for breach of the terms forbidding assignment *but does not render the assignment ineffective* . . .

Restatement (Second) of Contracts § 322 (1981) (emphasis added). The Court distinguished between an assignment provision's effect upon a party's "power" to assign, as opposed to its "right" to assign. A party's "power" to assign is only limited where the parties clearly manifest a different intention. According to the Court:

> "[t]o reveal the intent necessary to preclude the power to assign, or cause an assignment violative of contractual provisions to be wholly void, such clause must contain express provisions that any assignment shall be void or invalid if not made in a certain specified way." Otherwise, the assignment is effective, and the obligor has the right to damages.

Garden State Buildings L.P. v. First Fidelity Bank, N.A., 702 A.2d 1315, 1321 [(N.J. Super. Ct. 1997)] (quoting *University Mews Assoc's v. Jeanmarie*, 122 Misc. 2d 434, 471 N.Y.S.2d 457, 461 (N.Y. Sup. Ct. 1984)). The Court concluded that the parties had sufficiently manifested their intent to limit Midatlantic's power to assign the loan because the anti assignment clause clearly provided that assignments without the other party's written consent "shall be void." *Id.* at 1322.

> In adopting § 322, New Jersey joins numerous other jurisdictions that follow the general rule that contractual provisions limiting or prohibiting assignments operate only to limit a parties' right to assign the contract, but not their power to do so, unless the parties manifest an intent to the contrary with specificity. [citations omitted.] To meet this standard the assignment provision must generally state that nonconforming assignments (i) shall be "void" or "invalid," or (ii) that the assignee shall acquire no rights or the nonassigning party shall not recognize any such assignment.

Although the court referred to an "assignment," it applied the concept to an agreement that both assigned rights and delegated duties. While this approach may seem unsatisfactory in that it fails to put any teeth into a contractual prohibition, note that the parties are free to contract around the rule if they do so clearly. They could, for example, state: "Duties under the contract may not be delegated and any delegation without the other party's written consent is void."

Answer (A) is incorrect because it does not address the question of remedies. The issue is, when the parties have used their freedom of contract to restrict assignment and delegation, what is the remedy for violation of that provision?

Answer (B) is incorrect because it does not correctly answer the call of the question. The question asked is whether the homeowner has to allow XYZ to perform. While it is true that ABC has breached the contract, the question does not ask for the consequence of this breach on the contract between the homeowner and ABC. My guess is that since the only consequence of the delegation in the face of the prohibition is damages, then it is not a material breach by ABC and the homeowner could not cancel the contract between them for that reason. The parties were undoubtedly free to make it material. They could have added a provision to the contract stating, "Any delegation of duties by ABC constitutes a material breach of this contract, resulting in its immediate cancelation."

Answer (D) is incorrect because while delegation is important in construction contracts, freedom of contract is also important and a prohibition on delegation would be enforced, even if it was enforced only to the extent of allowing the other party to recover damages for its breach.

PRACTICE FINAL EXAM:
ANSWERS

169. **Answer (C) is the best answer.** The rule on unilateral mistake is found in Restatement § 153, which provides:

    § 153 When Mistake of One Party Makes a Contract Voidable

    Where a mistake of one party at the time a contract was made as to a basic assumption on which he made the contract has a material effect on the agreed exchange of performances that is adverse to him, the contract is voidable by him if he does not bear the risk of the mistake under the rule stated in § 154, and

    (a) the effect of the mistake is such that enforcement of the contract would be unconscionable, or

    (b) the other party had reason to know of the mistake or his fault caused the mistake.

    A unilateral mistake may be grounds for avoidance of the contract if the other elements of mistake are satisfied and the other party had reason to know of the mistake. Here, where the next lowest bid was almost 50% more, the contractor should probably have known. *See, e.g., Drennan v. Star Paving*, 333 P.2d 757 (Cal. 1958) (contractor not excused when it bid $7,131 and other bids came in at around $10–$11,000). Alternatively, the contract may be avoided if enforcement would be unconscionable. Making the contractor lose about $45,000 on a $112,000 contract may well be unconscionable. **Answer (A) is incorrect** because there is probably a mistake defense in this case. **Answer (B) is incorrect** because *actual* knowledge is not always required; constructive knowledge of a material mistake may be adequate to avoid a contract. **Answer (D) is incorrect** because the test is one of the objective intent of the parties. If a reasonable person in the contractor's shoes would not have known of the mistake, it doesn't matter what the subcontractor actually intended. And besides, an answer containing the misleading phrase "meeting of the minds" can never be a correct answer.

170. **Answer (D) is the best answer.** This contract is governed by the UCC, since widgets are goods. Under § 2-209(1), no consideration is needed for a modification, so **Answer (A) is incorrect**. If the modification was not entered into in good faith, it might nevertheless not be enforceable, but here the buyer's conduct does not rise to the level of breach of the covenant of good faith. According to § 2-209(2), the parties are free to enter into a No Oral Modification (NOM) clause, so **Answer (C) is incorrect** because it is too broad.

    Although parties are permitted to include an NOM clause in their contract, this does not mean that every subsequent oral modification is unenforceable. The Code anticipated that parties were likely to make oral modifications in spite of the NOM clause. Subsection 2-209(4) provides that even if the modification was not enforceable under subsection (2), it could act as a waiver. A waiver is a knowing relinquishment of a legal right. Here, the seller had the legal right to insist on the NOM clause, but by his conduct in agreeing to the modification, he gave up that right. According to subsection (5), once the other party relies on the oral modification, it is too late to retract it. Here, the buyer relied on the oral modification by turning down the better deal. Under these circumstances, the seller's waiver of the NOM clause is effective, and **Answer (B) is incorrect**.

171. **Answer (C) is the best answer**, although this result may be counter-intuitive. The default rule is that a material breach by one party discharges the obligations of the other party. There is not much doubt that the wrongful discharge of an employee is a material breach of an employment agreement. Normally, this would discharge all obligations of the employee. But here the parties specifically agreed that the employee's promise would be enforceable in spite of breach by the employer. In other words, the promise is unconditional or independent. Because the employee has to perform even if the employer does not, **Answer (B) is incorrect**. It does not matter whether the breach by the employee is material or not since the employer is making a claim for breach of a promise. Therefore, **Answer (A) is incorrect**. It is true that an employee owns an employer an implied duty of loyalty, but that obligation would normally end with the termination of employment. Because the employer's claim is based on the contractual provision and not on the common-law duty, **Answer (D) is incorrect**.

172. **Answer (C) is the best answer**. A recovery in restitution (*quasi*-contract) requires that the person conferring the benefit have a reasonable expectation of compensation; otherwise, it is conferred as a gift. Here, that would be a question of fact, because the doctor knew the Ski Patrol member and may have participated as a mere volunteer without an expectation of payment. **Answer (A) is incorrect** because, while it is true that there is no contract, that is not a defense to the doctor's recovery in *quasi*-contract. **Answer (B) is incorrect** because it is overly broad; while it is true that rescuers generally may not recover for their services, this is not true of a professional who is generally compensated for rendering similar services. *See* RESTATEMENT (THIRD) OF RESTITUTION AND UNJUST ENRICHMENT § 20. **Answer (D) is incorrect** because consent to professional services is not necessary for *quasi*-contractual recovery.

173. No. Under the parol evidence rule, once the parties have reduced their agreement to a writing that they intend to be final and complete, no evidence may be offered to supplement or contradict it. Here, the merger clause is a good indication that the parties intended the writing to be final and complete. Therefore, no evidence will be admissible to add or vary the terms. Note, however, that even if it were determined that the writing was not final and complete, the evidence would still likely not be admitted because it contradicts the writing and evidence is only admissible if it supplements or adds to the writing, not if it contradicts it.

174. It depends on the jurisdiction, but most jurisdictions would still not allow it. Most courts applying a "four corners" rule would look only at the writing to determine whether the language is ambiguous. Here, there is no "patent" ambiguity (an ambiguity that is apparent from the language of the agreement), and most courts would conclude from the face of the agreement that no evidence was necessary to determine the meaning. If the court applied the "plain meaning" rule, it would likewise probably conclude that the plain meaning of "non-exclusive" is not "exclusive."

Other courts will admit extrinsic evidence to determine whether the language is ambiguous.

In that situation, many courts will allow *objective* evidence but not *subjective* evidence. But even under that rule, they might disagree as to whether evidence of the parties' agreement is objective or subjective. Some authorities define *objective* as what reasonable parties would do, and admit only evidence such as trade usage that would demonstrate ambiguity. Others might say the evidence here is objective because it is not based on what a person has in his or her mind, but was objectively manifested by the parties.

For example, Judge Posner, an advocate of the objective view, said in *AM Int'l, Inc. v. Graphic Management Assoc., Inc.*, 44 F.3d 572 (7th Cir. 1995), that he would admit the idiosyncratic meanings of the parties. Curiously, in that diversity case he was applying Illinois law as he thought the Illinois Supreme Court would determine it. In a later case, the Illinois state court repudiated his conclusion, stating that it would stick to the "four corners" approach. *See Air Safety, Inc. v. Teachers Realty Corp.*, 706 N.E.2d 882 (Ill. 1999).

If a court applied the broad "context" approach to ambiguity found in *Berg v. Hudesman*, 801 P.2d 222 (Wash. 1990), then the evidence would probably be admissible because the court might determine that the meaning of language can never be determined without seeing the whole context in which it was used.

175. **Answer (D) is the best answer.** In an *accord*, the parties agree to discharge the debt when the agreed-upon *payment* is made. In a substituted contract, they agree to discharge the debt when the *promise* to pay is made. Here, it is an accord rather than a substituted contract because John agreed to accept Mary's payment rather than her promise to discharge the debt. Therefore, **Answer (C) is incorrect.** At the time of the settlement, it appeared that the debt was disputed, and therefore there was consideration for the accord. However, it later turned out that John was mistaken and Mary had not in fact owed him any money at the time she paid him the $50. Even though it looks like this undermines the consideration requirement, the rule is that a debt is considered disputed if the dispute is raised in good faith. Here, John honestly believed he had a claim against Mary, so the debt is considered disputed. *See Consolidated Edison Co. of New York v. Arroll*, 66 Misc. 2d 816 (N.Y. Civ. Ct. 1971), in which an accord was upheld because, even though there was no basis for the dispute, "the defendant honestly and in good faith believed that he owed less than the amount Con Edison claimed." Therefore, **Answer (A) is incorrect.** It is true that John was enriched by the payment of money he was not owed, but the law would say he was not *unjustly* enriched because he made the claim in good faith and the money was paid for the purpose of resolving a dispute. Therefore, **Answer (B) is incorrect**

176. **Answer (D) is the best answer.** This is the classic third party beneficiary situation. In the case that established the doctrine, *Lawrence v. Fox*, 20 N.Y. 268 (1859), Lawrence had loaned money to Holly. Holly then made a loan to Fox, promising Holly that he would pay the money that Holly owed to Lawrence. When Lawrence asked Fox to pay him, Fox claimed that he did not have a contractual obligation to pay Lawrence. The court nevertheless held that Fox was obligated to Lawrence because Lawrence was a third-party beneficiary of Fox's promise to Holly.

According to Restatement § 302(2), an incidental beneficiary is not a third-party beneficiary. Rather, he is simply a third party who benefits from a contract between two other parties. Therefore, he has no claim against the promisor. Since Baker is a third party beneficiary, and not an incidental beneficiary, **Answer (B) is incorrect.** In a novation, one party to a contract is replaced by another person, and the original party has no further obligations.

Here, Charlie remains a party to the contract, so **Answer (C) is incorrect**. Able has a duty to pay Baker $100. However, Able is not delegating that duty to Charlie; rather, Charlie is paying to Baker the $100 he owes to Able, not the $100 Able owes to Baker. Therefore, **Answer (A) is incorrect**.

177. **Answer (A) is the best answer.** The offeror, the student, was bargaining for a unilateral contract in which acceptance is rendered by performance of the act requested. **Answer (B) is incorrect** because the offeror was not bargaining for acceptance by a return promise. While it is true that the seriousness of the offer is measured by what a reasonable person hearing it would think, under these facts it would be reasonable to think she wanted the responsible person identified and the book returned. Therefore, **Answer (C) is incorrect**. **Answer (D) is incorrect** because a good test for determining whether a statement is an offer is to ask whether anything is required of the offeree other than to accept by giving the requested performance. Because performance would be acceptance, this statement looks more like an offer than an invitation to make an offer.

178. No. The acceptance must mirror the terms of the offer. Under the facts, the student who lost the book promised to pay for the return of *her* book and the student who purported to accept did not comply with the terms of the offer when he tendered a book that was not hers. Note that the fact that the amount of the offer exceeded the price of the book is not relevant. As our economist friends would say, if the book had $50 worth of utility for the offeror at that moment, it does not matter what its reasonable price was.

179. **Answer (B) is the best answer.** U.C.C. Article 2 applies to "transactions in goods." *See* § 2-102. "Goods" is defined in § 2-105(1) as "things . . . which are movable at the time of identification to the contract" and specifically included within the definition are "growing crops and other identified things attached to realty as described in [§ 2-107]." Section 2-107(2) specifically states that "[a] contract for the sale . . . of timber to be cut is a contract for the sale of goods within this Article."

Answer (A) is incorrect because an attorney's advice is a type of service, and a service is not goods because it is not movable. **Answer (C) is incorrect** because a contract to purchase a building is a real estate transaction, and real estate is not goods because it is not movable. **Answer (D) is incorrect** because a contract for intellectual property involves an intangible that is not movable.

180. **Answer (B) is the best answer.** The U.C.C. "firm offer" rule, § 2-205, provides:

§ 2-205. Firm Offers

An offer by a merchant to buy or sell goods in a signed writing which by its terms gives assurance that it will be held open is not revocable, for lack of consideration, during the time stated or if no time is stated for a reasonable time, but in no event may such period of irrevocability exceed three months; but any such term of assurance on a form supplied by the offeree must be separately signed by the offeror.

The provision specifically states that the offer must be made "in a signed writing which by its terms gives assurance that it will be held open." **Answer (A) is incorrect** because only the offeror must be a merchant. **Answer (C) is incorrect** because if no time is stated, the UCC imposes a "reasonable" period of irrevocability on the offeror. **Answer (D) is incorrect** because the offer can be made by a buyer or a seller as long as the offeror is a merchant.

181. **Answer (D) is the best answer.** This is a contract with the quantity measured by the requirements of the buyer. *See* U.C.C. § 2-306. Requirement contracts are valid and enforceable without specifying a particular quantity as long as there is a reasonable basis for measuring the quantity. A reasonable quantity would be imposed based, for example, on the needs of prior years. **Answer (A) is incorrect** because a requirements contract is enforceable without a specific quantity. **Answer (C) is incorrect** because a requirements contract is enforceable and consideration is present due to the exchange of promises. The modern view is that as long as the requirement of consideration is satisfied, there is no additional requirement of "mutuality of obligation." *See* RESTATEMENT § 79. Therefore, **Answer (B) is incorrect**.

182. **Answer (A) is the best answer.** This is a misunderstanding in which each party attached a different meaning to the language "my sailboat." Because the friend had sailed on both boats, in the language of Restatement § 20, "neither party knows or has reason to know the meaning attached by the other." Therefore, there is no contract because there is no manifestation of mutual assent. A court could not say which meaning the parties actually intended or which meaning is more reasonable. **Answer (B) is incorrect** because it is contrary to the facts. **Answer (C) is incorrect** because this is a case of misunderstanding rather than a case of mutual mistake. A "mistake," according to Restatement § 151, is "a belief that is not in accord with the facts." In fact, there was a 32-foot boat and a 37-foot boat, so there was not a mistaken belief. There was a misunderstanding about the meaning of the language used. **Answer (D) is incorrect** because misunderstanding prevents the formation of a contract.

183. **Answer (C) is the best answer.** In the famous case of *Kirksey v. Kirksey*, 1845 Ala. LEXIS 320 (Jan. 1845), the court determined that there was no bargain struck when a brother-in-law wrote to his sister-in-law, "If you will come down and see me, I will let you have a place to raise your family." Even more so than those facts, this language does not sound like a bargained-for consideration. The parents said "we hope," and "we plan," which is not language of commitment. **Answer (A) is incorrect** because the parents probably did not bargain for the daughter's performance when they said "if you do." **Answer (B) is incorrect** because even if she had reasonably relied on the promise, the daughter's remedy would probably be limited to the extent of the reliance. **Answer (C) is the best answer** because if there was no bargained-for consideration, then there was a promise to make a gift on condition. **Answer (D) is incorrect** because if there was a requested performance, it was returning to Spokane, and the daughter did that prior to their claimed revocation.

184. **Answer (D) is the best answer.** Tracking the elements of Restatement § 90, there was a promise that the promisor should reasonably have expected to induce action. There was nothing to indicate that the parents were not making a serious commitment. Therefore, **Answer (A) is incorrect**. The daughter substantially relied on the promise by returning to Spokane and forfeiting the deposit. And injustice can be avoided by enforcing the promise.

However, in accord with the rule that "[t]he remedy granted for breach may be limited as justice requires," rather than allowing her to recover what was promised, a court would probably limit recovery to the out-of-pocket expenses the daughter incurred in reliance on the promise. Therefore, **Answer (B) is incorrect**. It is true that the parents only requested the move, but the promise reasonably induced the daughter to give up the deposit on the apartment. Because that was a reasonable expense incurred in reliance on the promise,

Answer (C) is incorrect.

185.   **Answer (D) is the best answer.** The contract was illegal and thus unenforceable because the attorney was not admitted to the Kansas bar nor properly licensed under Kansas state law. Since the reason the contract is illegal is to protect the public, it is unlikely that a court would create an exception. **Answer (A) is incorrect** because while on occasion a party to an illegal contract may recover in restitution, here public policy would not allow the attorney to recover. *See* RESTATEMENT § 197. **Answer (B) is incorrect** because typically, no portion of an illegal contract may be enforced unless the contract is divisible into a legal and an illegal portion; here, the contract is not divisible. **Answer (C) is incorrect** because it is overly broad.

186.   **Answer (D) is the best answer. Answer (C) is incorrect** because the forum state (the jurisdiction where the case is heard) provides the choice of law rule that will be applied, but that rule does not necessarily point to the state's own law. There are two different default choice of law rules for contracts. If Idaho had the "old rule," then Answer A would be correct since Washington is the place where the acceptance occurred. If Idaho had the "new rule," then Answer B would be correct because in a real estate transaction, the location of the property is probably the most significant contact. But the facts say that the parties used their freedom of contract to contract around the default rules. They are permitted to do this if they choose the law of a state that bears a reasonable relation to the transaction. Since the chosen state — Idaho — meets this standard, then **Answer (D) is correct.** Since the parties' choice of law trumps the default rules, **Answer (A) and Answer (B) are incorrect.**

187.   **Answer (B) is the best answer.** There may be some jurisdictions that refuse to enforce all exculpatory clauses, but this is not the majority rule, so **Answer (A) is incorrect.** Most jurisdictions follow the rule of *Tunkl v. Regents of the University of California*, 383 P.2d 441, 444–46 (Cal. 1963), and look at the following aspects of the contract to make the determination:

> (1) It concerns a business of a type generally thought suitable for public regulation. (2) The party seeking exculpation is engaged in performing a service of great importance to the public, which is often a matter of practical necessity for some members of the public. (3) The party holds himself out as willing to perform this service for any member of the public who seeks it, or at least for any member coming within certain established standards. (4) As a result of the essential nature of the service, in the economic setting of the transaction, the party invoking exculpation possesses a decisive advantage of bargaining strength against any member of the public who seeks his services. (5) In exercising a superior bargaining power the party confronts the public with a standardized adhesion contract of exculpation, and makes no provision whereby a purchaser may pay additional reasonable fees and obtain protection against negligence. (6) Finally, as a result of the transaction, the person or property of the purchaser is placed under the control of the seller, subject to the risk of carelessness by the seller or his agents.

Applying these factors, a court would likely determine that medical services are an area of public interest, and that the patient entered into a contract of adhesion, so **Answer (C) is incorrect.** A court would also not expect a person to shop around on the basis of the contract terms for these services, so **Answer (D) is incorrect.** In fact, *Tunkl* itself involved hospital services.

188. **Answer (A) is the best answer.** A minor who enters into a contract may disaffirm it while he or she is a minor or within a reasonable time period after reaching the age of majority. **Answer (B) is incorrect** because there is no requirement that the disaffirmance be written. **Answer (C) is incorrect** because on disaffirming, the minor need only return what the minor received and does not have to make further payment. **Answer (D) is incorrect** because absent factors that are not present here, the minor who disaffirms a contract has to return only what the minor has left, even if what is left is damaged.

189. No. The company's argument would be based on impracticability. However, normal market fluctuations are not the kind of event that excuses nonperformance. *See* RESTATEMENT § 261 cmt. b. The company should have anticipated this event and put a term in the contract addressing what would happen if it occurred.

190. **Answer (C) is the best answer.** The statute of frauds requires that contracts that cannot be performed within a year from the making must be evidenced by a writing in order to be enforceable. RESTATEMENT § 130. Therefore, **Answer (D) is incorrect. Answer (B) is incorrect** because to satisfy the writing requirement, the writing needs to be signed only by the party against whom enforcement is sought; here, that is the company and therefore Answer (C) is the correct answer. **Answer (A) is incorrect** because partial performance takes only the performed portion out of the statute's purview. Presumably, the manager was already compensated for the performed portion of the contract, which renders the applicability of the statute to that portion irrelevant. She cannot recover for the unperformed portion because the statute does apply to that portion, and that portion was not evidenced by a writing.

191. **Answer (B) is the best answer.** Under the parol evidence rule, evidence that contradicts the terms of the writing will be excluded whether the writing is integrated or not; evidence that supplements the terms will be excluded only if the writing is integrated, and this contract appears to be integrated. **Answer (A) is incorrect** because evidence of a subsequent modification is not governed by the parol evidence rule. **Answer (C) is incorrect** because mutual mistake would prove a formation defense, and formation defenses are another exception to the parol evidence rule. **Answer (D) is incorrect** because in most jurisdictions evidence to prove a patent ambiguity (an ambiguity that is obvious from the face of the contract) is also an exception to the rule.

192. **Answer (B) is the best answer.** Section 2-313(1)(c) states that an express warranty may be created by "any sample or model which is made part of the basis of the bargain." When the seller showed the buyer a sample, he in effect promised that the goods would conform to the sample. Because he did not make the promise *verbally,* **Answer (A) is incorrect.** Because the sample creates an express warranty, and the language of the contract does not effectively contradict or disclaim it, **Answer (C) is incorrect.** Because a buyer can reasonably rely on an express warranty, **Answer (D) is incorrect.**

193. **Answer (D) is the best answer.** A merchant with respect to goods of that kind gives the buyer of those goods an implied warranty of merchantability. *See* § 2-314(1). The seller is free to disclaim that warranty, and used car dealers usually do. However, there are no facts indicating disclaimer in this case, so **Answer (A) is incorrect.** The warranty is given even if the goods are used. Therefore, **Answer (B) is incorrect.** However, the warranty does not promise that the goods will perform for a reasonable period of time. It promises only that

the goods "are fit for the ordinary purposes for which such goods are used." *See* § 2-314(2)(c). Therefore, **Answer (C) is incorrect**. To determine what the warranty encompassed, we would have to determine what the buyer can reasonably expect from a vehicle that has 80,000 miles on it. Furthermore, the buyer might have lower expectations depending on the price paid for the car. See Official Comment 7, which states in part that "[i]n cases of doubt as to what quality is intended, the price at which a merchant closes a contract is an excellent index of the nature and scope of his obligation under the present section."

194.   **Answer (B) is the best answer**. The duty to disclose is a duty associated with fraud and it arises only in limited circumstances that are probably not applicable here. *See* RESTATEMENT § 161. Therefore, this situation is best analyzed as a matter of good faith rather than fraud, and **Answer (A) is incorrect**. "Good faith" is defined in U.C.C. § 1-201(b)(20) as "honesty in fact and the observance of reasonable commercial standards of fair dealing." To act in good faith, it is not enough for the seller to simply perform the contract if it had reason to know the goods were no longer acceptable. Therefore, **Answer (D) is incorrect**. Here, the wholesaler acted honestly but good faith requires that it act both honestly and reasonably, and it probably did not act reasonably since others in the trade did not supply the oranges under similar contracts. Therefore, **Answer (C) is incorrect**.

195.   **Answer (C) is the best answer**. If a debt is disputed, then there is consideration for an accord. But the dispute must be raised in good faith in order to constitute consideration for an accord. If the owner made up the claim that the work was shoddy, then he did not raise the dispute in good faith, and the contractor would have a good argument that there was no consideration for the accord that led to the agreement on a price.

Alternatively, if a debt is unliquidated, then there is consideration for an accord. Therefore, **Answer (A) is incorrect** because if the parties had not originally agreed to the amount due (which is the definition of an unliquidated debt), this would not help the contractor's claim. Rather it would further the owner's claim that they had made a valid agreement to settle an unliquidated debt for the payment of $8,000.

An accord must be free of formation defenses. If the contractor claimed that the owner took advantage of his need for money to obtain a better price, this would be an unlikely basis for a claim of duress since the owner did not cause the situation. Therefore, **Answer (B) is incorrect**.

Because there is no requirement that an accord be in writing, **Answer (D) is incorrect**.

196.   **Answer (D) is the best answer**. The consideration is the promises to buy and sell the house; there does not have to be a separate consideration for each term in the contract, so **Answer (C) is incorrect**. It was expressly agreed that performance of the promises is subject to the buyer obtaining a mortgage. Because the buyer's promise is not immediately performable but is subject to the occurrence of an event, **Answer (A) is incorrect**. Although the buyer's performance is subject to a condition, the buyer cannot make the event occur or not occur at his whim, so the contract is not illusory. Remember, an illusory contract is one that gives one party a free out, and is therefore not binding on the other party either. Therefore, **Answer (B) is incorrect**.

197.   No. This term is an express condition. However, whether the event occurs or not is within the control of the buyer. Therefore, the buyer can't do nothing and claim that his

performance is excused when the event did not occur. Since he had the power to bring the event about or not, the court will find an implied obligation on the part of the buyer to make a good faith effort to bring it about. *See Billman v. Hensel*, 391 N.E.2d 671 (Ind. Ct. App. 1979).

198. **Answer (C) is the best answer.** The retailer clearly had reasonable grounds for insecurity when sufficient progress had not been made by September 1. Therefore, **Answer (A) is incorrect**. At the September 1 meeting, the retailer clearly demanded assurances and asked for those assurances within one month. Therefore, **Answer (B) is incorrect**. It appears that the manufacturer was unable to make adequate assurance during the October 1 meeting, so **Answer (D) is incorrect**. The best argument for the manufacturer is to claim that the demand was not made in writing, as required by § 2-609.

These facts are based on *AMF, Inc. v. McDonald's Corp.*, 536 F.2d 1167 (7th Cir. 1976). In that case, the court held that it was not necessary to comply with the writing requirement because according to U.C.C. § 1-103, the Code should be "liberally construed." That seems to me a bit of an overstatement — I don't think under the most liberal construction that "in writing" means "not in writing." Nevertheless, I think the court was right. The purpose of the writing requirement is probably partially evidentiary and partially cautionary — to warn the recipient of the demand that something serious is happening. I think the oral statement at the October 1 meeting was sufficient to satisfy that purpose and the manufacturer knew terrible things were going to happen if it didn't respond with adequate assurances. Incidentally, the common law version of the demand for assurances in Restatement § 251 does not require that the demand be in writing.

199. **Answer (C) is the best answer. Answer (B) is incorrect** because under the Code, evidence of usage of trade, course of dealing, and course of performance are admissible even if the agreement is fully integrated. *See* § 2-202(a). If it were not for its acceptance of the first three deliveries, the buyer would have a claim for breach based on the trade usage. However, its acceptance of the first three deliveries constitutes a course of performance that trumps trade usage. *See* § 1-303(a) and (e). Therefore, **Answer (A) is incorrect. Answer (D) is incorrect** because course of dealing is based on what the parties did under previous contracts between them; there is no course of dealing evidence in this question.

200. **Answer (C) is the best answer.** As the non-breaching party, the contractor is entitled to be compensated in the expectancy — an amount sufficient to put her where she would have been had she been allowed to perform the contract; expectation damages are also referred to as compensatory damages or the benefit of the bargain. Here the facts state that the contractor would have made a profit of $1,000 upon completion of the contract with the homeowner. **Answer (A) is incorrect** because while she would have been paid the full contract price had the work been completed, she would have had to incur costs to fulfill her part of the bargain. Therefore, the expectancy is the amount she would have been paid, minus her costs, which is her profit — here, $1,000, not the $5,000 contract price. **Answer (B) is incorrect** because although she would be entitled to recover her actual costs incurred in performing the job, the non-breaching party must mitigate the damages. It was not reasonable for her to incur costs after she had been informed of the breach. *See Rockingham Co. v. Luten Bridge Co.*, 35 F.2d 301 (4th Cir. 1929). Similarly, **Answer (D) is incorrect** because this amount includes costs that the contractor incurred after she had actual knowledge that the homeowner had canceled the contract. Such an award violates the duty

to mitigate the damages.

201.   **Answer (C) is the best answer.** This question involves the sale of goods, so we look to Article 2 for the applicable rule. Section 2-718(1) specifies that the amount of the liquidated damages stipulated in the contract must be reasonable in light of either the anticipated or actual harm flowing from the breach. **Answer (A) is incorrect** because any contract can contain a liquidated damage provision as long as it complies with the rule stated above. **Answer (B) is incorrect** because if liquidated damages are so large as to constitute a penalty, the clause will not be enforceable and the company will only be able to recover actual damages. Section 2-718(2) states that a deposit will not be treated as liquidated damages beyond a limited statutory amount unless the parties designate it as such, and if they do, the company will run the risk of having the provision disallowed under this principle. **Answer (D) is incorrect** because there is no percentage limitation as to the relationship between the liquidated damages and the actual damage. The test is one of "reasonableness."

202.   **Answer (D) is the best answer.** The wholesaler sent a definite and seasonable expression of acceptance with an additional term. Under § 2-207(1), a contract was formed and under § 2-207(2), the additional term is a proposal. We can deduce that these parties are both merchants because of the quantity involved. Between merchants, the additional term is deemed part of the contract unless one of the three exceptions applies. The exceptions in (a) and (c) don't apply because the offeror did not object in the offer or after it received the acceptance. The exception in (b) does not apply because "weight to be evidenced by a city scale weight certificate" does not materially alter the offer. **Answer (A) is incorrect** because, between merchants, additional terms become a part of the contract unless one of the three exceptions applies, and here none of them do. **Answer (B) is incorrect** because § 2-207(1) and (2) state that between merchants, there is a contract without any affirmative acceptance of the additional term by the offeror. **Answer (C) is incorrect** because that is the common law rule, but it is changed in a Code case and here the Code applies because the contract deals with chicken, which is a good.

203.   **Answer (C) is the best answer.** An assignee is subject to all claims and defenses by the obligor (the one who is obligated to pay). *See* RESTATEMENT § 336(2). Therefore, **Answer (A) is incorrect.** The neighbor has a claim for breach of warranty, so if that claim can be asserted against the obligee (the one to whom the obligation is owed), then it can be asserted against an assignee as well. Therefore, **Answer (D) is incorrect.** According to U.C.C. § 2-717, a buyer, on notice to the seller, may deduct damages when paying the seller. Therefore, **Answer (B) is incorrect.**

204.   **Answer (B) is the best answer.** Because the delegator remains liable when the duty is delegated, the obligee cannot show prejudice or increased risk, even when the delegatee is not creditworthy. **Answer (A) is incorrect** because the parties are permitted to prohibit the delegation of a duty. **Answer (C) is incorrect** because delegation is not allowed where a material variance in performance would result. **Answer (D) is incorrect** because generally personal service contracts involving personal skills are not delegable. *See* RESTATEMENT § 318(2) and cmt. c.

205.   **Answer (D) is the best answer.** According to Restatement § 71(3)(c), there is consideration if the bargained-for performance consists of "the creation, modification, or destruction of a

legal relation." When the parties mutually rescinded the contract, that was the "destruction of a legal relation." Therefore, there is consideration and **Answer (C) is incorrect. Answer (A) is incorrect** because the consideration for the original contract was in the form of the bargained-for mutual promises to buy and sell the house. **Answer (B) is incorrect** because it is not relevant. Once the parties rescinded the contract, it was too late for one party to change his mind.

206. **Answer (B) is the best answer.** This is an Article 2 transaction since a baseball is a good. Section 2-201 requires that transactions for the sale of goods for a price of $500 or more be evidenced by a writing. Since this transaction is within the statute of frauds, **Answer (A) is incorrect.** Section 2-201(1) requires that to be enforceable, the writing must be "signed by the party against whom enforcement is sought." Since the writing does not need to be signed by both parties, **Answer (C) is incorrect.** To be a sufficient writing, it must "indicate that a contract for sale has been made between the parties." The email constitutes such a writing. The Uniform Electronic Transactions Act (U.E.T.A.) § 7(c) provides that "[i]f a law requires a record to be in writing, an electronic record satisfies the law." Since the email is an electronic record as defined by UETA, it constitutes a writing for purposes of the statute of frauds. Therefore, **Answer (D) is incorrect.**

207. The company should demand assurances. An anticipatory repudiation is a clear and unequivocal refusal to perform in advance of the time for performance. The language used by the seller here is not clear and unequivocal. Therefore, the company should not treat it as a breach. On the other hand, the company does not have to wait until July 1 to determine whether the seller is going to perform. Because the language of the notice gives the company reasonable grounds for insecurity, it can use the procedures established by § 2-609 to demand assurances from the seller. If it gets reasonable assurances, it should be secure. If it does not get reasonable assurances, then it can assume that the seller has repudiated, and according to § 2-610, it can, if it wishes, resort to remedies for breach.

208. **Answer (C) is the best answer.** This contract should be governed by the C.I.S.G. The U.S. and Mexico are both signatories to the C.I.S.G.; Tempus knew or should have known from the faxed acknowledgment and the shipping documents that FC's place of business is in Mexico; Tempus's place of business is in the U.S.; Tempus did not purchase the precision gear works primarily for personal, family, or household use; and the fact that the gear works may be custom-made, rather than ready-made, does not take the contract outside the scope of the C.I.S.G. *See* C.I.S.G. arts. 1(1)(a), 1(2), 2(a), and 3(1). The twist in this question is that Tempus (the U.S. purchaser) did not contact FC (the Mexican manufacturer). Instead, Tempus contacted Gearz, which is located in New Mexico. Can Gearz's Albuquerque office be considered a "place of business" for FC? If so, we would have to consult C.I.S.G. Article 10 to determine FC's "official" place of business for this transaction. Article 10 provides that, when a party has more than one place of business, that party's place of business for purposes of Article 1(1) is that "which has the closest relationship to the contract and its performance, having regard to the circumstances known to or contemplated by the parties at any time before or at the conclusion of the contract." Here, unless Tempus had no reason to know that it was ultimately contracting with FC (and that should have been obvious when it received the confirming fax from FC's Nuevo Laredo factory), the place of business with the closest relationship to this contract is FC's Nuevo Laredo factory.

Because this contract falls within the scope of the C.I.S.G., the U.C.C. and common law all yield to the C.I.S.G., to the extent that the C.I.S.G. addresses a particular issue, because these are both state law sources of law, and the C.I.S.G. is a treaty of the United States. As such, under the Supremacy Clause, it trumps contrary state law. *See, e.g., Filanto, S.p.A. v. Chilewich International Corp.*, 789 F. Supp. 1229 (S.D.N.Y. 1992) (holding that the C.I.S.G. trumps Article 2 in cases where the CISG applies), *appeal dismissed*, 984 F.2d 58 (2d Cir. 1993). Therefore, **Answers (A), (B), and (D) are incorrect** — Answer (A) doubly so because, even if the C.I.S.G. did not govern, U.C.C. Article 2 rather than common law would apply because this is a sale of goods.

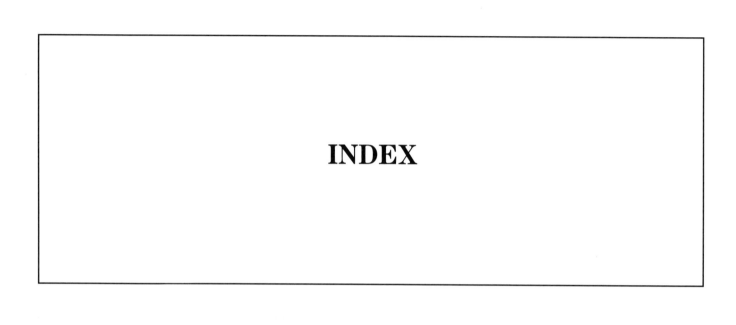

INDEX

INDEX